Pet Purpose

Pet Purpose

Your Unspoken Voice

Xanthe Wyse

Cover art, *Snowball* by Xanthe Wyse

Cover design by Xanthe Wyse

Independently published.

New Zealand.

bipolarcourage.com

ISBN 978-0-473-57214-3 (Softcover – POD)

ISBN 978-0-473-57215-0 (EPUB)

Your unspoken voice will be heard.

Table of Contents

Introduction

Pet Purpose: Your Unspoken Voice is a pet-themed story about how love hurts with bipolar disorder and post-traumatic stress disorder (PTSD). It is semi-autobiographical fiction with memoir and fiction woven together. All characters, including the pets, are composite characters. Place names are fictitious.

The early parts of the story are necessary to help the reader understand how much pain the main character (Heni/Larissa) is carrying. Also to provide context as to why the character did certain things in the later chapters which mainly depict bipolar mania with post-traumatic stress disorder (PTSD), from trauma.

Most of the story focusses on the character's adult life. The first chapter sets the scene in adulthood, followed by two chapters on childhood experiences. The story of the character's adult life then resumes. The character is attempting to get closure on grief and trauma.

The song titles which are mentioned throughout are included in a reference section at the end, to clarify which song and version. The songs chosen are linked in some way, whether by mood, lyrics or themes.

Some artworks by the author are included after the story. The artworks were therapeutic processing as well as visual mind maps that helped develop the storyline.

The author shares diagnoses of bipolar 1 disorder and post-traumatic stress disorder with the main character in this novel. The author strongly sees patterns, so has woven symbolic metaphor throughout.

The author aims to provide a unique perspective of processing complex trauma and grief through the art of storytelling.

1. No Rainbow Bridge

'My cat died today,' announced 4-year-old Alexandria Hertz-Kopf to the barista.

'And she's in the ground turning into dirt,' added Alexandria's twin brother Xavier.

'Really?' replied the barista, trying to suppress a laugh, glancing at the twins' mother, Heni Hertz. Even Heni, who had been crying all morning, cracked a hint of a smile.

Heni and her children had bright turquoise eyes which seemed to change colour in different light like iridescent avian feathers. The children's eyes seemed too big for their curious golden faces framed with honey locks. Xavier's hair was a tumble of soft curls and Alexandria's hair was fine and straight.

The twins each sat on a café breakfast bar stool, each dipping a long spoon into their chocolate milk fluffies. The barista was making coffee for their father, Richie Kopf, a police officer. Heni poured camomile tea into a white cup.

'It looks like pee,' said Richie with an Australian accent.

'I doubt it tastes like pee,' said Heni in her New Zealand accent. She had retained her Kiwi accent despite living in Australia since before the twins were born.

'You'd know from the smell, knowing you,' said Richie. 'I've never known anyone to have such a hypersensitive sense of smell as you.'

'Coffee smells like cat poop and Tripod agreed.' When Tripod, the three-legged black cat was alive, she had scratched around Richie's coffee cup as though it were a cat litter tray.

Richie reached across and clasped his wife's hand. Richie was called 'Rig' by his colleagues in the police force because they said he was built like a truck – tall and solid with muscular arms. Handsome, with striking emerald eyes and dimples.

Heni hadn't wanted to go out for coffee and would have preferred to have been left alone or to be comforted by an embrace from Richie's strong arms, where she felt safe and protected.

Heni wasn't wearing makeup and her glossy raven hair tumbled in natural waves. Richie preferred for her to wear little or no makeup. Heni looked beautiful without it. She was often mistaken for Italian or Spanish with her deeper skin-tone from her blended Maori and German ancestry.

Richie hadn't expected on his day off to be digging a grave. Heni had agreed to go out as a distraction from her sadness.

Heni had adopted Tripod from a shelter. She knew that older cats and dogs, especially those with disabilities are less likely to be rehomed. At first, Tripod was very timid, sitting in the corner of a cage, head dropped and not moving. She'd had one leg amputated, presumably after an accident. Her history was unknown.

After initially hiding in a drawer in the bedroom, Tripod came out and started to appear relaxed. One day, when she was asleep, sprawled out across the back part of the sofa, Richie joked, 'Cats are nature's way of showing us that not everything has a purpose in life.'

Despite having three legs, Tripod was a very fast runner – she'd zoom out of the room faster than a cat with four legs when a stranger came to visit.

Tripod was raised as an indoor cat and Heni trained her to use a human toilet. She scratched at the toilet seat briefly before pushing the flush button. Richie had built an outdoor area with cat netting and access via a cat door so Tripod could sun herself outside. Richie was annoyed when Tripod climbed the insect screens to chase lizards. The only way Tripod could leave the property was to go out the front door.

The attendants at the animal shelter had advised Heni to raise Tripod as an inside cat because of the risks of cats killing wildlife and wildlife killing cats.

4

'That's Stralya for ya,' joked Richie. 'Where everything's out to kill you.' He pointed to an article in the newspaper with an x-ray of the inside of a python, clearly showing the skeleton of an entire cat wearing a cat collar with a bell still attached.

The day Tripod died, Heni woke up with a feeling of dread. She could see that the new lizard enclosure had arrived. The enclosure was in the middle of the lounge, still covered in wrapping. 'Where's Tripod?' she asked.

'Dunno,' replied Richie, tugging off the protective wrapping. There were also boxes with lamps and a thermostat and other accessories to simulate basking in the sun. The twins were asking about when their lizard would arrive. They had chosen a frilled dragon and had already named it Lucky. They would be going to collect Lucky with Richie after the enclosure was set up.

Tripod had been playing with a redback spider that had gotten into the house a few days earlier. The neighbour had threatened to kill Tripod if she ever went over the boundary of the fence. He'd seen her peeking out the window. 'I'll wring its bloody neck,' he'd muttered as he mowed the dried up tufts of grass during a drought.

'Triiii-pod,' called Heni. Tripod was nowhere to be seen and her breakfast was untouched. Heni checked Tripod's favourite places like the linen cupboard. She checked under the bed. Tripod would have been frightened when the delivery people had arrived with big boxes. She was supposed to have been locked in a bedroom during the delivery of the lizard enclosure.

Heni's feeling of dread grew. *Did she slip out the front door? Is she hurt?* were Heni's thoughts. Heni went outside. She could see something writhing on the driveway and she went closer to investigate. It was a brown snake, a small yet highly venomous snake. It was injured with some small puncture wounds likely from an altercation with a cat. She ran back indoors to let Richie know and he confined the snake and made arrangements with a wildlife rescue and rehabilitation organisation.

Heni called for Tripod and started searching around the house and started asking the neighbours. The neighbours across the road came out and helped her search. Their lawnmower was outside under the eaves with the catcher beside it. Heni knew she'd find Tripod there. She just knew. She looked inside the catcher and Tripod was there, breathing – just. She was weak and lethargic. Heni pulled her out gently and Tripod was unable to stand on her three legs. She collapsed. Heni scooped Tripod up in her arms and ran back across the road to home.

'Richie…I found Tripod…she's been bitten by the snake. I have to get her to the vet urgently. Can you call the vet to let them know I'm on my way.'

Heni bundled Tripod up in the car and drove to the vet. When she arrived, Tripod's breathing was very shallow and barely there. Tripod started twitching all over and she stopped breathing. The vet urgently resuscitated her and administered anti-venom.

'The source of the bite was near the heart,' said the vet. 'Which is why the venom was absorbed and distributed so quickly around the body. It will be very touch and go whether Tripod survives the next twelve to twenty-four hours.'

The next morning, a vet nurse called to say that Tripod was responding to the anti-venom.

'She's not out of the woods yet but she's starting to stabilise,' she said. 'You can come see her anytime now.'

'Thank-you. That's such a relief,' said Heni. 'I'll come down now.' She still felt anxious.

Heni arrived at the vet and Tripod was resting but looked much improved. Her breathing was more normal. Heni stroked Tripod's fur.

'You get better, okay?' she said. 'You'll be coming home soon.'

The vet nurse said, 'She was probably playing with the snake then got bitten. You're a Kiwi? Where from? I've been to New Zealand.'

'A little town called Kanuka by a freshwater lake, an hour from a snowy mountain and an hour from the sea.'

'So people can surf, ski and waterski?'

'Yep. It doesn't get as hot though as here.'

'So what brought you to this stinking hot place of Jellybroome?'

'Love. I married an Australian. I used to be a vet nurse in New Zealand. We don't have exotics like lizards and snakes there.'

'There is a specialist vet for exotics in the next city. There is a lot more to worry about for pets here. Paralysis ticks are a big killer of cats and dogs. Snake bites and cane toads are also something you wouldn't have to deal with in New Zealand. A lot of pets get poisoned after licking a cane toad. It's quite addictive for them as they can get high and start hallucinating but a little too much can be lethal.'

The vet came out. 'We'll give you a call later to let you know how Tripod is getting on.'

The children had been to collect Lucky who was now in her new home.

'Lucky is a boy,' said Xavier.

'Lucky could be a girl,' said Alexandria.

'The breeder isn't one hundred percent sure,' said Richie.

The vet phoned.

'I'm so sorry but Tripod had a delayed allergic reaction to the snake bite. We did everything we could, but we lost her.'

'You mean....she's dead...?' asked Heni, her lip trembling.

'Yes. I'm sorry for your loss. When you're ready we can discuss what arrangements you would like to make for Tripod. We have cremation options.'

I'm sorry I wasn't there, Heni said over and over in her head. *I wasn't there to comfort you.*

She had been there so many times when other people had said goodbye to their pets, when she'd been a vet nurse. It was always hard to deal with and one of the main reasons she changed careers. Because it was so painful forming a bond then saying goodbye.

As a vet nurse, part of her job was to give a card with a poem about Rainbow Bridge on it to anyone whose pet had died. The poem was about how their beloved pet was waiting for them in a meadow, waiting to be reunited to cross Rainbow Bridge together. Some people loved the Rainbow Bridge poem. Other people were irritated and even upset by it. 'I don't believe in no stinkin' Rainbow Bridge,' a man had muttered throwing the poem on the floor after his beloved dog was euthanised.

Heni didn't want to talk about Heaven or Rainbow Bridge to the children. She didn't know what she believed anymore and the Rainbow Bridge story seemed so clichéd. So did Heaven. She didn't want to say that Tripod was sleeping as she didn't want the children to be afraid of going to sleep and never waking up. The only thing she knew for sure was that with a natural burial, Tripod's body would decompose and be recycled. Heni could compartmentalise and be matter-of-fact.

'Do you want to see Tripod?' asked Heni. 'It will be the last time you see her.'

The twins nodded. They had never been exposed to death before and Heni didn't want for it to be scary.

Heni opened the box and Tripod lay there curled up as though she were sleeping. Her fur hid the rash on her skin from the allergic reaction. Heni and the twins stroked Tripod's fur for the last time. Richie finished digging a hole in the back yard, just like when Heni's father did back in New Zealand when it was time to say goodbye to a beloved pet.

There were so many questions as the twins helped Richie fill in the hole. Then they pressed the dirt down wearing their gumboots.

'Is the snake a bad snake for hurting Tripod?' asked Xavier.

'No, snakes are not bad,' said Richie.

'What will happen to Tripod now?' asked Alexandria.

'Her body will break down and she will become the dirt to make the grass and flowers grow,' replied Heni.

'Will she ever wake up?'

'No. She has died and won't wake up.'

'Are we going to die one day too, Mummy?'

Heni couldn't lie. 'Yes, one day but I hope to be here for a long time and so will you.'

'Why are you crying, Mummy?'

'I'm sad because we won't see Tripod again and I'll miss her.'

Heni answered their questions without mentioning Heaven or Rainbow Bridge. With the truth, in a way that the children could understand.

Richie said nothing and went inside and turned on the stereo. *Somebody to Love* was playing through the newly installed surround sound speakers. *Queen* was one of Richie's favourite bands.

Richie took out two frozen rats from the freezer to thaw. Feeding time was exciting for Richie. If anyone were visiting, he'd feed his pet green tree pythons, Donner and Blitz, in front of them like a form of entertainment. He'd dangle a dead rat in front of each python. Lightning fast, the rat would be strangled and then engulfed whole over several minutes. Heni didn't like watching it as she had had a pet rat called Honey when she was a teenager. Honey had been very affectionate and intelligent. Heni had been sent home from school when Honey died, because she couldn't stop crying.

Heni cut three branches and arranged them in a tripod shape to mark the place to later plant a native tree with blossoms. 'Goodbye Tripod.'

She wiped her tears and gave her twins a big hug then took their hands and walked inside to get to know Lucky.

2. Rotten Egg

It was the eve of Heni's fifth birthday which coincided with fireworks festivities. Heni was invited next door to Kathryn Payne's house for fireworks. Kathryn was affectionately called Kat and Heni's nickname was Mouse, because she was so quiet. Kat and Mouse wrote their names in the air with sparklers. Kat's father, Lindsay, let off rockets then hammered a Catherine wheel to a wooden fence and lit it. It spun frantically then fell off, hitting the ground hard with sparks still spraying.

'Are you looking forward to starting school, Heni?' asked Kuini, Kat's mother. Heni nodded but didn't speak. She only spoke to her own family and to Kat. Kuini was a primary school teacher. 'You're in Kat's class,' said Kuini. 'Kat will look out for you'.

On Heni's first day of school, students were required to line up for story booklets made from pieces of A4 newsprint paper folded in half and stapled down the spine. They were fresh off the spirit duplicator machine. The other students were eagerly taking the booklets and pressing them against their faces to inhale the aroma of methylated spirits from the pages.

Heni's teacher, Mrs Castle, held one in front of Heni. 'How do you say your name?' she bellowed. Heni stood frozen and no words came out. Kat spoke on her behalf: 'Hen-ee, Mrs Castle'.

'Henny?' said Mrs Castle gruffly. 'Like Henny Penny?' Heni still did not move. She was frozen.

Mrs Castle tried to shove a booklet into Heni's hand. Heni didn't take it. She stood there very still and unresponsive. Mrs Castle scolded her.

Suddenly, Heni grabbed the booklet, threw it onto the floor and stomped her feet. She didn't want the booklet from this strange adult she had never met before. This booklet with the purple ink and the strange, yet intoxicating smell.

Mrs Castle slapped Heni's hand while continuing to scold her. Kat picked up the booklet from the floor and in a gentle voice led a sobbing Heni to a little chair at a table where they sat down.

Heni took a yellow crayon from the ice-cream container and angrily scribbled in the baby chick on the front of the booklet through hot tears. She didn't care that she scribbled outside the purple lines.

Heni didn't speak to Mrs Castle for a whole month. When she finally spoke, she said 'Can I have a bickie?' in a tiny whisper.

'It's not a bickie it's a biscuit!' retorted Mrs Castle harshly. Heni withdrew into silence again which frustrated an authoritarian-style teacher like Mrs Castle. Heni did her work but she wouldn't speak at school.

Ava Manu brought a treasure box to school. Heni was fascinated with it, opening and closing the little wooden drawers lined with velvet. Ava invited Heni to stay on the farm.

One of the first things Heni noticed when she visited the farm was a stag head trophy on the wall and a stuffed baby fawn mounted to a wooden base with its legs folded under. They were hard to the touch, not soft like Heni's pets and were lifeless with their glass eyes. 'They're creepy,' whispered Heni to Ava.

'Mouse, did you like going to the farm with Kent and Ava?' asked Daniel, her brother, who was a year older. Daniel had darker skin than Heni with sun-bleached blonde hair. Ava's brother, Kent, was in Daniel's class.

'Yes, we rode the horses and jumped on the trampoline.'

'Is Kent your boyfriend?'

'No.'

'Heni and Kent up a tree...K-I-S-S-I-N-G! Heni's got a boyfriend,' taunted Daniel.

Aroha Hertz turned the dryer off connected to the cap puffed up over her hair rollers. She took a few whiffs of her cigarette then tapped the ash into a natural paua shell used as an ashtray. 'Stop bickering and hurry up and finish the dishes!'

'Heni's got a boyfriend,' Daniel whispered.

'La-la-la I can't hear you!' Heni flicked the tea towel at Daniel's legs.

'Mum! Heni flicked the tea towel at me!'

'Telltale,' said Heni.

With a flicker of cheekiness in his eyes, Daniel scooped up dishwashing foam and dumped it on Heni's hair. Heni grabbed a cup, ran to the laundry to fill it then tossed it in Daniel's face.

Daniel cupped his hand over the tap and sprayed the kitchen with water.

Aroha took off her cap and started pulling out the T-shaped plastic pins from the rollers in her hair, releasing set curls. Aroha spent a lot of time making herself look pretty for Klaus, even though he said she didn't need to.

Aroha yelled, 'Get that water out of my kitchen!' Her yelling amped up the play more, like turning up the flames on the stove. 'Wait till your father gets home!'

The water was taken outside – mostly. But the windows were open on a late summer's evening and the children grabbed buckets with water and turned on the hose and were having a full on water fight. Water sprayed in though the windows and the yellow and brown patterned lino floor was drenched.

Klaus Hertz arrived home in his electrician's van. The children stopped playing and Aroha stubbed out her cigarette and hid the paua ashtray in a box with her embroidery threads. Klaus didn't know that Aroha smoked as he had lost his sense of smell after a concrete mixer exploded and he had inhaled cement dust.

Very quietly, without emotion in his steel grey eyes, he instructed in his hybrid German-Kiwi accent: 'Mop that water up, wipe the bench down and take the scrap bucket out to the compost'.

The water fight was over and Heni and Daniel did exactly as they were told. Heni didn't like conflict even though her will was as strong as her father's. Klaus needed order in the household.

The next morning, Heni was looking out the window. 'What is he doing?' she asked. The neighbour across the road had a sack and a tub of water.

'Don't watch that. He's drowning kittens,' said Aroha.

'Why?' asked Heni.

'Because he won't get the cats fixed,' said Aroha.

Heni didn't understand exactly what was involved with getting cats fixed but she knew it was a trip to the vet and the cats wouldn't have any more kittens.

Soon after, Heni and Klaus found a stray cat in a scruffy condition in the woodshed. On closer inspection, there were three kittens.

'Please don't drown the kittens,' pleaded Heni to Aroha and Klaus.

'We'll look for homes for them,' said Aroha. 'We'll get the mother fixed too so she doesn't have more kittens.'

Heni spent time with the kittens. The smallest white one looked like a fluffy snowball. 'Can we keep this kitten and call her Snowball?' asked Heni. Klaus agreed.

When they were old enough, homes were found for the other two kittens and the mother. Snowball and Heni formed a close bond. Snowball snuggled in Heni's bed with Heni.

When school started again, Heni's teacher was Kuini. Kuini had students call her by her first name, pronounced 'Queenie' rather than more formal address like the rest of the teachers. She taught the children Maori action songs and told myths and legends and played the guitar. She wore a jade pendant around her neck.

Kuini explained to the children that she had diabetes and needed medicine called insulin to help balance out her blood sugar levels.

She demonstrated pricking her finger to take a drop of blood on a little strip to measure her blood sugar.

Kuini told traditional and contemporary stories including those about the local area of the town of Kanuka. Mount Whakapono was a beautiful goddess whose emotions were frozen in ice after a demigod raged at her. She was separated from her children, who became islands.

When the snow and ice thawed, her tears released great feeling, forming the streams, the springs, the lake, the waterfall and the river, finally going out to sea where they sweetened the salt water and the fish became abundant. The water also reached her children who were isolated.

Kuini explained that Whakapono is a Maori word meaning 'believe.' Heni also lived on Whakapono Road.

Kuini's stories would take Heni into a land of imagination, along with her love of music and art. Heni was very quiet and thoughtful and the children at school also called her by her nickname, Mouse, even though she was at times chatty at home.

Young Heni regularly went to Sunday school at the church with Kat. One day at home, Heni played on her swing with Kat. She wound the swing up by twisting the ropes, jumped up onto it and then let it go, spinning around until she was dizzy. Suddenly, Kat said, 'I asked Jesus into my heart and he's my friend.'

'How?'

'Jesus, please come into my heart.'

Heni did this but didn't feel any different. However, she thought it was cool to share an invisible friend with Kat.

The Hertz family enjoyed music and Daniel and Heni both liked to change the records over. They listened to music as well as children's stories. Sometimes a record was stuck so they would carefully lift the needle to a new part so the music could continue to play. Heni and Daniel found it amusing to turn a knob to change the speed. The laughed and tried to imitate both the high-pitched and low drawn-out sounds.

Aroha worked part-time sewing curtains. She also sewed ball gowns as she enjoyed ballroom dancing with Klaus. Aroha frequently talked about her dreams of Heni becoming a bride in a white dress one day and promised that she would sew her bridal gown and bridesmaids' dresses.

Klaus and Aroha went ballroom dancing one evening. Aroha asked a friend's teenage daughter Deborah to babysit. During the evening, Deborah decided to leave so she called her brother Paul in to babysit instead. They shared flame-red hair and they'd shown Heni their insulin vials for diabetes when she'd visited their house on the corner of Victoria Street which backed onto Heni's house. Paul played board games with Heni and Daniel.

They played *Hangman*. Paul choose a three letter word starting with 'S-E-' and Heni didn't guess correctly the last letter and lost the game. She was hung. Paul was grinning when he revealed the missing letter was 'X'. Heni looked to Daniel for reassurance and he gave a tense, awkward almost-smile. They also played a battery operated game called *Operation* which made a buzzing sound if the tweezers touched the metal.

After that evening, Heni blocked out any memories of Paul. She started being anxious for the first time instead of carefree. She wet the bed a few times but she didn't tell her parents. She washed the sheets herself in the old wringer washing machine. She also started having episodes of stomach cramps and diarrhoea. She had nightmares and sometimes cried out in terror. Snowball was her best friend and snuggling up with Snowball helped her feel safer.

Heni didn't feel safe when there were strong emotions expressed, especially anger. If someone got angry, Heni would freeze up and go to a different place.

One day Heni was sitting on the doorstep petting Snowball. Klaus came stomping out of the house swearing in German. Heni didn't know what he was saying but she felt afraid of the anger he expressed. Heni and Snowball sat very still on the doorstep, frozen. She couldn't move. The loud noise from Klaus became distant. Klaus stomped around back and forth ranting and then went back indoors, muttering in frustration, 'You kids don't listen'. Heni couldn't move or speak when she felt unsafe.

If Klaus asked her to do something in a quiet 'I-mean-business' tone of voice, she always did what he wanted as she was afraid he might get angry. Anger terrified her. She felt like it was her fault. She didn't like it when Aroha got upset either. Aroha was also quick to anger but she would also cry.

Heni avoided conflict by trying to be perfectly behaved. After some frustration, Klaus and Aroha figured out that a quiet voice was more effective with Heni than yelling. Heni just didn't respond at all to yelling. It was as if she didn't hear. Because she couldn't when she'd freeze.

Heni felt safe with her friends Kat and Ava. Living just next door, Kat frequently came over to play.

One day, Heni and Kat were playing a game where they threw themselves at a hedge, trying to bounce back out. Then something hurt Heni's foot. She looked down and the side of her foot was covered with red dots. She looked cautiously into the hedge and there was a hedgehog rolled up into a ball. Heni didn't say anything to anyone about it.

'What's that rash on your foot, Mouse?' asked Aroha. She inspected Heni's foot more closely. Heni didn't confess that she'd accidentally stepped on a hedgehog. She felt she wasn't allowed to tell about anything painful. 'Maybe it's hives from eating those strawberries,' said Aroha. 'No more strawberries for you.'

Kat had long, straight, dark brown hair and both girls liked to wear matching hair clips. Kat started missing school and wasn't able to play. When Heni saw Kat again, her right arm was amputated just below the elbow and her long hair was gone.

'Cancer,' she said. Kat was cheerful as always despite being very tired. She was fitted with a prosthetic hook with which she was learning to pick things up. Soon, Kat's hair started growing back and she seemed to have more energy. The girls sat outside on the concrete with hammers whacking strips of gun caps to make explosive sounds.

After they'd used up all the caps, Heni said, 'We have a colour TV.' They'd recently changed over from black and white. The girls went inside and watched *Wonder Woman*, their favourite superhero. Sometimes Kat stayed over and the girls shared a bed after they watched *The Muppet Show*. It was comforting having Kat around.

When she was alone, Heni was afraid of the dark, or rather who might be in the darkness and drew the purple curtains of her bedroom early. Snowball would come to her bottom bedroom window to be let in and out. She'd open the window just long enough for Snowball to go through.

One weekend morning, Heni slept in. When she woke up, her furry friend was not with her. She ran outside to look for her and saw blood on the windowsill and the ground outside her bedroom. A lot of blood. *Snowball must be hurt!* How did she not wake up for her?

Aroha, Klaus and Daniel joined in the search. From the amount of blood, they guessed Snowball must have been injured in a road accident and gone somewhere to die. They looked in all the possible hiding places including the lawnmower catcher in the garage. They went next door and shone a torch under the house. They saw two glowing eyes. Snowball was under Kuini's house.

Aroha crawled under the house and tried to pull Snowball out. Snowball bit Aroha on the finger when she tried to pick her up. It was the first time Snowball had been aggressive with anyone. Somehow making a sling with a sheet, Aroha and Klaus got Snowball out from under the house and carried her home where she was put in a shallow box with the sheet.

Her rear end looked a mess and there was so much blood staining her white fur. Heni stroked her friend's fur and Snowball stayed still in the box, comforted by Heni's touch while they waited for the vet to open.

At the clinic, the vet raised Snowball's tail up. Where her anus used to be, there was a gaping hole where she had been ripped apart. 'Her back is broken,' said the vet. Even if I manage to keep her alive, she will suffer terribly for the rest of her life. She won't be able to walk or go to the toilet properly. She will be in constant pain. I recommend euthanasia.'

Heni went to the waiting room where there was a distinctive smell of vet disinfectant. A motionless Snowball was brought out in the open box. All the way home, Heni cried and petted her fur, knowing that she wouldn't see her friend alive again. Snowball wasn't even a year old. Heni's best friend. Her first euthanasia.

Klaus dug a deep hole in the back garden near the fence below an overhanging tree. Snowball was lying in a cardboard box with a hessian sack over her. Heni watched quietly but did not cry when Klaus filled the hole with dirt. He pressed the dirt down with his boots. When Heni looked up, the sky was dark grey with an intense rainbow in the distance.

The following year a big digger arrived to connect the houses to the town sewage supply. They dug a very deep, narrow ditch from the house to the end of the property where Snowball had been buried. It got steeper and steeper as it descended down to the mains sewer line that was being laid.

Indoors, Heni was baking. Heni loved to bake, especially cakes and desserts. After finishing up a batch of butterfly cupcakes, Heni decided to bake a lemon Madeira cake, Klaus's favourite. She finely grated the zest and squeezed the juice of a lemon. She had used the mixer to cream the sugar and butter together.

Then she cracked an egg into a cup before tipping it into the bowl slowly alternating with flour. She reached for another egg and as she touched it, the top half of the shell broke off revealing something ghastly. There was something black, damp and feathery curled inside the shell. Heni didn't want to open any more eggs in case there were any more nasty surprises. She threw the carton with the remaining eggs in the outside bin then walked to the backyard to see how the digging was progressing.

The digger was now at the end of the section. She ran out pleading, 'Please don't dig Snowball's bones up! She was distressed and didn't want to see her friend as bones. She was now anxious imagining Snowball as bones. Heni was relieved she didn't see Snowball's bones in the huge piles of dirt.

The pipes were laid and the huge trench was soon filled in. Grass soon grew over the dirt seam and Heni resumed practising her gymnastics leaping and tumbling in the back yard.

She often stayed after school to practice gymnastics using apparatus. Her favourite was using the springboard to leap over the vault during practice at school. She was constantly active – both mentally and physically. Aroha said she didn't give either her body or brain a rest.

Shortly after the rotten egg incident, the Hertz family acquired three hens so they always had fresh eggs. Heni could distinguish the hens apart and she and Daniel named them Lemon, Apricot and Butter and taught them to come when their names were called.

Heni's job was to feed and water 'The Saucy Chooks' and to collect their eggs. They became very tame and when Klaus turned over the compost heap revealing rich, dark soil full of earthworms; the hens soon figured out that worms were tasty to eat.

Heni was put off eating eggs on their own after the rotten egg incident but noticed the yolks were deeper yellow than the yolks of store-bought eggs. Marbles, their black and white speckled dog with mismatched coloured eyes got on well with the hens and chewed on chicken poop like chewing gum.

Heni enjoyed supervising the chickens when they were out of their coop having free run of the garden. Klaus fenced off an area with chicken wire and stakes so the chickens could enjoy the sunshine unsupervised as well.

Heni and Daniel arrived back from the movies. Heni was humming the tune to *Rainbow Connection* after they had watched *Kermit the Frog* singing. Heni went to check on the hens.

There was a gap in the chicken wire and feathers everywhere. Heni was distressed. She could only see Apricot. On the ground was an egg without a shell. It was as though someone had cracked an egg directly onto the ground, with the yolk still intact neatly inside the raw egg white. The fence and hedge were tall – surely too tall for a chicken to fly over but perhaps Lemon and Butter had escaped?

She went around the neighbourhood with Daniel. Daniel asked, 'Have you seen our chickens?' A woman looked puzzled but decided to take a look in her back yard on Victoria Street. There on the compost heap, scratching around, was Butter. Heni picked Butter up, tucked her wings in under her arm and walked around the block to take her home. Lemon was never found and was presumed killed by a dog Aroha had seen roaming.

Did Lemon suffer like Snowball? Heni didn't understand suffering and Sunday school and church provided inadequate explanations for it.

Heni had lots of questions at Sunday school after learning about the Noah's Ark Bible story but she was too shy to ask the teacher, so Kat asked on her behalf. They'd been taught that after they die, people can go to Heaven, was supposed to be a very nice place.

Unless they were the people in the Noah's Ark story that God drowned along with nearly all the animals, or they did not obey God. Those people went to Hell which sounded like a terrible place.

'What about animals like cats and dogs and chickens?' Heni whispered to Kat. 'Do they go to heaven?'

Kat asked the Sunday school teacher, Mrs Justice just before they were about to break up for church potluck lunch with casseroles and cold roasted meat, bread and coleslaw.

'Do cats, dogs and chickens go to Heaven?' asked Kat on Heni's behalf.

Mrs Justice replied, 'Animals don't have souls, so they don't go to Heaven.'

No pets in Heaven? Heaven doesn't sound like a very nice place, thought Heni. Heni had more questions but didn't get satisfactory answers. She had difficulty speaking up and speaking out loud, so all her confusion stayed inside her head.

She didn't understand suffering. Even as a young child, it made no sense to her that God would drown nearly everyone because some people ate some fruit from a tree which was only the very first thing they did wrong.

Not long after Lemon died, Kat started missing school again. Aroha told Heni. 'I have some sad news. Kat died this morning.'

Heni was stunned. 'Like Snowball?' she stammered. Snowball had suffered so much. Had Kat? She'd never complained.

'They'll be a funeral for Kat in a few days. Then she'll be buried in a cemetery.' Heni had never been to a cemetery before.

'Did God kill Kat?' Heni had recently read the Bible in full at eight years old. God ordered the killing of a lot of people which Heni found to be terrifying.

'God has taken Kat's soul to Heaven,' replied Aroha.

But there's no pets in Heaven. Why can't she stay here?! It's not fair! The words would no longer come out.

21

'Would you like to see Kat to say goodbye? She looks like she's sleeping.' Heni was already detached from the conversation and was silent and no longer interacting. She was shut down. She didn't see Kat.

The coffin was up the front of the church and Heni sat silently on a pew. She didn't take in any of the words that were said. The strong emotions from other people were so overwhelming that she shut them all out when she sat very still.

She also blocked out unpleasant memories by keeping busy, practising gymnastics with Ava and Daniel. Daniel did very well competitively with gymnastics but Heni was too terrified to go backwards on her own to do a walkover or backflip, so she quit and moved onto several other activities to keep her mind constantly busy. So she didn't have to look back.

Heni liked to play marbles during school breaks. One day after winning some new marbles, she was walking past the toilets going back to class and dropped her marbles, her treasures. They scattered everywhere and other children scrambled excitedly to take them like a lolly scramble. Heni did not show any emotional reaction to watching the children steal the marbles.

When she arrived back to class after losing her marbles, she was glad that the teacher, Mr Knot allowed the students to do art. It was soothing.

She was drawing a picture of a cat, trying to make the ears look realistic. Daniel had shown her how to do ear creases. He was good at drawing. Art, music and patterns helped Heni go into her own little world where there was no pain, no suffering and where pets go to Heaven.

Mr Knot stood at the front of the class to make an announcement. Heni was still drawing.

'Mouse, you won!' the other students were saying excitedly.

'What?' Heni hadn't heard what Mr Knot had said. She was often very quietly elsewhere. Aroha told her she was always daydreaming.

Heni looked up. 'Heni, you won the regional poster competition for the fireworks display,' said Mr Knot.

Heni's prize was a bookshop voucher, tickets to the local fireworks display and a meeting with a well-known local professional artist, Mrs Hutchings. One of the teachers drove Heni to town to have her photo taken for the local newspaper. It was all very strange and confusing. Heni didn't smile for the camera, wearing her blue-grey tracksuit with messy hair.

She met Mrs Hutchings who had dozens of posters pinned to a wall selected as the finalists from hundreds of children from all the participating schools in the region.

'Yours stood out above all the others,' she told Heni. 'Your layout and the colours you used.'

Aroha took Heni to spend her bookshop voucher. Heni picked out an invisible ink book and some fruit-scented felt-tip pens. Brightly coloured felt-tip pens were like treasures in Heni's world. She could draw her patterns to escape whenever she wanted. She also practised piano and violin. She immersed herself in books. It was an effective escape from any uncomfortable feelings and thoughts.

School summer holidays were spent swimming in the lake or the sea. 'Last one in is a rotten egg!' yelled Daniel as he leapt into the water first. 'Mouse is a rotten egg!' he taunted. Earlier that day, Daniel had told Heni excitedly that he had seen Aroha run over a dead mouse with the lawnmower. There were no signs of the mouse in the grass clippings.

'Don't call me Mouse anymore,' said Heni firmly to Daniel. 'My name is Heni.'

3. Broken Wings

Heni made a new friend, Filly. Filly gave Heni a soap with a poem about friendship on it for her twelfth birthday. Klaus took Filly and Heni to ride a rollercoaster. The girls wanted to ride again and again.

'Guess what?' said Filly. 'I've got a boyfriend.'

'Who?'

'Ollie.' Ollie was a quiet boy in class and also was a member of Ava's swimming club.' Ava was one of the fastest swimmers at her club.

When Heni got home from school, she wondered if Ollie would like to have an extra girlfriend. She saw a boyfriend as a good friend who happened to be a boy.

Heni looked Ollie up in the white pages of the chunky telephone book. She dialled the number. Ollie answered.

'Hi, it's Heni,' she said shyly. She wrapped her fingers around the curly telephone cord.

'Filly said you're her boyfriend. Do you want to be my boyfriend too?' Heni didn't see an issue with a boy having two girlfriends. Especially two girls who were good friends.

'Sure, I'll be your boyfriend as well as Filly's boyfriend. That sounds cool.'

'Okay. See you at school tomorrow.'

'Bye.'

Heni hung up. She couldn't wait to tell Filly that they both had the same boyfriend. The following day was mufti day. Heni wanted to look really nice so she wore a red tartan dress with her new shamrock green stockings. She had never seen anyone wear brightly coloured stockings before.

Filly was late to school as she had an appointment. The bell rang for recess and Heni couldn't wait to tell her the news.

Filly had already found out and she was upset. 'You little bitch!' she yelled in front of the other students. 'You rang Ollie!' This was not the reaction Heni was expecting. They'd never had a disagreement before.

Heni started to cry. The other students laughed. 'Heni is a crybaby wearing ugly green stockings!' one of the students mocked. Heni cried all the way home alone. Filly dumped Heni as her best friend and also dumped Ollie. Ollie didn't seem bothered.

Heni took the friendship soap Filly had given her and tearfully used it in the bath. The poem about friendship dissolved in a pile of suds.

A few days later, Filly forgave Heni and they became friends again. 'You used the friendship soap,' didn't you?' she asked.

Ollie gave Heni a gold heart locket with a piece of polished paua shell in the centre of the heart. It had a tiny hinge on one side and the locket opened and closed. 'Paua shell like the colour of your eyes,' he said shyly. He also handed Heni an ice-cream container. Inside was a grass skink he'd caught. Klaus made an enclosure for Heni's new pet lizard, Dino.

Heni and Filly were art monitors preparing materials for art class at recess. Filly had a new boyfriend, Damion, and half a dozen students let themselves in including Ollie. Heni was slicing paper with the guillotine.

The students enthusiastically shuffled Heni to a secluded area by the kiln and art storage materials - an out of bounds area to students. They wanted to see some action.

'Heni, you're going to pash Ollie. I'm going to pash Damion,' announced Filly. Everyone's going to watch.

Filly kissed Damion with lots of tongue. Heni screwed her nose up as it looked so wet and slobbery. Filly laughed triumphantly.

'Your turn.'

The other students grabbed Ollie and Heni by the arms and stood them in front of each other. Heni and Ollie had never made any physical contact before.

'Now pash!' Filly ordered. She pushed Heni towards Ollie. Heni and Ollie looked awkwardly at each other. Heni was too embarrassed to kiss Ollie with everyone watching. Ollie was humiliated and reacted by whacking Heni on the forehead. Heni burst into tears and ran away from the spectators.

'Heni got duuummmpped' the students chanted as she ran away. Their chants seemed to fade into the background as her tears blurred her vision. She opened the door and let it slam behind her. She ran all the way home.

Heni's friendship with Filly was confusing. Sometimes friends, sometimes not. She walked to Filly's house to walk together to school. *Total Eclipse of the Heart* was playing on the radio. Filly went through her mother's handbag and stole money and medication. She emptied the contents of some capsules into a cup then mixed them with water. She offered the cup to Heni. Heni shook her head. Filly swallowed the mixture.

Then Filly filled the water bowl for her family's German Shepherd, Tyler who was chained to the garage. She placed the bowl of water on the ground. Then she kicked Tyler in the chest and laughed. Tyler whimpered and cowered. *Why did you do that?* Heni felt so hurt inside but she couldn't get the words out.

Shortly afterwards, Filly moved away. Heni walked to and from school by herself.

'Heni, wait up!' Daniel ran to catch up. They walked together and noticed a cat on the road on the curve of Victoria Street opposite where Butter the hen had flown over the back fence some years before.

Daniel went up to inspect a cat lying on the road. 'Is it asleep on the road? Maybe it's dead? It might get run over?' The cat was indeed dead but didn't have any obvious injuries. Daniel decided to remove the cat from the road so cars wouldn't run over it. He picked it up.

'It's as stiff as a board,' he said. He dropped the dead, slate-grey cat onto the ground and it made a dull thud and there was a whirl of dust. He stifled a chuckle.

'Hopefully the owners will find it soon,' said Heni.

They walked past a playground next to where Daniel had left the cat. Heni had never seen children play there. She felt uneasy whenever she walked past that park but didn't know why.

'That park gives me the creeps,' said Heni.

'Why?'

'I don't know. It's like something bad has happened to children there.' She didn't know why she felt uneasy.

Ava continued to do well in swimming, representing the school. She was also a very capable horse-rider. Heni continued to visit the farm at regular intervals and became more confident at horse riding.

'Let's do a lifesaving award,' said Ava when the girls were fourteen.

'I dunno. I'm not as good a swimmer as you.'

'You'll be fine. I'll teach you to swim better.'

Heni was very slim and didn't float very well. It was a huge effort for her to swim the distance required for the award. Despite this, with Ava's encouragement, she put the effort in and the girls were ready to be evaluated for their Silver Star Award.

'Would you like to stay on the farm this weekend?' asked Ava.

'Yes, I'll ask.'

The teenagers played music from cassette tapes in Ava's room. *Broken Wings* was playing.

'Did you know my name can mean *bird bird* – so two birds?' said Ava.

'No.'

'Ava means *bird* or *living one*. Manu means *bird* or *butterfly* or *kite* in Maori.'

'My name means *Jane* in Maori. How boring is that? Although I would spell *Jayne* with a *y*.'

'Mum said I have two sets of wings.'

A teardrop prism hanging in the window projected rainbows on the walls. Heni felt relaxed and happy on the farm with Ava.

Kent took Heni for a ride on a trail bike. He sat behind her with his arms on either side also holding the handlebars. Heni felt a current between them when they accidentally touched hands. She had never felt that before.

'Just turn the throttle to go faster,' Kent instructed. 'I'll help you with the gear changes.'

'Whoah,' said Heni, laughing as they neared a grassy wall. 'Look where you want to go,' said Kent, helping her steer away from crashing. That's it.' They picked up speed. Kent and Heni had been glancing and smiling at each other more often lately. Sometimes Heni wondered what it would be like to kiss him. But then she thought that would be weird as he was her best friend's brother.

Mrs Manu was making curried eggs to go with the roasted chicken legs and salad for lunch. She had hollowed the yolks out of boiled eggs and was mixing them with seasonings and mayonnaise ready to pipe back into the egg whites. 'Go feed the horses before we have lunch. Watch out for Storm. She's a bit friskier than normal.'

Heni had only ridden Pegasus before. She was a quieter horse than Storm. The sky was starting to look grey in the distance and there was electricity in the air.

Ava was confident, perhaps overconfident around the horses. She'd walk behind the horses when grooming them.

Heni fed apple wedges and carrots by hand while Ava went into the paddock and filled the feeding troughs. Pegasus seemed more interested and curious than usual and came over into Storm's space just as Ava walked behind her. There was a clash of thunder and Storm kicked out. Her hoof struck Ava in the head and Ava fell back unconscious.

Heni stood frozen staring. Was Ava dead? She tried to run inside or call out for help but she couldn't move. Kent saw what had happened and sprung into action. He yelled out, 'Mum! Ava's hurt!' He shooed the horses into another paddock. He stayed with his sister. 'I'm here,' he said. The rest was a blur as the brand new rescue helicopter service transported Ava to hospital where she was kept in an induced coma.

After she came out of her coma, it would be several weeks before Ava was permitted to have visitors from non-family members. Heni was told Ava had a traumatic brain injury and she would need to learn to talk and walk again.

Heni was assessed for the Silver Star Award on her own, which she passed.

Heni took a flower picked from her garden in a little bottle as a vase to school. At lunchtime she walked to the hospital which was nearby.

Ava was with an occupational therapist and Heni was allowed to say 'hello' briefly. Ava was in a wheelchair and she couldn't sit up straight and her eyes were crossed. She was very thin and looked like she had no control over her body. She was barely recognisable with her shaved head and a scar from Storm's hoof. The occupational therapist was talking to Ava normally and even though she was floppy like a rag doll, she seemed to respond even though she couldn't yet talk.

'Hi Ava,' said Heni. Ava made jerking motions in Heni's direction. Heni sensed she recognised and understood her, even though her body wasn't co-operating. 'I brought a flower for you,' she said putting it on the table. Then she sat quietly and watched the occupational therapist do a few exercises as part of Ava's rehabilitation before Heni had to go back to school.

Ava was very determined and after several months, she started back at school. She was walking, but more stiffly than before. She was no longer cross-eyed after a surgery and her hair had started to grow back, covering her scar. She started gaining back the weight she had dramatically lost. She looked a bit dazed, had jerky movements and couldn't write with her right hand anymore so she learned to write with her left.

After the accident, Ava started having epileptic seizures. She'd fall to the ground and her whole body would convulse and she'd wet herself. Most of the students seemed afraid of her now that she was different to how she was previously. They avoided her. Yet they talked about her behind her back. She was popular previously but now Heni was her only friend.

Ava resumed swimming, although she was no longer fast enough to swim competitively. She also resumed horse-riding, despite her parents' concerns. Riding seemed to be therapeutic and was more natural for her than walking.

Mrs Manu insisted she only ride Pegasus from now on, not Storm. Pegasus seemed to sense when a seizure was coming on and would stop, wait and look back. Ava had a brief aura letting her know she was about to have a seizure, so she'd dismount. Pegasus would wait quietly and nuzzle her face when Ava came to.

Ava was very positive about adjusting to her disabilities. She wasn't allowed to get a driver's licence and she struggled in class and had to repeat a year.

'The hardest thing,' she confided in Heni, 'is when people say "Oh what a pity. She had so much potential. She used to be such a good swimmer. She used to be a top student." People avoid me now but talk about me.'

'You're still a great swimmer. You had to fight to walk and talk again. Your determination is inspiring.'

Heni's favourite subjects at school were science and art.

In science, her teacher Miss Fletcher asked for the curtains to be drawn then she turned out the lights and put a half glass of water on the overhead projector. A full circle rainbow was projected. 'Rainbows are not actually bows. They are circles. But the horizon blocks the view from seeing the full circle.'

Heni arrived to art class early and only a few other students were already there. They were talking about Ava. 'Oh, what a shame. Ava wanted to be a scientist, but she'll never be one now,' said Annette.

'Yes, she's brain-damaged,' said Mrs Sharp.

Stop talking about her like that! She's a person! Heni's fists were clenched and she was screaming inside her head but no words came out. She sat there frozen in silence, her mouth and body not in sync with what was in her head.

Then, still unable to articulate anything, she picked up some paints and vigorously applied them to paper.

'You always paint something different depending on what mood you're in,' said Mrs Sharp, standing behind Heni. *Isn't that the point?* thought Heni, irritable, yet looking outwardly calm. Still no words would come out.

'You're going to have a nervous breakdown one day,' continued Mrs Sharp.

What are you on about? Heni looked at her puzzled.

'It's because you're always so busy, non-stop. Doing extra sessions for your art portfolio, competing in an arts scholarship for music, staying at the top of your classes, busy with swimming and running....' Recently Heni had started running cross-country. She was trying to do something with all the excess energy she had.

'I'm going to have a nervous breakdown because I like to keep busy?' asked Heni, baffled, finally finding some words. She wasn't really sure what a nervous breakdown was but she thought Mrs Sharp was being ridiculous and horrible. She decided then that she wouldn't be taking art further. She had loved art since kindergarten but Mrs Sharp annoyed her. She would be quitting art at the end of the year because of what Mrs Sharp said.

Back at home, Heni climbed up onto the woodshed. She stretched out her arms like wings. She wanted to fly. She leapt off the roof and landed on her feet before rolling onto her side, hugging one leg, saying, 'Ow ow ow – jarred my leg,' while laughing. A shooting pain lingered from her heel up the whole length of one leg. She didn't tell anyone she had jumped off the roof.

After completing school and getting near the top of her classes, Heni was accepted to start a veterinary science degree course.

Kent was working on the farm which had converted to dairy and he started skydiving training. Ava was volunteering to help people with disabilities ride horses. Daniel was doing an electrician's apprenticeship under Klaus.

Heni and Kent's friendship deepened. He confided in Heni how he felt about having dyslexia.

'I felt like a dummy because I had difficulty reading and didn't finish school. You did so well at school. Ava, too, until her accident and then suddenly she was struggling. My greatest achievement is that I can do a back flip on a snowboard.'

'You are also an amazing musician.'

'I can't read music. I just play by ear.'

'You play piano better than just about anyone I know who can read music. I wish I could play drums like you.'

'Really? You want to play drums? I could teach you drumming and you could teach me reading.'

'Deal.'

Kent started giving Heni drumming lessons and then also bass guitar. 'You'd make a great bass woman,' he said. They often played music together.

Heni continued having stirrings of romantic feelings for Kent but she pushed them away. She'd never had romantic feelings for anyone before. There had only been a very mild interest with Ollie but not enough to want physical contact. She had avoided boys since. Experiencing romantic and sexual feelings for the first time made her feel anxious.

She was doing well at university and got A's in her first year. Her mind was sharp and she was readily absorbing information. At the end of her first year, she was presented with a joke award, 'Mouse of the Year.' The other students said it was because she was quiet. They didn't know that her nickname used to be Mouse.

In her second year at university, she seemed bubblier than her usual quiet self. Everything seemed faster. She was sprinting from class to class. Talking faster than usual. She made new friends and debated with lecturers. She was getting good at playing the drums and she was always busy tapping rhythms. It helped discharge the constant energy.

'You're more talkative than usual, but I don't mind listening,' commented Kent. 'I think you're amazing that you have so many interests and you do everything so well.' Sometimes Heni wanted to hug Kent and she wondered what it would be like to rub her hand through his hair, but she held back. She noticed for the first time after several years that his eye colour was actually hazel. They were just good friends, she told herself.

During the mid-year holidays, Kent and Ava invited Heni back to the farm. Kent and Heni rode trail bikes across the farm to the top of a hill that overlooked the sea. They sat down to chat. They were making more eye contact and smiling and laughing more.

Kent leaned across and kissed Heni. Her first kiss. She felt excited, then anxious.

She pushed Kent away. 'What did you do that for?!' snapped Heni.

'What did I do wrong?' Kent was confused. Heni was irritable.

'We are not going out. Okay?!'

Heni got back on the bike and rode back to the farmhouse. She was very quiet and distracted and avoided Kent. She wanted to go home. When she got home, she hid in her room as much as possible.

'What's wrong?' asked Aroha. Heni wasn't herself. Intrusive thoughts had been bothering her since Kent kissed her. She was noticeably anxious. Horrible memories were tormenting her.

Heni was quiet at dinner, trying to shut it all down.

'Michaela is pregnant and unmarried. A huge disappointment to her parents. Gone off the rails,' Aroha said in a judgemental tone. 'I hope you're not going to go off the rails.' Michaela was Kat's younger sister who had been at high school but had since left now that she was pregnant.

Church had been part of Heni's life since she was very young. Aroha listed other young people from church who were 'going off the rails' because they were 'living in sin' or pregnant as unmarried teenagers. Heni imagined herself on a rollercoaster falling off said rails. Her mind was racing with confusion but she didn't say anything at dinner. She definitely wasn't herself.

She held herself together until she got to the sleep-out, then burst into tears. She was overwhelmed with foreign thoughts and feelings. She needed someone to talk to but didn't feel she could tell Aroha how she was feeling. She called Michaela.

While she was waiting for Michaela, she heard a strange noise outside. She turned on the light and saw a hedgehog burrowing in the dirt outside.

'Michaela, I don't know what's wrong with me,' Heni said, sobbing. 'My head's all confused and I feel like getting drunk and having sex with a stranger.' Heni had never been drunk before. She had only tasted wine once and she had felt sleepy. She avoided thinking about sex – she shut down even the tiniest thoughts about sex. It had been taught in church that thinking about sex was the same as doing it. Her first kiss had made her freak out. She'd never wanted to lose control. She didn't want her parents to disapprove of her.

'My parents are very disappointed with me,' said Michaela. They threatened to disown me but seem to be coming round now. I'm going to run home and get something for you.' Michaela returned a few minutes later holding a framed poster of a kitten clinging to a rope with its hind legs dangling. 'Hang in there,' she said, giving the poster to Heni.

Heni felt comforted by Michaela accepting her and not judging her but she still felt tense and had difficulty sleeping. She had developed a migraine and was off her food. She tried to lie down but was constantly restless. Distressing images kept flashing through her head.

'I think you need to go to church and have deliverance,' said Aroha, in her judgemental tone. 'This looks like demonic activity.'

'Resist the devil and read your Bible,' added Klaus.

Heni felt hurt that her parents believed she was possessed by demons. She just wanted to be loved and understood, not condemned. She was too exhausted to pray and resist the devil. She didn't understand what was happening to her.

Terrified and feeling tortured, she decided to tell Aroha and Klaus what was distressing her. She felt so ashamed but couldn't keep it in any longer. She had horrible images going through her mind. Distressing memories. She spoke with urgency and pain in her voice.

'Remember when you went ballroom dancing and a teenage boy with ginger hair babysat me? Around the time Snowball died. I've blanked out his name and his face apart from his smile. His sister was Deborah and his mother was Nancy Nixon. Nancy was a netball and basketball coach. They lived on the bend of Victoria Street where the grey cat as stiff as a board was, that Daniel and I found. Their house was down a long drive next to the park. I've been to their house. Deborah and her brother had insulin vials for diabetes.'

'What about it?' asked Aroha with a suspicious tone of voice.

It was very tense and Heni was distressed and felt ashamed, but she told her parents what she remembered. She was talking fast and crying.

'He offered to read me a story so I felt happy and climbed into his lap. He was smiling then he unzipped his jeans and pulled out his penis. He made me play with his penis. I didn't know what it was and I thought his erection was silly so I laughed. He took me to the bedroom and told me to take off my panties so he could look at me. He smiled in a weird way and I felt scared and whispered, "I'm going to tell Mummy". He said "Don't tell Mummy. It's our little secret." We played hangman and I couldn't guess the "X" in "SEX". Daniel was there for the hangman game but I don't remember where he was for the rest of it.'

Klaus and Aroha had stern looks.

'It was only one time! It wasn't that bad!' exclaimed Aroha.

'I think he's dead now anyway,' added Klaus.

Heni felt like they both acknowledged her memories were true yet dismissed her at the same time. She felt very distressed and didn't feel heard.

'What's his name and how did he die? How old was I? How old was he?' Was he in his late teens? I've blanked out his name and his face but I can remember strange details.'

'It doesn't matter,' said Aroha. 'Forgive and forget'.

Aroha and Klaus were irritable and wouldn't tell her any information that they knew. Heni was upset they seemed so dismissive.

'Why wait to tell us after all of these years?' asked Klaus.

'I buried it. It came up and I felt ashamed,' replied Heni.

'Well bury it again,' said Aroha.

In her distress, Heni asked Klaus, 'Why didn't you hug me? If you'd hugged me, maybe it wouldn't have happened!' Klaus started to cry. It was the only time Heni had seen Klaus cry. He told Heni he'd always found it hard to give and receive affection as he'd been a child in Germany during the war and his family had been unaffectionate. His stoic family was about survival, not affection.

Heni was so anxious, she lost a lot of weight in a short time and her ribs were protruding. She couldn't sleep and was constantly restless. It felt like her whole world was cracking apart. Aroha said it was a nervous breakdown and she could be healed if she went to a certain visiting pastor. The pastor ordered that demonic spirits were cast out of Heni, but this made her feel worse. She felt misunderstood and unloved. Friends abandoned her. She started to question her faith in God.

Heni's brain had always been so sharp but now she could no longer focus when she tried to go back to university. The buildings seemed to loom down at her, screaming 'Failure!' Unable to concentrate on her studies, she quit. The doctor wrote 'Decompensation state' on the medical certificate for her to withdraw from her studies. He did not investigate Heni's mental health further or give her any information about what was happening to her.

Aroha kept insisting that God would heal her if only she believed hard enough. Heni was exhausted yet she was getting into arguments with Aroha.

She was still going to church occasionally but felt disillusioned. She felt so alone, curled up in the foetal position on the floor of her bedroom, crying out to God. But there was no answer to her desperate pleas. She confided in a young woman from church that she wanted to die. 'If you kill yourself, you'll go straight to hell,' said the young woman. Heni felt she couldn't tell anyone how she really felt. She had to bottle it up, stuff it down.

She was tempted to open the case of wine leftover from Daniel's wedding and drink straight from the bottle. To try to sleep, as she remembered how sleepy she had felt with just a few sips the one time she had tried wine.

Her despair was deeper when her period was due. 'I hate being a woman,' she sobbed to herself in the shower. In a few days, she would be bleeding heavily. She went to the doctor, asking if anything could be done. He said a contraceptive pill should help.

He also diagnosed her with haemorrhoids that had emerged since her since her breakdown. Heni was a bit embarrassed when he asked to see her bottom. 'If it makes you feel better, I've seen hundreds of rear ends,' said the doctor. He prescribed an ointment.

Heni felt very unwell starting the contraceptive pill. She tried starting a job. A few weeks later, she quit as she was crying and couldn't concentrate.

She didn't see Kent and Ava for several months. She didn't want them to see her this way. No longer smiling. No longer achieving. A university dropout. Can't keep a job. She felt like a huge disappointment to her family and to herself.

What gave her slight relief from her pain was to ride her bicycle to the lake or to the river and sit and watch the patterns in the ripples of the water. Away from traffic and people. She sat there with a journal and wrote poems. Poetry that didn't rhyme and that she kept to herself. She was very quiet and solitary.

Months went by and then she enrolled in a veterinary nurse course, despite lacking the focus and drive that she previously had. She was determined to work with pets somehow, even if it wasn't her childhood dream to become a veterinarian.

4. Cracked Pot

Heni had been sleeping a lot while trying to keep up with her veterinary nurse studies. Still low in energy and quieter than usual, Heni finally met up with Ava.

'Kent told me what happened,' said Ava. 'He didn't mean to upset you. He really likes you and I know you like him.'

'I do like him. I freaked out. It's weird starting to have feelings that are more than for a friend. I've never had those kinds of feelings before.' Heni told Ava about how distressed she was when she remembered the abuse.

'I'm so sorry you went through that,' said Ava.

'Please don't tell Kent.'

'I won't. You can tell him yourself if and when you're ready. It might help him understand your reaction though. Perhaps the attraction you shared triggered memories of the abuse?'

'Maybe? I don't know what's wrong with me. After cracking apart, I've had no energy.'

'You've definitely become withdrawn. I'm glad we're talking again even if it feels like your emotions are all confused.'

'I don't think I have the energy to see Kent. It's hard for me to even put on a smile. I don't want anyone to touch me.'

'You do what's right for you. Shall I let Kent know that you're not ready to date him?'

'I'm not ready to date anyone.'

'So you'd be okay if Kent dates someone else?'

'I guess. I can't stop him living his life just because I feel screwed up.'

Heni focused on completing her veterinary nurse qualifications despite her low mood. She heard that Kent had a girlfriend. She wished it had been her but she was chronically exhausted. It was a struggle to get out of bed. She had never been so extremely fatigued in her life. In body and mind.

She started a job at a veterinary clinic. On the first day of work, the smell of the disinfectant suddenly seemed to intensify and Heni's senses felt overwhelmed. Feeling panicked, she ran outside to the carpark, gasping for air. Her heart was pounding hard and she felt like she was going to throw up.

'Why did you bolt like that?' asked her new employer, Dr Bruce Davies. Heni tried to explain but she was confused herself as to what had happened.

'You're such a weirdo. I can't believe I've hired such a scatterbrain,' said Bruce with disdain. 'You'll be lucky to last out your three-month trial.'

Heni wondered if what Bruce said was true, because her brain no longer functioned as it used to. Bruce made daily insults, mainly of Heni's personality and intelligence, which made her feel more anxious, and then her mind would go blank when asked a question so she would believe that she was incompetent.

Heni put on a smile even when she felt low. It was exhausting wearing a mask, smiling and being pleasant to people. But on her way home, on her little blue scooter, she had to fight back an extreme urge to throw herself on the road and be run over. She arrived home, crying, unable to shake the intrusive thoughts.

Kent broke up with his girlfriend. He wanted to see Heni and even though Heni wanted to keep him at a distance, they started talking again. Gradually, Heni started to feel a bit more like herself, although her brain was no longer the same since the breakdown.

She felt like her memory was gone – everything she'd learned seemed to be forgotten. And everything that she wanted to forget, she could remember. Eventually, she started to feel more up to social contact instead of isolating herself.

Kent joked around a lot but only sometimes briefly showed a serious side. He told Heni about how he struggled at school because of his dyslexia. 'The reading recovery teacher wouldn't help me. I overheard her saying that I was a "cracked pot" and not to "waste resources" on me.'

'That's terrible,' said Heni.

'So I became the class clown. If teachers thought of me as a cracked pot, I figured I may as well crack jokes and smoke pot. I only turned up to school to socialise.'

'You've been making great progress with reading and writing.'

'You're an awesome teacher. I had a crush on you for years but you were so smart at school that I thought you would never see me as more than a friend.'

'You and Ava have always been important to me. Guess I'm a late bloomer. I don't even know how to flirt to save myself.'

'Oh, I think you may do it without your realising it. There's something about your smile.'

'We both like to improvise with music. You've been helping me turn my poems into song. You're a natural.'

'Not A natural. B natural. Get it? Just don't B flat. You're definitely not flat,' he added, glancing teasingly at Heni's chest.

'You can B sharp which is C. See?'

'Yeah, I can see alright. Looking fine. Maybe you can become a naturalist?' Kent winked.

'*That'll be the Day,*' replied Heni with a common phrase which also happened to be a song title. Kent launched into song, clowning around. Kent had the ability to remember song lyrics from many different eras and genres.

In addition to being a talented musician, Kent enjoyed adrenaline-filled outdoor activities. Kent qualified as a tandem master and invited Heni to do a skydive with him. 'Why would anyone want to jump out of a perfectly good aeroplane?' Heni asked, smiling. She was smiling more when with Kent.

'How about a bungy jump then?' asked Kent.

Heni figured that at least with bungy jumping she had more of a chance of survival if the bungy cord detached from around her legs than if a parachute failed.

She hadn't enjoyed herself for a long time, so she agreed to it. On top of a bridge, she stretched her arms out like a bird flying, just like the time she leapt off the roof of the woodshed. Then she let herself fall forwards and bounced upside down on the bungy cord. She nearly lost her top in the process, exposing her bra.

'Nice lingerie,' joked the man who pulled her into the boat on the river.

She felt exhilarated as the adrenaline surged through her body and she walked with a grin on her face up the several flights of stairs to meet Kent.

Along with all the fun adventures, there would be times when Heni and Kent would talk about deeper issues.

'I'm sorry I freaked out when you kissed me for the first time. I've been sexually abused and the memories came back,' she said.

'Thank you for telling me. Sorry you went through that. We can take things at your pace. If you feel uncomfortable at all, we can stop,' said Kent.

Heni started to feel safer with physical intimacy with Kent but she couldn't completely relax. Kent adored her and she started to let down her guard slightly but the hypervigiliance and aversion to touch persisted. She was always on guard with physical intimacy such as kissing. Always ready to run away. Her muscles wouldn't relax. Her mind wouldn't relax. She both simultaneously desired it and was fearful of it. She started to enjoy holding hands and sensual kissing.

Heni had loved Kent and Ava as treasured friends for years, yet falling in love with Kent felt terrifying. Heni's moods were like bouncing up and down on the bungy jump. Elated, then irritable, melancholic with crying. Her moods and conflicted emotions became like a non-stop rollercoaster when they started having sex.

Heni had been indoctrinated in her teens to stay a virgin until she married. Pastors had used analogies of women being like used chewing gum if they had sex with more than one person or sex before marriage. The same judgements did not seem to apply to men.

Heni avoided going to church because of judgemental attitudes from people in the congregation. It hurt being told she was demon possessed. Some people from church also said that Kent wasn't a 'true' Christian. Kent said he didn't see a problem with sex before marriage. Kent adored Heni yet he said he wasn't in a hurry to get married.

Kent gave Heni rainbow rose buds on her birthday. He also bought home a bottle of Rosé wine. Heni had never been drunk because she didn't want to lose control or be sick.

As they sipped wine together listening to music, Heni went into a trance with the song *White Wedding*. After less than half a glass of wine. Heni kissed down Kent's neck to his chest then towards his navel.

'Are you sure?' asked Kent.

Heni wasn't sure. She had internal conflict from the beliefs she'd been raised with plus her past trauma. Right now, she felt so terribly lonely despite being with her best friend. Tears streamed down her face as she pleasured him but Kent didn't realise that Heni was crying because of the low lighting.

They continued with intercourse. Penetration hurt and tears continued to stream down her face. Even though she loved Kent, sex did not feel enjoyable. It was like she wasn't really there. The emotion she felt was overwhelming sadness. She stuffed that emotion down as she didn't want to upset Kent by giving the impression that she didn't like sex.

The next day they drove to the beach and ate fish and chips. Kent bumped into his ex-girlfriend, Lacey, who was wearing a bikini. There was overt flirtatious exchange between Kent and Lacey. Heni simmered quietly while feeling like scratching Lacey's eyes out. She hated the unfamiliar intense feelings of jealousy that steamed inside her. Kent didn't seem to respect that sex needed to be meaningful for her. Had she made a mistake?

When they were alone, her jealousy erupted to the surface and she had an irritable outburst at Kent. Kent was apologetic. He was besotted with Heni. Even though she was deeply in love with him, she was frequently crying but didn't know why. She tried to keep her tears to herself as she didn't want to upset him.

Heni and Kent moved in together, despite objections from Heni's family. Her family were opposed to 'living in sin.'

'My parents are happy for us to be together whether we are married or not,' said Kent. 'We'll get married if and when we're both ready. We're too young for marriage and children.'

'I wish my parents weren't so uptight about it,' said Heni.

Heni was still crying frequently after they moved in together but now she was unable to hide it.

'I don't know what's wrong with me,' she sobbed. She managed to mask her low mood at work but when she got home, the tears flowed.

'I'm taking you to my doctor,' said Kent. 'We need to sort this out.'

Kent went along to Heni's visit. Dr Kyle said, 'You have clinical depression. Most likely for years. I'm going to prescribe an antidepressant. It may take weeks before you start to feel a difference. Take a month off work to rest.'

After getting past side effects such as nausea, Heni started to feel like she had more energy.

Kent was very patient and helped Heni feel more comfortable with intimate touch. Heni discovered that she enjoyed massages. Massages felt sensual but didn't have to be sexual. Instrumental music, especially the piece, *The Rain Must Fall* by *Yanni,* helped Heni go into a trance to feel relaxed enough to receive intimate touch. Perhaps it was the strong back beat, her favourite instruments of piano, drums and bass guitar. It calmed her and took her out of her constant state of hypervigilance temporarily.

Kent didn't pressure her to continue on from a massage to sex and he respected her wishes when Heni wanted to stop. Heni felt safe with Kent. Gradually she learned to enjoy sex but she couldn't fully let go.

Kent arrived home with a black puppy. 'What shall we call her?' he asked.

'What about Zoey? Zoey means life', said Heni.

Zoey went to a puppy class led by a retired police dog handler, Todd. Then she progressed to obedience training classes.

'I don't like that,' whispered Kent to Heni when Todd gave Zoey a firm leash correction when she was learning to heel, which was walking with her shoulder close to the handler's left leg. Todd had taken the leash from Heni because he said her attempts at corrections had been too hesitant. Todd popped the leash firmly. Zoey vocalised with a 'yip' after the correction by Todd.

'It's because she was startled', said Todd. After that initial correction, Zoey needed very few corrections with only a light touch and she didn't vocalise again. The training was mostly reward-based and included food, praise, play and affectionate touch.

A long-line with set up distractions was used as an intermediate step before advancing to off-leash. Food was quickly phased out when it was used. Zoey was taught both word commands and hand signals. Zoey loved playing fetch with a toy that bounced in all directions.

Heni practised training Zoey including heeling on and off-leash while changing directions frequently so that Zoey was focussed on her. Then, after a few minutes of training exercises, she released her to play her favourite game again. This is what Todd had instructed Heni to do. To keep rewarding her with more play after signalling her 'recall' which was a hand signal or command to 'come'.

Zoey was very reliable with her recall and Heni and Kent enjoyed taking her to the beach, the creek and the park. Zoey came running immediately with either the words 'Zoey, come,' or a sweeping hand signal. She sat in front of Heni, attentive until released with a word or hand signal.

Zoey enjoyed a lot of freedom, going on holiday with Kent and Heni all around New Zealand. They stayed in camping grounds and pet-friendly hotels. Training Zoey to pee on command was very handy before ferry trips and for a urine sample for the vet.

Zoey was affectionate and gentle. She slept in her own bed and jumped onto Heni and Kent's bed each morning and gave them kisses.

Even though Zoey was so reliable, Heni put her leash back on around busy roads. Just in case something went wrong. Zoey had been trained to 'wait' or 'down' at different distances and in distracting environments and this was practised with all her walks.

Zoey was now a year old with long legs, floppy ears and a glossy black coat. Heni clipped on Zoey's leash before they exited Queen's park to cross a busy road after an evening walk. Zoey was walking calmly beside her and Heni noticed a grass verge had stakes with string and plastic tied to it. The plastic was flapping in the wind.

Then, Zoey did something she had never done before. She leaped into the air like she was spooked. They made it home but something didn't seem right. She told Kent what had happened.

Heni was making dinner and Zoey was with Kent. Heni was jolted out of her dream-like state by Kent calling out.

'Heni! Something's wrong with Zoey!'

Heni ran into the lounge. Zoey was thrashing around crashing into things. She was frothing at the mouth.

'She's having a seizure,' said Heni. Heni grabbed the phone and called the after-hours vet.

She tried to explain to the vet what had happened. Kent started crying. He said Zoey was still and he thought she had died. Then Zoey leapt to her feet and barked at Kent like she didn't recognise him and saw him as a threat.

The vet, Dr Marsha Adams confirmed that Zoey was having a seizure but further investigation was needed. Even though Heni had encountered pets with seizures before, Dr Adams reminded Heni to speak calmly when Zoey came to as she would be unaware of where she was at first, so she might react aggressively when disorientated.

Zoey exhaled heavily as she came back to the present. Kent went to finish cooking dinner while Heni gently talked to her. Zoey lifted her head, looked up at Heni like she was asking 'What happened?' then her head dropped back to the floor and she fell into a deep sleep. Then she got up, went outside and ate her own dog poop.

Zoey continued to have seizures and Dr Adams confirmed a diagnosis of canine epilepsy. Zoey started on medication but she did not respond well and continued to have seizures. Like Ava, Zoey knew when they were coming on. She'd seek out Heni in a disorientated state before she started thrashing. Sometimes she'd take a chunk out of her lip or nose if she had seizures on concrete surfaces. Then, when she'd recover, she'd go looking to see if there was any dog poop to eat.

Kent said, 'I find it more distressing when Zoey has seizures than when Ava does. I think it's because she shows all her teeth and jerks so violently that she climbs up the wall. It makes her look like she's possessed.'

'She's not possessed,' said Heni. 'Just like Ava's not possessed. She has a neurological disorder. It was upsetting when people told me I was possessed for having depression.'

Even though she was still in her twenties, Heni's haemorrhoids became much worse. There was a lot of blood every time Heni went to the toilet so she was sent to a specialist surgeon, Dr Lance Hackett. 'You have three large internal haemorrhoids which will need surgery,' said Dr Hackett.

Heni was too embarrassed to tell her workplace the reason for her surgery, so she didn't specify what the surgery was for. Dr Hackett instructed her to apply for six weeks off work to recover post-surgery.

Heni told Aroha she was having surgery soon.

'But you haven't given birth yet,' said Aroha. 'How can you have haemorrhoids? You're only young. Are you constipated?'

'No, I've never been constipated. I get diarrhoea at times,' said Heni.

As she was waking from general anaesthetic, still under the influence of morphine, she became aware of clanging noises, a peg on her fingertip and something on top of her puffing up. 'It's just a warming blanket,' said a nurse, noticing she was waking up. 'Your blood pressure was low.'

Later, when she was fully awake, Dr Hackett told her, 'We had to remove a lot more tissue than expected.' She was sent home the same day of the surgery with a cocktail of medications.

She was back that evening though, for more morphine as the spasms were extremely painful. Like a leg cramp but more intense, very painful and concentrated in the anus.

The first time Heni tried to go to the toilet, she felt like she was trying to pass shards of glass the size of dinner plates. Excruciatingly painful. She screamed. Kent came running into the bathroom then retched over the sink as it smelt so awful. Diarrhoea mixed with medications. Heni collapsed onto the floor, faint, with her heart beating fast and shallow. She was in shock.

Perhaps it was a reaction to the medications but Heni soon started vomiting too. She felt like she was being torn apart each time she tried to go to the toilet. She could detect on her own breath a smell like nail polish remover as she burned up all her fat stores from her already slim frame.

She talked to Dr Hackett on the phone and he was concerned that if the vomiting and diarrhoea didn't stop, she would have an electrolyte imbalance. She was unable to keep down electrolyte solutions.

A week after the surgery, she was lying in bed in extreme pain that the pain killers couldn't take the edge off. She was very thin and felt faint. Very weak, she phoned Kent, 'I love you,' she whispered. 'I don't think I'm going to wake up.'

A song was playing on the radio in another room that she hadn't heard before: *Fly Away*. As the song played it seemed to become louder and completely immerse her as she went into a trance and felt herself lift up high outside her body, floating away from the pain. She was barely conscious but the dissociation eased the pain more than the morphine did. She drifted in and out of consciousness.

Heni was rushed back to hospital by ambulance. Inside the hospital, she was too weak to acknowledge Dr Hackett. Dr Hackett barked orders for urgent blood tests for electrolytes. Then Heni started trembling and went into cardiac arrest.

When she woke up, she was receiving intravenous fluids of saline and potassium. 'I feel revived,' she said to the nurse. She had lost a lot of weight and was still in pain, but she felt very much alive. She went on to suffer months of severe pain going to the toilet.

In her postsurgery follow up, she asked Dr Hackett, 'Why didn't you tell me it would hurt so much?' She felt like her bottom had been ripped apart, like Snowball.

'In case you were too afraid to go to the toilet,' Dr Hackett replied. 'Nearly everyone has a painful time the first few times they poop after the surgery. Two out of five people have pain for an extended time.'

'I think I would have put up with the damned haemorrhoids with all the bleeding if I had known how painful it would be.'

'I've been told going to the toilet after surgery is like a poker red hot hedgehog – going backwards,' said Dr Hackett calmly.

'Yes, that's a good description of what it felt like. I had a look in the mirror. My anus looks weird.'

'It's not like it's going to be on display, is it?' said Dr Hackett with a smile.

After the surgery, Heni struggled with depression. She pushed Kent away and felt like he was smothering her when he was trying to show he cared. It really hurt him when she told him she didn't know if they were meant to be together and if she still loved him. People at work noticed her dramatic weight loss. She struggled at work. Euthanasias were particularly hard to deal with – so much death.

The doctor put her back on antidepressants and suggested a relationship counsellor. The counsellor said it was usual for couples to go through a period of disillusionment after initial infatuation. Heni was restless with more energy after starting back on antidepressants. She started several new hobbies at once and was thinking about a career change.

Kent arrived home with chocolates in the shape of rose buds covered with red foil.

'They're beautiful...I'm so sorry I hurt you,' said Heni. 'I don't know why I pushed you away when I was in so much pain.'

'I understand,' said Kent. 'Let's go for a walk by the lighthouse with Zoey.'

Kent and Heni enjoyed walking in nature and there were plenty of places in New Zealand were Zoey was allowed to go. Sometimes Kent took his ukelele and they sang together.

They walked past the lighthouse and sat on the top of the rocks where they could see and hear the waves crashing below them.

Kent played the ukulele and sang *Truly Madly Deeply* with much expression. It was hard for Heni to make eye contact with anyone, but she reciprocated with Kent.

When he finished singing, Kent held Heni's hand and said, 'When you nearly died, I realised that I could not live without you. I don't want to lose you. Heni Victoria Hertz, will you marry me?'

'Yes, of course I will.'

Kent presented Heni with an engagement ring he'd chosen. 'It's rose gold with a star-cut diamond,' said Kent. For the most beautiful star under the Southern Cross.'

They decided to get married the coming summer, on New Year's Day on Kent's parent's farm.

Ava agreed to be Heni's bridesmaid and Daniel agreed to be Kent's best man. Heni chose medium purple-blue for Ava's bridesmaid dress like the colour of forget-me-nots with pink rose buds as bouquets. Aroha was delighted to be making the dresses. Ever since Heni was a little girl, Aroha had talked about her dream for Heni to become a bride.

Heni was accepted into an introductory graphic design course which would be completed just before the wedding. She'd been continuously ground down by Bruce but now she felt like she had a way out. Previously Bruce had called her stupid because she didn't complete her veterinarian degree and because he didn't like the way Heni expressed herself when she was speaking. 'You rabbit on and don't get to the point!' he said when Heni was talking. Heni was either very quiet or very chatty. There was not much in between. Since going back onto anti-depressants, Heni was very talkative.

Bruce said he'd like a plaque on a dedicated carpark space with 'Dr Bruce Davies - Senior Veterinarian.'

'Gold-plated?' asked Heni. Some of the other staff stifled a giggle.

Bruce looked flustered. His face expression seemed to say *How dare you mock me!* He looked disgusted with Heni. 'You stupid, stupid, stuuuu-pid girl!' he sneered, stomping his feet. The other staff stopped to watch.

Instead of feeling intimidated like she usually did, Heni started to laugh. Bruce had no power over her anymore. He looked ridiculous having a tantrum like a two-year-old.

'Get into my office!' ordered Bruce.

'I'm not going into your office for you to yell at me in private,' replied Heni. She felt empowered standing up to him.

Bruce turned around, stalked to his office and slammed the door.

'He said you were a mouse. You're definitely not a mouse,' said Dr Jeff Hart, another vet. Heni had never told them her nickname used to be Mouse or about the 'Mouse of the Year' award at university.

'Why a mouse?' asked Heni.

'Because you were so quiet. He was also against giving you the job because you are a young woman and he thought you'd leave to have kids.'

'This mouse has bite,' replied Heni. 'And I'm going to leave without having kids.' Then she handed in her notice.

Heni enjoyed the graphic design course while she was preparing for the wedding. She applied to go back to university, this time to study graphic design.

She also borrowed cassette tapes from the library to teach herself how to speak German, Spanish and Maori. She read books on numerous subjects and she decided to take up painting again for the first time since she had quit art at school. She enrolled in a summer oil painting class.

5. Depth that Varies

'Did you realise it was my birthday today?' Heni asked Kent.

'Oh, crap. I'm always in the shit…it's just the depth that varies,' joked Kent. 'I'll make it up to you. I promise.' Kent had been distracted with work.

Somehow the conversation steered towards cemeteries.

'If I die before you, don't put me in a cemetery,' said Heni.

'Why not?'

'I dunno. Can't stand the places. Give me the creeps.' Heni could only remember going to a cemetery one time to visit Kat's grave.

'What do you want me to do with you instead?'

'Cremate me and sprinkle me somewhere in nature, near some water perhaps?'

'What if I put you in a cemetery?'

'I'll come back and haunt you.'

'When I die, I'll come back as a bee.'

Kent gave Heni a late birthday present. A pair of deliberately mismatched earrings. One was a jandal in yellow and the other was a high heel in pink.

'These are cool,' said Heni.

'I can't believe my aunt Edna is your art teacher,' said Kent. 'I call her 'the purple people-eating monster,' because she only wears purple and she's as nutty as a fruitcake. She needs to be in the loony bin.'

'Do you think I should be in a loony bin too?'

'Of course not. Sorry, that was so insensitive of me. Sometimes I get carried away with my jokes.'

At the class, Edna was wearing purple.

'Circles and sausages…everything can be drawn as circles and sausages… there are no straight lines in nature,' shrilled Edna as she plonked a dried-up cow's skull on the table as a subject for a still life. 'There is no pure white in nature either…white is really shades of cream, beige and grey'.

Heni squinted her eyes at the skull. She didn't like skulls. They reminded her that something had died. But Edna was right – she could see several shades other than white – including pale purple and pale pink.

Edna seemed to notice Heni's new earrings. 'There are jandals people and there are high heels people,' she said in a snobby voice. 'If you know what I mean.'

Heni wasn't quite sure what she meant other than she seemed to imply that people who wore high heels were better than people who wore jandals. Heni rarely wore high heels. She considered them to be modern foot torture devices. She preferred comfort over style.

'In the new year we will have life models,' announced Edna. 'Two male models and then two female models'.

Heni told Kent about the art class and that she was disappointed that she was going to miss out on the male life models as they would be on their honeymoon. She had never painted nudes before.

'You're just disappointed you're not going to paint their circles and sausages,' quipped Kent. Don't worry, I'll be more than happy to pose as your nude model anytime you want.'

They went to a restaurant, *Twin Flames*, the following night to celebrate Heni's birthday.

'One of your earrings is missing,' said Kent.

Heni touched her earlobes and took out a lone jandal earring. 'Oh, no, I've lost the high heel.'

Heni struggled to finish her meal then excused herself to go to the toilet. She had been feeling nauseous recently. When she arrived back at the table, she was very quiet and wanted to go home before their desserts arrived.

'You were gone a long time,' said Kent. The colour was gone from Heni's cheeks. They went home.

'Are you okay, Heni?' asked Kent. 'You can talk to me, okay?'

'I think I had a miscarriage at the restaurant,' said Heni in almost a whisper.

'Are you sure?'

'No, I'm not sure. I've been feeling unwell and my period was late and it's never late. Then I had all this cramping at the restaurant and started bleeding.'

'Could you do a pregnancy test?'

'I was going to but there's no point now. If I was pregnant, I'm pretty sure I'm not now. There was a lot of blood in the toilet.'

'Do you feel sad?'

'I don't know what to feel. I feel nothingness. I don't even know for sure if I was pregnant. How can I feel sad about losing a baby that might not have even existed? I don't want to talk about it anymore, okay?'

'Okay.' Kent rubbed Heni's back and then left her alone. Heni was quiet and withdrawn for several days before focussing on the wedding again.

Zoey's seizures continued to get worse. Longer in duration and intensity. Medication had failed to control them. A week before Christmas, Zoey had twelve seizures in less than 24 hours. She was so exhausted, that she couldn't even turn her paws up to stand. She was in a state of collapse.

Heni and Kent pulled her onto the bed and held her while she whimpered. She was in distress.

Heni phoned the vet.

'It's time,' Dr Adams said. 'When they are continuous like this, we can't stop them.' Heni already knew that.

Heni had found it very hard to deal with euthanasia when she was a vet nurse but she had kept her emotion inside. But now with Zoey, her tears were flowing. Kent was crying too. He carried Zoey to the car and then into the veterinary clinic. Zoey was whining constantly.

57

Kent carried Zoey and lay her down on the consultation table. Zoey tried to lift her head despite being exhausted. Dr Adams injected a needle into a vein in Zoey's leg. Zoey slumped within seconds into Heni's arms. Then she was gone.

On Christmas Eve, Heni and Kent went to a beach where Zoey used to swim in the sea. Heni scattered Zoey's ashes and said, 'Wherever there is water, I will remember you. Be free, my beautiful girl.'

A week later, Kent and Heni were strapped together in a small aeroplane, with the coastline visible below.

'Are you ready?' asked Kent.

'Now or never, right?' replied Heni, nervous with excitement.

'I've got your back,' yelled Kent as they were in the doorway about to exit the aeroplane.

Heni planned to change into the bridal gown Aroha had painstakingly made once they landed. Plus tidy up her hair a bit – she wanted her hair pinned up with some loose curls around the front without too much fuss.

'I love you!' shouted Kent as they leapt out of the plane. Heni would have shouted 'I love you back,' but she was too busy screaming as they hurtled towards Earth during her first ever skydive. If only the descent would slow down so she could take time to admire the view of the coastal farm were they were to be married.

The ground was getting scarily closer and the chute hadn't opened. This was more terrifying than falling in love.

'Fuck!' shouted Kent. *What's wrong?*

There was a flapping of fabric as the main chute was cut away. Kent had deployed the reserve chute but they were still falling fast. The reserve chute was tangled and didn't fully open.

'I'm sorry Heni. I love you.'

Then Heni was in brownish-green liquid, trying not to drown, while being pulled under from behind. She tried to stand up but the sludge was like quicksand pulling her under. She could hear shouting but only faintly, like in a far-off dream. Then she blacked out.

She woke up in hospital, heavily sedated. Aroha was crying. Klaus looked worried but held back tears. 'What happened?' she asked groggily.

'Your chute didn't open properly,' said Klaus, holding back emotion as he usually did. 'You landed in an oxidation pond.'

She started to remember now, it was her wedding day. 'Where's Kent?' she asked hesitantly.

Aroha and Klaus said nothing.

'What's wrong? Is Kent okay?'

Aroha started to sob. Klaus started crying too. It was rare for Klaus to cry.

'We're sorry love, but Kent drowned.'

What? Drowned? In cow shit?

It was too much to comprehend. Heni shut down.

She sat staring without expressing emotion and without speaking.

Then after a break, Aroha and Klaus had more bad news.

'Heni, Ava died too. She had a seizure shortly after Kent's death and died.'

Heni showed no expression of emotion. She refused to eat and didn't speak.

Had she killed Kent falling on him, pinning him down? She felt like she was to blame. Her mind was racing but then she shut down again – the sedation helped her to shut everything down. Heni refused to go to the funeral. She was supposed to get married, not be going to a funeral.

Heni didn't want to see the wedding dress Aroha had made. Aroha put it in a box lined with tissue paper and into storage in case Heni wanted to see it again. Heni didn't care what happened to the cake Mrs Manu had made. She was also supposed to also become Mrs Manu, Kent's wife. Now she was alone.

Heni didn't start the graphic design degree. She didn't feel creative. She couldn't afford the rent and she felt terrified being alone after Zoey and Kent died so she moved back in with her parents. She was frequently tearful and anxious but mostly shut down, unresponsive and unable to socially engage.

She was put back on antidepressants and after several months briefly saw a psychologist. The psychologist wanted Heni to name her emotions and identify patterns of thoughts. She said it was called Cognitive Behavioural Therapy (CBT).

'I don't know what my emotions are called,' said Heni. 'It's like either nothing or like a video recording in my head but I don't know what the names of my emotions are.' Heni struggled learning and applying CBT as she had difficulty identifying and naming emotions.

Heni didn't want to socialise but Aroha insisted it would be good for her to go to church. Heni just wanted to stay away from other people. She isolated herself. When Heni arrived at church, some members of the congregation were discussing Kent.

'Kent's gone to Hell for living in sin,' someone said. Heni ran out the door and didn't go back. She tossed her Bible into the bin.

Months went by and her mood was still very low. She tried starting another job, but was irritable and extremely anxious and quit. She'd felt so irritable with her supervisor, that she'd stormed out of the workplace and walked briskly, muttering her frustration out loud until the energy started to calm.

Yet when she walked back into the workplace, she felt anxious again to the point of panic. She was put on some anti-anxiety medication short-term and referred by her doctor to a psychiatrist.

'I see you've been diagnosed with treatment resistant depression. Do you have highs?' said the psychiatrist, Dr Margaret Wilson.

'What do you mean, 'highs'?'

'Happier moods than normal?'

Happy? Normal? What did normal feel like? Heni hardly ever felt happy. Not since she'd been plagued by depression since her late teens. There'd been some happy times with Ava and Kent.

'I don't think so,' said Heni. Some temporary feelings when I went to church. Everyone was doing it. They said we were getting high on God's spirit. I felt a bit high when I fell in love.' Heni started to cry.

'How have you been on the latest antidepressants?'

'I felt like I needed to run and run and I was still restless. I came off them after quitting my job after two weeks because I kept having distressing thoughts.'

'I'm going to try switching you from an antidepressant to lithium,' said Dr Wilson.

'What's that for?'

'It's a mood stabiliser for bipolar disorder. Bipolar disorder has highs and lows.'

'Really? I'd love to have some highs. Even to feel 'normal' happy, whatever that is.' She followed Dr Wilson's advice and started on lithium.

Very soon after she was stumbling around having difficulty walking, was slurring her speech and started vomiting but then she felt ravenously hungry immediately after. She felt like she was going to fall into a very deep sleep and never wake up. She stopped the medication and went back to Dr Wilson.

'This medication made me really sick. How can you diagnose me with bipolar after only seeing me for five minutes?' Heni was irritable.

'Sorry for poisoning you. I'll switch you to another antidepressant. You may have to stay on antidepressants for life.'

Heni started a job doing accounts administration. She found it boring entering invoices into the computer, but it didn't require too much concentration. She didn't feel like she had the energy to pursue a graphic design career. She'd quit going to painting class. She didn't socialise. She felt like a hermit crab, withdrawn into its shell. Her life was going to work, which took huge effort, and sleeping.

Aroha and Klaus's heavy emphasis on church and God grated on her so she went to live with her brother.

The only joy that came into her life was in the form of Ziggy. Daniel wanted to get Heni out of the house and suggested they go look at the animal shelter for a dog or cat for Heni. He knew how much Heni loved pets. Ziggy was an older puppy that was happy in Heni's presence. He ran playfully around her with his leash in his mouth in the meeting area. It was the first time Heni had smiled in a long time.

Daniel and Heni signed the adoption papers for Ziggy. When Heni went back a few days later to collect Ziggy who was freshly washed, the shelter staff made a confession. 'Ziggy has fear aggression.'

'Fear aggression?' Several dogs had been put down when she was a vet nurse for fear aggression. Ziggy had shown no signs of it when she'd met him.

'This is our fourth attempt to rehome Ziggy. He's not very good with children.'

Daniel didn't want to have children. Heni wasn't even thinking about a partner, let alone children. Daniel said that if it made Heni happy, he was willing to go through with the adoption.

Ziggy came home and helped Heni open up her heart to love again. Ziggy helped her get out of the house because Heni took him for walks. Ziggy was uncomfortable with his nails being clipped and showed his teeth when his tail was touched.

To help Ziggy overcome this, Heni used relaxing touch like Kent had done with her to help her be more comfortable with touch. She had Ziggy lie on his side then groomed him except for his tail, until he was in a state of deep relaxation. Then she would gently and briefly touch his tail. Ziggy's body would tense up, so she'd resume long strokes to other parts of his body. Gradually, Ziggy built up a tolerance of his tail being touched and groomed.

Pairing clipping of Ziggy's nails with food was also helpful. What helped most was to train Ziggy to go into a relaxed state on command. Heni pointed a finger at him and said 'Bang'. Ziggy flopped down onto his side and his breathing slowed. Heni clipped his nails and then announced, 'You're alive!' and Ziggy bounced back up again ready for play.

Heni couldn't imagine life without Ziggy, her best friend and companion. Ziggy was helping her heal. The shelter said Heni saved Ziggy. But Heni felt like Ziggy saved her.

6. Bonfire

Heni didn't date following Kent's death. She didn't talk about the accident or any other painful experiences in her life. She refused counselling after the few sessions of CBT. She pushed painful memories away in her mind and focused on getting through work.

She didn't socialise. She only left the house to go to work and to take Ziggy for a walk. This was her life for a few years. Just going to work and spending time with Ziggy.

Daniel gifted Heni surfing lessons for the week of her birthday. He thought it might be a way to encourage Heni to meet new people and perhaps have fun. He couldn't remember the last time he'd seen Heni laugh. It would have been before the skydiving accident. She had started to smile with Ziggy in her life.

Daniel thought Heni might refuse the gift but to his surprise she accepted and seemed almost enthusiastic about it. Heni hadn't swum in the ocean since scattering Zoey's ashes. Heni had never tried surfing other than catching waves with a body board when she was a teenager with Daniel. It had been fun.

The surfing class was a small group of beginners all wearing spring suits. Heni didn't have a scrap of makeup on. Her hair was pulled back with some messy curls escaping. After some practice on the boards in the sand, they made their first attempts in the sea.

Coming in for a break, with wet hair, Heni unzipped her spring suit and pulled it down to her waist revealing two cat's eyes she'd had tattooed onto her shoulder blades not long after Kent and Ava died.

Richie, one of the other rookie surfing students noticed and admired Heni's elongated curves. Richie smiled. Heni returned Richie's smiles in a subtly flirtatious exchange with fleeting eye contact.

Richie seemed confident when he introduced himself and they started talking. Richie's Australian accent was obvious. He told Heni he was on holiday.

'Look,' called Richie as they paddled out deeper. Heni turned to look where he was pointing. Two dolphins were playing in the waves, not far from them.

Flirting had been foreign to Heni previously but today she felt more daring, confident and attractive. She smiled a lot and had a glint in her eyes. When they came back in, Heni and Richie sat next to each other on a secluded part of the beach, out of reach from where waves smashed against the rocks.

Richie asked, 'How do you not have a boyfriend? You're gorgeous.'

'It's been three years.' Heni didn't want to go into the details. About how Kent died. She didn't want to deal with pain. Instead she smiled playfully.

'Three years! I don't believe you,' exclaimed Richie, playfully nudging her arm with his fist. 'I haven't had a girlfriend for a while. I have a stressful job. I'm a police officer. So are you a good girl or a naughty girl? You have such a pretty smile and I noticed you have tattoos.'

'I was always a good girl but perhaps I'm now a naughty girl,' smiled Heni. 'I was raised in a strict, religious family,' she added.

'I'll happily let you sin with me,' joked Richie.

Heni said something she usually wouldn't. 'Would you let me handcuff you? With real handcuffs?' She gave Richie a naughty smile and stroked one finger down his bicep to his wrist. She had never overtly flirted with anyone like that. Not even Kent.

Richie was grinning. 'I'd willingly let you handcuff me,' he replied, holding his wrists together before surrendering one hand to Heni. Heni took his hand and gently stroked his palm then brushed his hand against her full lips. She felt an unfamiliar hunger and yearning and she sensed Richie felt desire too.

She missed Kent so much and had vowed never to fall in love again because it hurt so much that he was gone. But now she was experiencing desire for someone she had met just hours ago.

Richie scooped his hand around Heni's waist. As the waves crashed on the rocks, they leaned closer then kissed. Tender and sensual at first, then more passionate. Heni had never felt that intensity of attraction before. Deeper kissing was in that moment no longer disgusting to her.

She'd had a friendship and romance with Kent but she'd never experienced passion before. It was like a thrilling ride she didn't want to get off from and most definitely a distraction from pain.

Later the surf school set up a bonfire on the beach to finish up. Heni and Richie sat on a piece of driftwood, snuggled together, sipping cider.

'I'm going back to Oz in two days,' said Richie. 'Come with me.'

Heni had never been to Australia before. She usually thought things over, but she strongly wanted to be with Richie, even though they barely knew each other.

They held each other's gaze. Their eyes had reflections of flickering from the fire.

'Can my dog Ziggy come too?'

'Of course.'

'Okay,' said Heni. 'I'll come over in the next few weeks, as soon as I can arrange Ziggy's flight.' She was bored with the accounts job and felt like a new adventure. Perhaps she could get back into graphic design?

'Brilliant.'

Richie picked up a towel and holding hands, they walked off to a secluded dune on the beach.

'Are you nuts!' exclaimed Aroha, when Heni told her parents she was moving to Australia to be with Richie.

'You've only just met this joker!' said Klaus. 'You're going to quit a good job, sell everything and move to Australia for some virtual stranger? You've always been sensible. This is not like you, Heni.'

'We're in love,' insisted Heni, twirling the broken seashell temporary engagement ring. 'I don't have much stuff to sell anyway.'

'In love?' scoffed Aroha. 'More like in lust! You need to get right with God, Heni.'

'We're getting married.' Previously the thought of marriage made Heni very anxious but now she felt excited.

'How can you be in love with someone you just met? It's infatuation,' said Klaus. 'If you would do the proper thing, you'd introduce us to him. He could be dangerous for all we know.'

'He's a police officer. I feel safe with him.'

Heni knew her parents had a 'not under our roof' rule when it came to men. Even though there'd only been one man until now. Kent had never been allowed to stay over. Klaus and Aroha were extremely disapproving when they had moved in together before marriage.

Heni didn't have time for their disapproval. She had too much to do. She was a whirlwind of energy as she handed in her notice at work, sold her car and organised Ziggy's vet checks and flight.

Heni had saved most of the money from her job. Klaus had said that he was proud of how his daughter 'could live off the smell of an oily rag' just like himself. 'Low maintenance' is what Kent had called her. Heni didn't spend money on expensive clothes, shoes and makeup.

While Heni was organising moving to Australia, Richie emailed some photos. He looked so strong and confident standing wearing his police uniform with his legs apart and chest out like a superhero. He also sent her nude selfies.

Usually Heni was turned off by nudity and sex but now she was aroused by it. She felt like a completely different person. She wondered if this is what 'normal' felt like for other people. Experiencing sexual attraction and having a libido. Most of the time she'd been depressed with no interest in sex.

Heni already had a recent passport as she was considering going on an overseas holiday at some stage in the near future. Possibly to a tropical island. She hadn't expected to ever fall in love again, especially so quickly. Less than two weeks later she was reunited with Richie. Ziggy was booked for a flight a few days after her arrival.

Richie picked up Heni from the airport with just one suitcase and a wad of cash from selling her car.

'Wow, it's so hot over here,' said Heni. 'I feel like my eyeballs are going to cook.'

'It'll get over forty degrees Celcius in late summer,' said Richie. 'You'll be needing the air-conditioning going in the house and in the car.'

'What's winter like here?'

'Like a New Zealand summer. It doesn't really get cold here.'

'Let's get married in winter then. There'll be snow on Mount Whakapono in winter back in New Zealand.'

'Mount fuck-a-what?' asked Richie, laughing. 'Fuck-a-porno?'

'Far-Car-Paw-Naw,' Heni said. 'Whakapono is a Maori word for 'believe'. It's the name of the mountain and the street where I grew up in a little town called Kanuka.'

'Kanuka? Like Manuka honey?'

'Yes, only a different tree, so Kanuka honey. Manuka is the name of the nearby city where I went to uni.'

When they arrived back at Richie's house, Heni heard a strange noise outside.

'What's that?' It was an unfamiliar sound like hysterical laughter.

'Oh, that's our wildlife,' said Richie.

Heni ran back outside. There were two kookaburras sitting on a powerline cackling away. In the background there was the sound of a woman's voice making loud orgasmic noises, presumably from a house down the street.

'I've never heard anything so ridiculous in my life,' said Heni, barely stifling a giggle.

The rush of Heni's decision to move to Australia and get married had resulted in a rift with family.

'You're running away,' said Aroha.

'No, I'm not,' insisted Heni. She didn't want there to be friction with her family but she felt like she was making a fresh start. She thought her family should be happy for her, but they weren't.

'You make your bed, you lie in it. Don't come crying back to me when it all falls apart,' were Aroha's parting words to Heni as she left New Zealand.

Heni bought a car straight away – a station wagon with tinted glass windows and air-conditioning as Richie had recommended. It felt good spending money for a change. A stark contrast to how she usually saved it.

The roads were a lot busier than she was used to but Heni managed to get to the airport on her own to collect Ziggy. She could see Ziggy standing quietly in the crate, waiting for the quarantine officer to sign a release. She was glad there were not weeks nor months of quarantine time. Ziggy was pleased to see Heni and hopped into the back of the car looking relaxed after having his first pee on Australian soil at the airport.

When Richie arrived home from work, Ziggy backed into a corner and barked with his hackles up. This was the first time Heni had seen any signs of the fear aggression the shelter had mentioned. Heni had had no problems until now, apart from helping Ziggy overcome his aversion to his tail being touched and his nails being clipped. Ziggy was very affectionate with Aroha, Klaus and Daniel. Although he hadn't had much opportunity to meet other people with Heni isolating herself so much.

Richie wasn't impressed. 'Oh great. Your dog hates me.'

'Just sit down quietly and I'll get some treats. Just toss some on the floor and let him come to you in his own time.'

Richie did as he was instructed. When he reached his hand forward, Ziggy growled.

'Don't stretch your hand out or stare at him. Avoid eye contact as that can be threatening. No loud or low, growly voices. Be quiet, or use a softer, higher tone of voice than usual.'

'Is your dog gay?' asked Richie. 'He does look effeminate. I don't want to sound gay.'

'Well then shut up!' snapped Heni looking unimpressed.

Heni pointed to Ziggy's new bed. She'd bought him a soft bed for indoors and a trampoline style bed for outdoors. 'Ziggy, bed,' she said pointing at the bed using a more authoritative tone of voice. Ziggy climbed into the bed.

'Ziggy and I are part of a team,' Heni explained to Richie. 'To accept me, you need to learn to accept Ziggy. He's like a child to me. It's either use a tone and volume of voice that helps Ziggy feel less threatened or you need to be quiet. Your deep voice sounds like a growl to him. He will get used to your regular voice but it will help when talking to him to use a softer, higher voice.'

When Ziggy was looking more relaxed, Heni invited Ziggy out of his bed and Richie tried tossing food onto the floor again as directed. Ziggy got closer and closer.

Richie tried putting on a gentle, higher voice. 'Hey there, Ziggy,' he said. 'I feel silly but I will do this to please your mummy who will soon be barefoot and pregnant and giving you lots of brothers and sisters.' Richie winked at Heni.

'One or two kids. I'll be a working parent if I want to. Just let Ziggy touch you when he wants to. Don't reach out and pat his head,' instructed Heni. She remembered how Kent helped her overcome her aversion to being touched. Touch had to be on her terms. Just like Ziggy. He needed to be given some space and time to trust.

Ziggy nuzzled Richie's hand and took some treats.

'Just let Ziggy lead where he wants to be touched without moving your hand forward,' said Heni. 'That's it.' First Ziggy nudged his rear end into Richie's knee, then he pressed his head into Richie's hand.'

'You're making a new friend,' said Heni. Ziggy started to felt relaxed around Richie and adjusted to his lower voice, although he was startled if Richie used a louder or angry-sounding voice. Heni understood Ziggy.

'I didn't actually ask the landlord if we could have a dog,' confessed Richie. 'We'll have to keep Ziggy a secret until we can get a place of our own. I don't have enough for a deposit on a house yet. It's been hard saving while paying rent when my flatmate moved out.'

'How much would we need? I have savings.' Heni had hardly spent any money other than on board and Ziggy's care.

'Probably need around thirty grand?' said Richie. 'I don't have that kind of money.'

'I have over thirty thousand dollars saved that I can get transferred over from New Zealand. Let's buy a house!' Just like moving impulsively to Australia to marry a man she'd just met, buying something big without thinking it through was not like her, even though saving for a house had been one of her goals.

'When we buy a house, I want to get birds in an aviary and pet snakes,' said Richie.

'Pet snakes?'

'Yeah, pythons. You're not going to make me choose between you and the snakes now, are you?' Richie said jokingly.

'You like exotic pets?'

'Yes, I do. You're my favourite exotic pet.'

'What kind of exotic pet am I?'

'A beautiful bird with brilliant colours and a unique song.'

'Will the snakes get big enough to eat a cat? I don't want for them to swallow a cat. I want to get a cat,' said Heni.

'Nah, they won't eat it whole,' said Richie. 'They'd spit that bit out.'

'Gross!' said Heni. 'What do the snakes eat?'

'Rats. I'd buy six-packs of rats frozen. Just thaw a rat for each feed.'

'I used to have a pet rat called Honey when I was a teenager. She was so intelligent and affectionate. You can do all the feeding of the snakes yourself.' It didn't appeal to her to feed the snakes.

Over the following weeks they went shopping for an engagement ring and a house. Instead of a traditional diamond ring, Heni chose a yellow gold band with a ruby heart. They purchased a house in a nice subdivision. The house had stone detail around the front and a granite bench. Huge slabs of sandstone formed a retaining wall around the edges of the property.

The cream colours of the walls looked a bit tired. Unlike Heni, who for the first time in years continued to have a lot of energy. She plastered, sanded and painted the walls and ceiling herself in natural rock colours to fit the rock bench and front of the house. She wished this energy would last forever.

Heni also started a new job as a photo editor for a pet art photography studio. She was fortunate to get the job as she'd had limited training, but her employer wanted someone with an artistic eye but not too much experience so they could train her how to edit studio photos their way. She got to look at pets all day on a computer screen whilst enhancing the photographs. Her employers were impressed with her enthusiasm and positive attitude.

Heni went to an animal shelter to adopt a cat. Tripod soon came to trust Heni. Tripod enjoyed sunning herself outdoors in the catio but also enjoyed sleeping on the bed and the couch. Heni checked Ziggy and Tripod daily for paralysis ticks and kept them indoors at night.

Richie set up reptile enclosures for his pythons Donner and Blitz which meant 'thunder' and 'lightning' in German. He wanted to breed snakes and sell them. After dinner, Richie got the snakes out for Heni to handle for the first time. Blitz squeezed Heni's hand tightly so she could feel her engagement ring crushing into her other fingers. Then Blitz uncoiled partially and hovered near Heni's face.

'I dunno Richie...she's eyeing me up funny. Maybe she can smell the food I've just eaten?' Suddenly, Blitz struck and latched onto Heni's bottom lip, then coiled up her body to wrap around Heni's face.

Heni screwed up her face and flapped her hands vigorously, frantically signalling for Richie to take Blitz off.

Richie laughed and gripped Blitz who released then wrapped firmly around Richie's arm. 'Your first snake bite,' he said, inspecting closer. 'You have puncture marks in your lip'.

'That felt so awful. I could feel her muscles contract around my face. It gave me the heebie jeebies.' Heni was flapping her hands again at the recollection and then she stopped and closely inspected her hand. 'There's a heart-shaped dent in my finger from my engagement ring being squeezed so hard,' she observed.

Richie was keen for some photos of the snakes so Heni got her camera. Donner struck out and scratched the lens of the camera with his tiny teeth. So every photo had a fine, barely noticeable line unless Heni edited them out. 'Crap, it's a brand new camera,' said Heni. She had bought her first camera, something she'd wanted for a long time but hadn't wanted to spend money on before.

Somewhere while busy setting up home and pets, Heni and Richie were getting to know each other more. Heni had still not mentioned the skydiving accident or the sexual abuse.

'I'm divorced, no kids,' said Richie. 'Was married for a year. Had a few girlfriends. What about you?'

'I've only been with one guy. We were going to get married. He died...on our wedding day,' said Heni, her voice quavering as she controlled emotion. She'd never let the grief out over Kent and Ava. She'd never even visited their graves.

'I'm sorry. Wait...only had sex with one guy? Are you serious?'

'Yes. I didn't want to date anyone after losing my fiance.'

'That's understandable. I'm a very lucky man then.'

After redecorating the house, Heni was still feeling creative so she decided to take a class. 'I want to make a stained glass hanging,' she said. She enrolled in a class making small ornaments using a copperfoil technique. She designed a round hanging with two dolphins and the tutor modified the lines to suit the cutting lines of glass.

'This is a challenging piece for your first time,' said the tutor.

'I really want to do it. It represents me and my fiance.' Heni didn't want to take baby steps. She wanted to run and leap and cartwheel like she used to do, practising gymnastics as a child. She didn't want to walk. She wanted to fly.

With guidance, she completed the piece which had a chain incorporated into the seams. The finishing touches were gluing small teal glass beads for eyes. It was soon hanging proudly in the house. She told her mother.

Aroha was critical the first time Heni talked on the phone after moving to Australia. 'Stained glass ornaments can have spirits,' she said.

'What?'

'Of the person who made it.'

'I made it. With help.'

'Everything has spirits and can have curses,' insisted Aroha in a particular tone of voice that Heni felt was judgemental.

Aroha was going on and on but Heni wasn't taking it in. Aroha had frequently talked about spiritual curses. Aroha was suspicious of the antidepressant medication Heni was on. According to her beliefs, depression was a spiritual affliction and she called the antidepressants 'the Devil's sweets.' Talk of evil spirits and curses made Heni feel anxious and irritated. She was sick of it. She'd had lifetime of it. Talk of curses, demons and Hell.

'Your stained glass ornament has spirits from the person who made it,' insisted Aroha.

'I made it though. Someone helped me.'

'It has the spirit of that person transferred to it. Including generational curses.'

'How ridiculous!' exclaimed Heni, unable to hide her irritation. 'Do you have to get rid of curses from everything you buy? Even buying a pair of shoes?! Your shoes could have curses then!'

'Come back to Jesus, Heni, before it's too late. You're being rebellious.' Heni knew that 'too late' meant that Aroha believed Heni would go to Hell.

Heni felt upset and ended the conversation. She wished she could talk to her mother without religion getting in the way. She'd believed in Jesus for years previously but she felt Jesus had let her down. Jesus didn't intervene when Paul abused her. She'd heard nothing when she cried out to God for help during her breakdown.

Talk about God and curses and Hell were distressing for Heni. She just wanted to be close to her family and wished that religion wasn't a part of it. To Heni, the stained glass represented love, and she wanted the unconditional love and acceptance of her family without the huge rift.

It was the first time Richie witnessed Heni in tears. 'The stained glass is beautiful,' he said. 'Like you. You're my dream.' He was often full of compliments. He wiped her tears and gently kissed her face. Then they had sex. Richie found it hard to believe when Heni told him she wasn't usually interested in sex. 'You're so incredibly sexy,' he said.

Heni's family had made it clear they didn't approve of the union and would not be attending the wedding. So Richie and Heni decided not to have family from either side. Just a celebrant and witnesses.

Richie's friends were limited to the police force, so he invited his friend and senior work colleague, Doug, and his much younger wife, Vanessa, to be witnesses. Vanessa was a fitness model with long blonde hair extensions, breast implants, long fake nails, and a mask of makeup. Her false eye-lashes looked like spiders around her brown eyes.

Heni had been keeping busy leading up to the wedding to try to distract herself from rising anxiety. Despite the disagreement with her mother, the tears had been a release from some of the internal stress.

There would be no jumping out of aeroplanes nor a traditional wedding this time. No bridal party nor guests. Just very low key. In the garden of their new house with their pets. Outside the catio, Heni had planted some native trees to attract birds.

Heni and Richie went shopping to try on rings. A ring in the shape of a snake with an emerald eye wrapped snugly around the ruby heart like the rings had been made to fit together. Since Richie was a snake enthusiast, they thought it would be a fun alternative to a traditional wedding ring.

When they were in the jewellery store, Heni was admiring the crystal ornaments in the display cabinet. She liked how they caught and reflected the light. The larger items were over a thousand dollars.

Heni chose a figure-hugging, chilli red dress which showed off her emerging baby bump. Richie chose a pine green shirt which had red in the shadows. 'Green silk shot with red,' was the description given by the shop assistant. His eyes looked even brighter green wearing the shirt. Heni held a simple bouquet of Australian native blooms.

After a very simple ceremony, Doug took some photographs of Heni and Richie smiling with their pets. Then Doug, Vanessa and the celebrant left.

Richie gave Heni a present. 'It's fragile,' he said.

Heni unwrapped a box which had a label with 'Exotic.' She lifted the lid and unfolded the tissue paper. Inside was a colourful crystal bird radiating light.

'This bird reminds me of you,' said Richie.

'It's beautiful,' said Heni taking it out of the box.

'Like you.' Richie took Heni's hand and looked into her eyes. 'Don't ever fly away from me, my beautiful bird.'

In these Arms was playing on the stereo.

Heni gave Richie a picture of a full back tattoo design of a mother elephant with two baby elephants at Richie's request after learning they were expecting twins.

'Wow, this is so amazing,' said Richie. 'It's even better than I expected. You are so talented.' Richie booked in right away with the tattoo artist.

Despite the conflict with her family, Heni decided to retain her maiden name, Hertz. Richie and Heni decided they would combine their surnames into Hertz-Kopf for the children.

Apart from Heni's family not approving of their union, life was good. Heni now had an adoring husband, children on the way, her beloved pets, a lovely home that she had redecorated and a new career. All within six months of meeting Richie.

7. Certified Nut

Immediately after the wedding, Heni was exhausted. The energy she'd had previously was gone and it was a struggle to get to work and do chores around the house. It felt like depression and she still had nausea with the pregnancy.

She was tearful at work and struggling to focus. She went to the doctor and they said her depression wasn't under control so she should increase the dose of her antidepressants. 'Will the meds harm my babies?' she asked, concerned. The doctor insisted that the risks of being unmedicated for what they called 'treatment resistant depression,' outweighed the risks to her unborn children.

The dose of the antidepressants was increased, and after the first trimester the nausea eased but the fatigue continued. Her brain still felt scattered, which made continuing with work very challenging.

Another ultrasound revealed that Heni and Richie were expecting a boy and a girl. To cheer Heni up, Richie took Heni jewellery shopping. Heni chose a gold band with two heart-shaped gemstones. One heart was an orange topaz and the other heart was a blue topaz. It was called 'fire and ice'.

Richie joked it could be her maternity ring instead of buying her an eternity ring. Heni liked that idea. To Heni, the two hearts represented the two beating hearts of her unborn children. She wore the ring on her right hand opposite to her engagement and wedding rings.

Richie was building a bird aviary in the backyard for the exotic parrots that he wanted to get. Heni heard an angry noise from Richie and then Ziggy came inside, very despondent, and curled up in his bed.

'Ziggy,' called Heni gently. Ziggy didn't respond. He was completely shut down.

Heni marched outside. 'What did you do to Ziggy?' she demanded.

Without looking up, Richie replied without any remorse, 'He was in my way so I kicked him and yelled at him to get out of my way.'

'You what? How dare you kick him. He's in his bed, depressed,' said Heni. Richie shrugged his shoulders like he didn't care.

'Don't you EVER kick, hit or yell at a pet again,' continued Heni with a tone of voice that meant, 'or else this relationship is over.' She felt vulnerable being heavily pregnant. She loved Richie. How could he do this? And not be remorseful?

Ziggy stayed curled up in his bed unresponsive for three days before he started coming back to life again. He was wary of Richie. His confidence and trust were knocked. Heni's too. She had invested her all in this man.

Very quietly, she said to Richie. 'I'm going to leave and take Ziggy and Tripod with me.'

'Where will you go?' asked Richie.

'I don't know but I can't live with someone who kicks dogs. I thought you loved pets.'

'I do love pets. Heni don't do this.' Richie got up and started pacing. He was angry. 'Heni don't leave me!'

Heni was sitting on the floor next to Ziggy. Very still and quiet. Whereas Richie was riled up. He smashed his fist into the wall, leaving a hole with bits of plaster falling to the floor. Then he stormed out, slamming the door.

Heni sat quietly, looking down at the floor, not moving other than barely perceivable breathing. As her mind was completely shutting down, her last thought was *at least he didn't put a hole in me.*

Heni sat frozen for hours before her brain started to partially wake up again. Her emotions were still shut down – it was too painful for her to feel. She struggled to think.

When her brain started activating with racing thoughts, she felt anxious. *Should I go back to New Zealand? But the trip would be too stressful for Tripod. I've got two children on the way. How will I support myself with two babies if I stay this tired?* It was too hard to think about it so she slowly climbed up onto her bed and lay her side with her knees drawn up as far as they could go, with arms wrapped around her bulging tummy.

Ziggy finally climbed out of his bed and lay up against her back and Tripod curled up on her pillow. She loved them and they loved her. She loved Richie but love was sometimes too confusing and painful.

Hours later, Richie came home and begged for her to stay and he promised never to do it again. Heni could smell alcohol on his breath.

Six weeks before the twins were due, Heni experienced a stabbing pain in her side and was clutching a bucket with nausea. Soon she started vomiting. She was admitted to hospital as the stabbing pain worsened. A nurse taking her blood pressure said, 'your pulse is only fifty beats per minute. Are you an athlete?'

'Do I look like an athlete?' asked Heni. 'I feel like a beached whale.' Heni's belly was very swollen and her tissues were puffing up.

Various scans and tests were done to investigate a kidney stone, but no stone was to be found, despite a swollen kidney that was unable to drain. The drugs administered intravenously did little to relieve the pain. The doctors said they could only give her certain medications because of her pregnancy, not the usual medications for kidney pain.

The stabbing pain continued all day and night and Heni started having Braxton-Hicks contractions. The doctors told her they would deliver the babies prematurely if she went into labour. They started making arrangements for incubators to be flown in from other hospitals.

Heni didn't know how she was supposed to give birth when she was so exhausted, having been awake for several days and nights because of the pain. The doctors said they couldn't give her any more painkillers because she'd already been administered three times the dose of a birthing woman and the drugs were classed as opioids which they said were addictive.

One very abrupt maternity nurse said condescendingly, 'I hope you've considered your pain relief for the birth, dear, because it's clear you have a very low pain threshold.'

Heni was in tears when that nurse walked away. Another nurse with a kind manner sat down with her and said, 'Don't listen to her. Renal pain has been described as more painful than childbirth, gunshot wounds, burns and stabbings. What you're experiencing is nothing like childbirth, which is a natural process. We going to give you a sleeping pill to try to help you sleep.'

Heni finally went to sleep after several days of no sleep. When she woke up, she needed to pee. The kind nurse held her arm as she walked groggily to the toilet. She felt like she'd been kicked in the back by a horse, but the pain had reduced significantly. The doctors concluded that her babies were compressing a tube from the kidney so the urine could not drain. Now, finally, she could relieve the fluid that had accumulated in her tissues.

Then the pain started up again but not as extremely. 'Your bowel has been turned to concrete from all the medications,' a nurse said. 'It's pressing on things again.' So the next stage was trying to unblock her with enemas and oral laxatives.

After a brief rest, Heni couldn't help but clean her house obsessively. It was a nesting instinct, she was told, so no one thought anything odd about the burst of energy. The pain from her kidney trauma gradually eased and her energy levels picked up.

When she gave birth, she felt safe with the kind midwife who helped ease her anxiety with reassuring words. This was after another midwife had told her that she was at risk of bleeding to death, and other worst case scenario stories, that had made Heni feel very anxious. There was a change in midwife just hours before the birth.

Heni went into a trance-like state while Richie held her hand. In the trance-like state, she felt very little pain. She didn't need any medical pain relief options. It felt a bit like when she floated away to escape her pain after the haemorrhoid operation. She tore but it was no more painful than smarting like a bikini wax or a bee sting which soon faded. Childbirth was uncomfortable but it wasn't extremely painful like the haemorrhoidectomy.

Alexandria was born first, soon followed by her brother Xavier on either side of midnight. Heni felt light-headed and dreamy. She held her babies immediately after the birth. Heni looked into their eyes which started off a teal colour but later changed to become like hers – a striking turquoise colour that seemed to change in the light like polished paua shells.

'Do you want to keep the placentas?' asked the midwife. 'Perhaps put them under a tree?'

Heni viewed the placentas. 'Nah, my dog would probably dig them up.'

Heni felt completely fine apart from feeling faint when she sat up. An electrocardiogram was conducted to check her heart which was fine. 'Mild shock,' the medical staff concluded.

The maternity suite was full so Richie and Heni went home with their newborn babies the same day as giving birth. A midwife visited at home to help Heni with breastfeeding and to check on the babies.

Aroha and Klaus visited Heni in Australia for the first time. They thought Heni's chattiness and euphoria was the excitement of becoming a mother.

'Hormones,' Aroha said. Richie's mother, Bernice agreed. She had moved to be local as she was keen to help out with babysitting.

A few weeks later, Daniel visited. Heni talked non-stop, very fast. Daniel joked that he 'Couldn't get a word in edgewise'. Heni seemed happy when she was chatty. She also sent long emails to friends and family. She could type fast and emails were an extension of the nearly non-stop chatter. Nothing was thought of as particularly odd about her fast speech and emails other than her lack of a filter about personal topics.

Richie thought it was a welcome relief from seeing her withdrawn and depressed. 'You could talk the ears off an elephant,' joked Richie. 'I cannot believe you were called a mouse because you didn't talk'.

The babies were feeding well but Heni had very little sleep. Especially because Alexandria was hard to settle.

Alexandria was crying inconsolably, even though she had been fed and her nappy was clean and dry. Richie yelled explosively at Alexandria at close range, 'STOP CRYING!' Alexandria cried even harder.

Heni felt afraid. *Is he going to hit my baby?* were her thoughts through the fog of her brain shutting down. Then Richie stormed out of the room leaving Heni in shock with a very distressed baby that she was unable to calm.

After that, when Heni couldn't calm Alexandria, Heni ran to the bathroom and put the shower on and cried. She felt so helpless that she couldn't help her newborn to stop crying. But apart from moments of distress like this, she felt like a contented, capable mother.

Richie was usually fun, friendly and affectionate but his eruptions of explosive rage terrified Heni. But she stayed with him because she believed love could help him overcome his flaws. In this big, strong man, she saw a vulnerable boy at times. Just like she was a woman but was also like a hurt girl.

No one outside their immediate family would guess that Richie had rage issues. Most likely no one would believe it. Richie's rage and Heni's depression were kept secret.

Richie didn't want to talk about his explosive rage but a few times he blamed the stress of his job. He refused to see a counsellor about it as he was fearful it would affect his career. He kept everything under control at work and unleashed at home. Heni kept forgiving him again and again for his outbursts and tried her best to please him to try avoid triggering unleashed anger.

One of the things that appeased Richie was sex. Heni rationalised that it was not that bad as he had not actually hit her or the children and he didn't hit or kick Ziggy again. Most of the time, Richie was a funny, outgoing guy. That's the side that everyone else got to see.

Daniel had noticed little put-downs of Heni framed as jokes. He had expressed his concern but Heni defended Richie.

Heni had never felt the expression of anger from herself other than occasional mild irritability. The only time she could remember feeling angry was when a teacher hit her on her first day of school.

She'd suffered terribly from depression. She didn't feel emotions as intensely as other people, most of the time. Usually she felt numb. It was rare for her to feel emotions passionately.

Heni did not yet have the language to label what was happening to her other than what the doctors had told her. They said she had depression and anxiety. Anxiety for Heni was more than worrying. It involved constant hypervigilance – she was constantly on guard for threats. So she could not fully relax.

Not long after giving birth, Heni tried to go back onto the contraceptive pill as Richie wanted to resume their sex life. She came crashing down from the brief high she'd been on since giving birth. She was irritable, felt nauseous and tearful and wasn't in any mood for sex.

'I can't go back on the pill,' she told Richie. 'It makes me feel sick. It made me feel sick when I first started it too.'

This time it felt even worse. The lack of sleep was finally catching up with her. It was exhausting breastfeeding two babies around the clock. Her breasts were painfully engorged so she'd wake up from only a few hours sleep at a time. Richie was back at work so she was mainly on her own with a bit of help from Bernice.

When the twins were nearly three months old, Heni was still struggling. 'I'm going to give up breastfeeding,' said Heni wearily to Richie. 'I need my sleep. I feel like a zombie. This is the most exhausted I've been in my entire life.' Her tone was flat and she couldn't mask anymore how depleted she was. Previously, with depression, she could still mask a smile for short periods of time.

Richie agreed she needed her sleep. Heni started weaning the twins onto formula which started to reduce her milk supply to more comfortable levels so she was able to finally get some sleep. Richie was pressuring Heni to resume having sex. Heni was so anxious about getting pregnant again as she felt overwhelmed with two babies.

'Hi, I'm doctor Paulson. I don't believe we've met before.' Dr Paulson extended his hand to shake Heni's. He looked like he was in his fifties and he had greying hair and pale blue eyes that sparkled. He seemed pleasant enough.

'No, we haven't met. My usual doctor has gone on holiday. He inserted an IUD last week but I've had non-stop cramping. I felt so sick on the pill so I stopped taking it. It's the first time we're trying an IUD.'

Dr Paulson looked on the computer. 'You have a history of treatment resistant depression? There's not much on your medical history.'

'I moved from New Zealand. Yes, I've been diagnosed with clinical depression. They call it 'treatment resistant' because the meds don't seem to help much. I get even more depressed before my period – it feels like I'm allergic to my own hormones.' Heni started to cry.

'There's no such thing as being allergic to hormones. I can write you a prescription to try something different for your depression. As for the IUD, I'll need to take a look.'

'It feels a bit awkward as we've just met.'

'If it makes you feel better, I can get a nurse to be present if that helps.'

'Oh, a nurse would make me feel better.'

Doctor Paulson called for a nurse who stood and observed while Dr Paulson investigated what the problem was.

'Your body is rejecting the IUD. It's trying to expel it. I'll need to remove it,' said Dr Paulson. 'It'll be a bit uncomfortable.'

Heni barely flinched even though it hurt more to remove the rejected device than to insert it.

'All done. You can get dressed now.' The nurse left the room.

Heni sat back in a chair.

'We'll need to look at other options for contraception,' said Dr Paulson.

'Richie doesn't like using condoms. I don't much like them either. But I don't want to get pregnant again and I don't trust condoms as the only form of contraceptive. I am feeling exhausted with two babies.' Heni started to cry. Dr Paulson stroked her hand soothingly.

Dr Paulson seemed very friendly and in no hurry to get to the next patient. He started to talk about his wife and children and hobbies. He said he was a musician. Doctors had never done that before – talk about their personal life.

Now and again Heni would cry. 'You're a mess. Your creativity is a gift and a curse,' said Dr Paulson soothingly, putting his hand on Heni's knee several times during the consultation.

Heni felt uncomfortable but had heard that Dr Paulson was a very respected doctor in Jellybroome, so she didn't speak up about her discomfort.

'Here you go,' Dr Paulson said to Heni as he handed her a prescription. 'I want you to try a different antidepressant. It's an older class of antidepressant.'

'Thank you,' Heni managed a smile under the tears and put the prescription in her handbag. She was feeling vulnerable and fragile.' Heni opened the door to leave.

'Wait!' directed Dr Paulson.

Heni stopped and turned around.

'Close the door,' instructed Dr Paulson.

Heni was confused but followed the doctor's instructions.

'Here...give me a hug,' he said with outstretched arms.

Heni felt uncomfortable and didn't know whether to step towards the doctor's embrace or open the door and flee. Alarm bells were going off in her head. She hesitantly closed the door and made an uncertain step towards the doctor and he embraced her firmly. She could feel his breath on her face. The cigarette smoke she had been able to smell on him at a distance now felt like it was smothering her.

'We'll get through this together,' said Dr Paulson leaning forward to kiss Heni's cheek. Then he kissed Heni firmly on the lips and slipped his hand inside her maternity bra. Heni stood frozen, unable to move or speak.

'Your milk smells delicious,' murmured Dr Paulson. 'I want some.'

Using all her willpower, Heni broke free and ran towards the door. Her mind was a whirlwind of confusion as she fought for clarity.

As she reached for the door handle, Dr Paulson snarled, 'No one will believe you. You're a certified nut. It's our little secret.'

Our little secret. Heni felt sick and had cramps like she was going to have diarrhoea. She opened the door, ran to the bathroom and made it to the toilet just before her bowels evacuated violently.

Her mind was racing. *Did I start it? Did I seduce him?* How was she going to tell Richie? Should she tell him? Should she report the doctor? Was he right? Would no one believe her? Heni didn't tell Bernice what had happened when she arrived home.

Heni vowed to never go back to Dr Paulson ever again. She blamed herself for what happened. Just like she blamed herself when she was sexually abused as a child.

She washed her face and made some dinner. She always did her best to please Richie. Richie arrived home from work and Heni was distant and restless.

They ate dinner, barely speaking. Heni had hardly touched her meal, just pushing it around on the plate.

'How did your doctor's appointment go?' asked Richie in an unemotional tone as though he were conducting an interview. 'Get that IUD sorted?' Heni burst into tears and told Richie what happened.

'Did you lead him on?' demanded Richie as he banged the table then paced back and forth.

'No,' replied Heni softly. She questioned herself internally, *Did I lead him on? Was it my fault?*

'Do you want him?' demanded Richie.

'No,' whispered Heni, barely able to get the words out. She felt like she was lying, as she was confused by unwanted feelings of attraction for Dr Paulson, along with disgust.

Richie's fists were clenched. 'I'll give him a couple of black eyes,' he muttered angrily. 'No one else is allowed to touch my bird.' Richie was still angry when he went to start an evening shift at work. Heni was alone with the twins who were asleep.

Heni went to the bedroom. She was sobbing as she picked up a pair of tweezers with the tips hovering in front of a power socket. She was fighting a war within to not insert the tweezers into the socket. The urge to kill herself was so strong.

The window was open and the smell of cannabis was wafting in from the neighbour who had just moved in. Along with the smell, there was music. A song she had never heard before, *Bring Me to Life*. The lyrics wafted over the fence and through her window, distracting Heni.

A tiny voice in her head said, '*My babies need their mother. Even a broken one.*' She wanted to believe that tiny voice, and used all her willpower to pull the tweezers away from the electrical socket, and drop them into a drawer. She still felt numb, yet felt convinced that a song she had never heard before had saved her. Heni never told Richie what happened.

Heni made an appointment the following week with Dr Finch as she didn't trust the prescription by Dr Paulson.

She told Dr Finch about doctor Paulson. Dr Finch recommended Heni make a formal complaint, which she did.

Heni told Dr Finch that she had nearly put the tweezers in a power socket.

'I'm referring you to a psychiatrist,' said Dr Finch.

'I don't want to see a psychiatrist,' said Heni. 'Last time I saw a psychiatrist, the meds they gave me poisoned me. It's not that bad. It's not like I have a life-threatening illness like diabetes.'

'You do have a life-threatening illness and it is that bad. If you refuse to see the psychiatrist, I will be admitting you to the new mother's unit. You will be contacted by the psychiatrist within the next few days.'

The psychiatrist, Dr Nadine, prescribed yet another change in antidepressants. During the changeover, Heni experienced increased irritability. 'It feels like static shocks inside my head,' she complained. 'It's worse when I turn my head. Like an electric fence but inside my head.'

'That's brain zaps. A discontinuation syndrome with some antidepressants. We're switching you to another class of antidepressants.'

Richie tried to initiate sex. Heni pushed him away, exhausted.

'Why won't you have sex?' asked Richie.

'I'm too exhausted and I don't want to get pregnant again,' said Heni. 'I know I can't cope with any more children.'

'I don't want to use condoms,' said Richie. 'You'll have to go back on the pill.'

'I don't trust condoms. I felt so sick on the pill. My body won't tolerate an IUD. I'm scared to try other hormonal options.'

'What options are there left?'

'Vasectomy? Or maybe I should get my tubes tied? Vasectomy is less invasive I think.'

'Get your tubes tied. I *need* to have sex. I can't help it if I have a high sex drive. I loved our sex life before you got pregnant.'

8. Death Row

Heni resigned from her job when she realised that it would be too exhausting for her to return to work full-time after maternity leave. She hoped that she could have the energy to do something part-time. She wanted to have some of her 'own' money.

She noticed another change in dynamics in the relationship when Richie was the sole income provider. Richie acted like he had all the power when it came to deciding what money was spent on. Which frustrated Heni.

When the twins were around nine months old, Heni taught them baby sign language. Bernice was sceptical, saying it would delay speech if the twins could sign. The first sign Heni taught them was 'milk' which was imitating milking a cow.

Teaching them sign language was amusing as Ziggy sat nearby watching and learning too. Ziggy wriggled with excitement when Heni signed 'eat' and 'car.' Heni remembered when she'd taught Zoey hand signals.

One evening Alexandria was distressed and kept crying, despite having been fed, wearing a clean nappy and having no temperature. Then Heni noticed her tiny hand doing the sign for 'milk.' She prepared another bottle of formula and Alexandria calmed down. Being able to communicate her needs before she could speak significantly reduced her distress.

The twins started crawling. Xavier started crawling first. Ziggy was in his bed and Xavier looked enthusiastic as he started crawling towards Ziggy. Heni noticed a subtle change in Ziggy's body language that he was not comfortable. Ziggy's body stiffened.

'Xavier, stop!' she called out. Xavier kept crawling at speed towards Ziggy. Heni ran towards them as she could tell from Ziggy's tense body that he was likely to lash out. Xavier reached out his hand to pat Ziggy. Ziggy snapped.

Xavier started crying as Heni swooped in and picked him up. There was a mark on Xavier's arm from Ziggy's teeth. Xavier's sensitive skin had raised marks but Heni was relieved the skin was not broken.

The twins had patted Ziggy before when being held by Heni or Richie and Ziggy had seemed fine. But now Ziggy was fearful when the twins were mobile independently. Ziggy's fear aggression had flared back up.

'I'm sorry if this is hard to hear, but Ziggy should never have been adopted out,' said the vet.

'But it's not his fault...he must have been abused...he's afraid of anything resembling a stick. The shelter said he wasn't very good with children but he's been fine with the children until now. He has a close bond with me.'

'We euthanise a lot of dogs for fear aggression. It's very sad but you need to strongly consider the safety of your children. They cannot be together.'

'It's not fair. Isn't there anything else we can do?'

'Here's a card for a trainer. I've heard he's not cheap but a trainer is your last resort before my recommendation of euthanasia.'

Heni had made progress training Ziggy herself but she had been less consistent since moving to Australia. Ziggy was a lot more challenging to train than Zoey had been.

The trainer was several hundred dollars for a single session with a guarantee to return for a follow-up session. It sounded a bit dodgy but the vet had recommended him. And Ziggy was on death row. Heni pleaded with Richie for the money for the trainer.

Richie was working out on his home gym equipment in the garage. He showed little emotion and was matter-of-fact. 'That's more than twice what we spend in a week on groceries,' he said.

'Please Richie, I love Ziggy. He's like a child to me.'

Richie started doing bicep curls. Heni loved his strong arms. She felt protected but all Heni could think of now was saving Ziggy.

'Please Richie. I can use barriers for now to keep him away from the kids. He was fine with the twins until they started crawling. I know Ziggy loves them but he just got a bit startled, that's all.'

'Barriers can fail and management is a pain. One snap to the face and we're looking at plastic surgery and scars for life. He could kill them.'

'I know he didn't mean to lash out. It's something from his past.'

'Ziggy's never liked me much anyway. The logical thing I see is to put him down. Too dangerous to pass onto someone else. He's a ticking time bomb.'

Pain was written all over Heni's face. 'Please Richie, I'm begging you. Can we please get the trainer before such desperate measures. He may be able to help your relationship with Ziggy too.' Ziggy was still wary of Richie after Richie had kicked him.

'Ziggy is a pansy. I don't know what you see in him. If I had a dog I'd have one with balls. A real man's dog. Or I'd get a bitch. Not an 'it'.'

'Please don't say that,' Heni said softly. 'I love him.' Her shoulders were slumped forward and defeated, she left the garage. She curled up on the bed staring at a fine crack on the wall.

Ziggy jumped onto the bed and lay with his body close to Heni. He always seemed to know her deepest feelings even when she tried to hide them from humans. Ziggy lay there quietly next to Heni like he knew.

'I'm sorry Ziggy,' Heni said quietly. Ziggy gently kissed her cheek.

Heni's body started to sob so hard her body was almost convulsing. The floodgates could no longer be held back. She reached behind her and stroked Ziggy's fur then fell asleep with her friend snuggled up beside her.

'They look like baby mice in tomato sauce,' Richie said about the baked beans on toast. Heni usually cooked amazing dinners but she barely had the energy to toast the bread and open a can. 'That was meant to be a joke,' said Richie, trying unsuccessfully to lighten up the mood. Heni gave a weak smile and stared at her little mice drowning in a sea of tomato sauce.

At times she had been vegetarian. She'd even tried being vegan and failed. She loved animals and it hurt when vegans on social media had told her she was a murderer for being a vegan apostate. Christians on social media had told her she was a murderer, too, for not believing in God anymore. She slowly scooped up the baked bean baby mice with a fork and put them on a lifeboat of toast. She wasn't hungry.

'Excuse me,' she said quietly as she left the table and headed towards the bedroom.

Richie didn't like for Heni to be depressed. When Heni was depressed, she was too exhausted to be the domestic and sexual goddess Richie wanted.

Richie turned on his bedside lamp and put his hand lightly on Heni's shoulder. 'I just wanted to tell you that I've reconsidered and I'll pay for the trainer.'

Heni opened her eyes. 'Really?' she asked. 'You'll give Ziggy a chance?'

'I'll pay for this trainer. But there are some conditions. If it doesn't work, you'll have to face up to the reality of what we said.'

'Of course, I understand Ziggy is on death row and I don't want for the twins to get hurt.' Heni started to come back to life.

'Contact the trainer tomorrow.'

'Thank you. Thank you so much,' said Heni hugging Richie tightly.

'I'm doing this because I love you,' he said. 'I know how much Ziggy means to you. He's growing on me too.'

'I love you too,' she said. In the dim light she saw the flicker in his eye of the passion of when they first met.

They started in engaging in a passionate kiss. Ziggy was still in the middle of the bed.

'Ziggy, off,' said Heni authoritatively. Ziggy jumped off the bed. She pointed to Ziggy's bed and Ziggy climbed into his own bed. 'Good boy'.

Richie started kissing Heni again and closed the bedroom door.

A few days later, Steve, the trainer arrived for Ziggy.

'You've got an anxious dog,' said Steve immediately. 'You need to give him structures and boundaries.' Heni agreed with that. She knew she hadn't been consistent since struggling with her energy levels. Some of Ziggy's behaviour had deteriorated since her pregnancy.

'Dogs need to be shown who's boss. Dogs must not sleep on the furniture.'

Ziggy was wary of Steve. Steve threw a heavy chain on the deck to make a loud noise and yelled at Ziggy. Ziggy cowered. This wasn't what Heni was expecting. Her way of helping Ziggy greet strangers seemed to work well. Ziggy didn't lunge at people when she had him go to his bed until he was more relaxed.

'Put this on Ziggy,' instructed Steve. It was a slip chain. Heni hadn't used one since Zoey's training.

Heni slipped the collar over Ziggy's neck and attached the leash as instructed.

Steve grabbed the leash. Heni stood there in horror as he performed extremely forceful corrections, over and over again. He yanked the leash so hard that Ziggy's feet lifted off the ground. Steve kept yelling at Ziggy in a guttural voice.

Was this the therapy to save Ziggy's life? The police dog handler had not been that forceful, despite using the same tool. Did it have to be so extreme? Heni wasn't sure how it would help to make Ziggy safe with the children.

Steve instructed Heni to yell in a low voice. Heni got a sore throat. She also noticed her relationship with Ziggy was eroded. So she ditched the training and did not have Steve come back for a repeat session.

Heni was very wary of trusting dog trainers after that experience. The only advice she accepted from Steve was that Ziggy was an anxious dog and needed consistent boundaries. But she thought Steve's methods were too harsh. Even abusive.

Soon after, Heni met Suzy, an amateur dog training enthusiast. Suzy did agility with her dogs. She said that dog trainers all have different philosophies and that dog training was unregulated. Anyone could call themselves a dog trainer. Suzy agreed with Heni that Steve's methods were overly harsh.

Suzy didn't see a problem with dogs sleeping on beds and couches, as long as they got off when instructed to without growling and showing teeth. As Heni incorporated more consistent structure and regular exercise in Ziggy's routine, his anxiety was reduced. Suzy said Heni had done a really good job earning Ziggy's trust, and using tone of voice effectively and her confidence was renewed with leading him more consistently.

Heni also noticed that the children did better with more consistency and structure, especially Alexandria. Alexandria had a very sensitive temperament and was sometimes feisty. Xavier was mostly laid back.

The twins went to preschool care a few hours per day while Heni worked part-time in variety of positions. The roles were typically short-lived. She got fired from one for questioning the authority of her employers. She got made redundant from another.

The preschool carer said that Xavier fitted in well with other children but Alexandria was struggling. She'd sometimes scream.

'She may not be able to come along to preschool as she's disrupting the other children. She screams so loud, she could shatter glass.' The preschool carer showed her the bruises all over her legs. 'These bruises are from when I restrained her.'

'Why did you restrain her?

'Because she was being disruptive with her screaming'.

'I don't see why she needed to be restrained. Why didn't you just take the other children away until she calmed down? Please don't restrain my child unless it is absolutely necessary, like if she is hurting someone.'

'I think you might need to take her to see a child psychologist.'

During the screaming episodes, Alexandria fell to the floor and paddled her arms and legs and she seemed to have no awareness of her surroundings. These weren't just tantrums. The episodes continued when she started school and teachers also expressed concerns that Alexandria was behaving differently to the other children.

Alexandria saw some specialists.

'No evidence of seizure activity,' the specialist said, after the electroencephalogram tests. 'Most likely is brain irritation.'

Alexandria was seen by a child psychologist and psychiatrist who both said that Alexandria was having meltdowns which were more severe than tantrums. The psychiatrist said 'I think Alexandria has ADHD – Attention Deficit Hyperactivity Disorder. I can prescribe a medication.'

'So you're not really sure? She can focus at school so I don't think your diagnosis is correct. I don't want her developing brain exposed to psychotropic medications if you are not even sure what she has.'

Heni refused the medications from the psychiatrist and instead opted for Alexandria to see a child psychologist to learn some skills to help reduce her anxiety and meltdowns.

The psychiatrist emailed a report to Heni for school. Heni contacted the psychiatrist, upset.

'You're accusing me of being a refrigerator mother?' she asked.

'What do you mean?'

'Reactive Attachment Disorder. I read that children in orphanages who have not been loved can get it. My children are very much loved.'

'I'm sorry. It is unlikely that she has Reactive Attachment Disorder. It was just a possibility I considered and I forgot to remove it from the report.'

In meetings with the psychologist, Heni was told that she had one child of an 'easy-to-parent' variety and one child of a 'challenging-to-parent' variety and that one learns so much more with parenting challenging children.

The psychologist said that 'challenging-to-parent' children require more routine and structure and they will test the boundaries more often by being oppositional. Boundaries and structures would help reduce Alexandria's anxiety and reducing Alexandria's anxiety would reduce meltdowns.

The psychologist also worked directly with Alexandria, teaching her to recognise early signs that a meltdown might be coming on and she had permission to take herself away to discharge the hyperarousal energy with repetitive movements such as jumping on the trampoline. This was proving to be very helpful.

She said that Heni would need to be very consistent with any fair consequences. She suggested that Heni pick her battles and give warnings that transitions are coming up to help Alexandria adjust to them. Heni would let Alexandria know ten minutes ahead that there would be a change. Then five minutes. It seemed to help. She tried to avoid meltdowns but she would risk them for something she felt was important.

Richie worked shifts so it was hard for any structure to revolve around him. Most of the care of the children was given by Heni. Heni and the children liked to create imaginative stories in a scrapbook.

One of the stories they called 'Larry the Letterbox Lizard' after a skink took up residence in the letterbox, to the delight of the children. Xavier and Alexandria invented the story, which Heni drew in cartoon outlines for the children to colour in. Larry the lizard travelled through tunnels to other rooms where he met up with friends to play cards or swim in a cave swimming pool. The underground caves were lit up with lightbulbs.

Heni treasured the art the children made. They expressed joy in painting on an easel with poster paints just like in her own earliest memories of painting when she was at kindergarten. Like Heni, the children loved books. They also started developing their own interests.

Socialising at school was easy for Xavier but challenging for Alexandria. She struggled to make friends. One girl, Missy, targeted her and frequently called her names, pulled her hair and laughed at her.

Heni went in several times to talk to the principal, trying to get her to do something about the bullying, but the principal made excuses. When Heni was helping Alexandria get dressed after a bath, she noticed bruises all over her body.

'What are these bruises from, Alex?'

'The principal grabbed me.'

Heni asked Alexandria exactly what had happened. Missy had spat in Alexandria's face after stabbing her with a pencil. Alexandria had screamed in distress. Then the principal had restrained her and Alexandria had gone into full meltdown.

There was a clear outline of a bruise in the shape of a hand. Heni showed the bruises to Richie when he got home from work. 'They're not listening to me. You'll have to come in.'

Richie arrived at school in his police uniform. Heni and Richie met with the principal and showed them photos of the bruises on Heni's phone.

'Please explain these bruises on our child's body. She said they were inflicted by you,' said Richie.

'She did them herself! She threw herself around like a wild animal.'

'Xavier said he saw it happen exactly as Alex said,' said Heni.

'Okay, I did restrain Alexandria. I put my hand on her shoulder to escort her to my office because she was disrupting the other students. I didn't expect her to go feral.'

'You didn't need to restrain her,' added Heni.

'She might have run out onto the road.'

'She was upset. She has never run away before when upset. She usually falls on the ground. She was nowhere near the road.'

Finally the principal apologised and stated that the school was proud of their zero-tolerance for bullying policy.

Yet the bullying persisted. Heni decided to take matters into her own hands. She walked onto the school grounds and confronted Missy. She said in a very quiet voice. 'You've been bullying my daughter, calling her names, spitting in her face, pulling her hair, pushing her around. Stop.' Heni used a quiet, yet authoritative tone of voice. She gave gave an intense look.

Richie said later, 'You can't go around threatening kids, Heni.'

'I didn't threaten her directly,' said Heni. 'I think I scared her a little with a very quiet voice Dad used which scared me. It was more effective than yelling. I gave her a look like *Don't mess with me kid because you don't want to find out what I'm capable of.*'

'You have scared the living daylights out of me with that look, too,' Richie joked.

Alexandria reported back that the bullying finally stopped.

But then Jackie, a girl who was starting to be Alexandria's only friend, called Alexandria a crybaby. For the first time, Alexandria lashed out and there was a full on fight with pulled hair, fists, ripped clothes and skinned knees. Then Alexandria hid under a table like a frightened animal and lashed out at anyone who came near. It was similar to Ziggy's fear aggression. Heni came to collect the children for the last time from that school as Alexandria was now afraid to go to school.

'I want to die,' said Alexandria. 'I have no friends.' It was so painful for Heni to hear. She took both her children out of that school and started Xavier at a new school. It took several months to transition Alexandria to the new school. The principal paired her with a non-authoritarian style teacher and she started to make some friends.

Alexandria still was seeing a child psychologist for anxiety. The psychologist said that Alexandria was now having meltdowns arriving home from school, because that's where she felt safe to let go, after holding herself together all day at school.

The following year, a teacher punished Alexandria for having 'fidgety hands'. Heni went in and told the teacher that it was petty and that there was no need to shame her and that it was ridiculous to expect children to stay completely still all day. Alexandria had always fidgeted to relieve her anxiety. If she didn't do it, she was more likely to have a meltdown.

Since the unfair restraint at the first school and the fight with Jackie, the meltdowns had changed. Instead of falling to the ground paddling her arms and legs, screaming, Alexandria had started hitting and kicking Heni. She would fight, yet she still had no awareness of what she was doing.

When Alexandria was calm, Heni asked her, 'During your meltdowns, can you not hear me when I tell you to stop?'

'No, it's like I'm in a dream and my head is under sand and your voice is so far away I can't hear what you're saying.'

'Do you realise you are hitting and kicking me during meltdowns?'

'No.'

It was very stressful for Heni to be attacked by her own child. It was more stressful than the loud screaming. Alexandria was now getting very strong.

Richie also unleashed his frustrations at home which added to the stress. It was unsettling when Richie admitted, 'I wanted to beat the shit out of a druggie who bit me. But I was professional and did the arrest.' Richie had to have blood tests for HIV and he was annoyed he had to refrain from sexual contact until the follow-up blood tests came back clear.

On one of Richie's days off, he took Heni and the children to a tiger sanctuary. Spectators were invited to pet Dewi, a female tiger. Heni felt in awe as she rested her hand on Dewi's shoulder. The family watched Raja, a male Sumatran tiger swimming. Heni purchased a photo of Raja in the pool, had it framed and put it above her bed.

On the news was a disturbing item. A man had been arrested after murdering his wife. He had confessed to hitting her on the skull with a hammer then raping her while she was barely alive. Then he killed her with an axe. He still had name suppression. Their children had been removed from the home for neglect prior to the murder.

'I know who it is,' Heni said to Richie.

'So do I but I'm not allowed to tell you.'

'It's Oliver Green from our anti-natal class.'

'How the heck did you know that?' Richie looked astonished.

'I'm right, aren't I? Remember when I told you when he stood next to me that I could tell he was a dangerous predator? I could sense it. I shut off my fear because I knew it would excite his prey drive.'

It later came out in the media that Oliver Green, dubbed the 'HAM' for 'Hammer Axe Monster' admitted that he had killed his wife Natalie. He said Natalie had been the only person who had ever loved him, and that he went into a rage when she refused sex. He also confessed that he intended to abduct the caseworker who removed their children from the home.

Heni felt grateful that she was married to a man who protected her and the community. A respected police officer who would keep her and the children safe.

9. Pet Purpose

Heni was having trouble finding a new job. She'd worked several part-time jobs and had recently been made redundant again. She decided that if no one would employ her, she would start her own business.

'I want to start a pet sitting business,' Heni told Richie after the twins were settled into their new school.

'You want to sit on pets?'

'I want to take care of pets in their own homes. It's popular in the United States but quite new to Australia. An alternative to boarding kennels.'

'That would be just like a hobby? Surely you wouldn't make any money from it?'

'I've researched it and talked to professional pet sitters elsewhere. I'd need to get insurance and register a business name, get a business tax number and stuff like that.'

Richie dismissed it as a hobby but he agreed to it.

So Pet Purpose was born a few weeks before Christmas. Heni applied for a business tax number, registered her business name and later applied for a trademark. She purchased pet sitting insurance and designed her own logo and marketing materials. She built her own website and hand-delivered flyers around the neighbourhood. She set up business cards in holders at the local vets. Her first Christmas brought a handful of clients, mainly from the flyers.

The following Christmas she hired employees for the summer holidays because she had hundreds of pets booked in for twice-daily visits. She had set up a pet and client database with scheduling software accessed via a phone app. Clients commented on how passionate she was about caring for their pets. She gave photo albums with client pets to her first few hundred clients. Some said her photos were the best they'd had of their pets. She'd captured their candid expressions and a connection through the camera without setting up poses.

The first pet was a rainbow lorikeet called Squirt who soon became a regular client. Squirt was very social so his owners asked if he could stay as a boarder. He was very affectionate and also very playful, tossing his toys off the table and watching them drop. He was possessive of his cage and Heni had to make sure he was out playing on his ropes before she could change his food and water.

One day though, Squirt didn't seem himself. It was subtle. He was a bit cranky at times and other times just snuggling into her neck but something wasn't right. She knew birds could go downhill quickly so she took him to the vet.

'He seems a bit docile but I can't see anything wrong with him,' said the vet. 'But then I'm not an expert on birds, especially exotic birds.' Most vets tended to specialise in cats and dogs.

As the hours progressed, Squirt got worse. He was puffed up and his feet started curling up so he could no longer grip his perch. Heni put him in a shoebox and kept the box warm. Squirt was still taking a small amount of fluids via a dropper. 'Something's terribly wrong,' said Heni. She didn't want a pet in her care to die.

She told Squirt's owners about an exotic bird and reptile specialist vet in the next city. Squirt was diagnosed with metal poisoning, most likely from his beloved bells which he licked when he played with them. He was treated for the metal poisoning and his bells were thrown out and replaced with stainless steel ones. Squirt made a full recovery.

Suzy started working for Heni as a pet sitter and she continued to mentor Heni with dog training and behaviour. Clients were pleased with Suzy after bad experiences with other trainers. They also were very impressed with how Heni could build a bond of trust with their pets. Especially the pets with a history of trauma.

Pet Purpose

One of the dogs Heni took on had a history of fear aggression and a lifetime of neglect. She was now in a new home. Heni dropped tiny portions of Pip's food on the ground as she entered the property. Pip stopped barking, ate the food then watched quietly from a distance. Heni avoided eye contact but she did not completely turn her back on Pip. She prepared food and water then sat down and ignored Pip.

Pip came closer and closer over the next few days and then finally nuzzled Heni's hand. After that, they were friends. Pip's owner was delighted when Heni sent a photo update of Pip being affectionate.

'What's your secret?' said a new client at their introductory Meet and Greet. Axel, their dog, came over to Heni as soon as she sat down.

'What do you mean?' asked Heni.

'Axel is wary of strangers, but has responded to you immediately. Even my cat runs away with strangers.' Molly the cat was sitting nearby watching curiously.

'I've always been a pet magnet. One of my secrets is to ignore dogs and cats at first. Don't talk to them or make eye contact. I just walk in and sit down while chatting to the owner about their care. Sitting down lowers my height. I stay standing if it's a bossy dog. The outgoing pets come over straight away and I give them attention when they calm down. Most pets like attention but some don't. I let them come to me when they're ready.'

The majority of new clients found Pet Purpose via Heni's website. She blogged regularly to keep her website ranked at the top of her area. She decided to try offer a stand-alone poop scooping service, so she phoned up some lawn-mowing contractors to do some market research.

'What do you do about dog poop on lawns?' asked Heni directly.

'I just mow over the top of it,' said a lawn mowing contractor in a drawling Australian accent.

107

'Doesn't it get stuck to the wheels of your lawnmower and transfer to another property?'

'It's usually all dried up.'

'Do you not mind getting particles of dog poop dust up your nose?' asked Heni.

'I wear a mask.'

'Yeah right,' laughed Heni.

Heni wrote a blog post about the conversation and other pet poop adventures. To her surprise, she was contacted by two local newspapers and two radio stations because they thought the blog post was hilarious.

During an interview with one of the newspaper reporters, she talked and talked and it was hard for the reporter to interrupt to ask questions. Heni couldn't help it. The reporter told her that the blog post was funny, but she looked at Heni a bit strangely when she was talking non-stop. Heni was either very chatty or silent. One extreme or the other.

Heni was nervous but did a live radio interview anyway. She tried her best not to talk too much but she had trouble reining herself in and ended up talking more than the radio announcer. She felt proud of herself for giving it a go, as public speaking was something she felt anxious about.

Another radio station emailed her, and asked her if she would like to take part in a weekly pet themed program. Based on the blog post.

'You won't want me to talk,' replied Heni. 'You'll know what I mean if you speak to me on the phone. I already did one radio interview.'

The radio announcer phoned her. 'I see what you mean,' he said, as Heni had difficulty with give and take and completely took over the conversation, whilst going off on numerous tangents. Heni was aware of it, yet she could not control it.

'I'm not that spontaneous really, either,' said Heni. 'At least if I write something down, my brain has had to slow down a little to think about it. Writing something amusing doesn't necessarily translate to speaking.'

Although sometimes, she had some people laughing and other people disgusted at her lack of a filter, when she told unexpected, amusing stories. She both entertained and offended others when she was in the energetic, talkative moods which were a contrast to her often quiet and serious moods.

Heni's clients voted for her for a business award. Her business was selected as one of the three finalists.

She phoned back a potential client who had enquired about their dogs.

'Do you still require pet sitting for your dogs?' she asked.

'I have a confession to make. I don't actually have any dogs. I am a mystery shopper for the finalists for the business award.'

'Oh wow. I hope I did okay.'

'I wrote a really good report for you. It's obvious you are passionate about what you do.' Passionate was a word people used frequently to describe Heni, especially in client testimonials. They also frequently commented on how Heni had a 'gift' with pets.

Heni rarely wore dresses so she bought a new black and red dress for the formal evening event. Richie was stunned when Pet Purpose was announced as the winner of Business of the Year, but Heni did not feel surprised. She had felt confident she would win. The announcer called Heni up onto the stage and said 'You're trained in pet first aid and CPR – so can you do mouth-to-mouth resuscitation on a dog?'

On stage in front of hundreds of people, Heni felt like she was in a strange dream with her head swimming, trying to keep her anxiety at bay, but she managed to reply with a smile, 'More like mouth-to-snout resuscitation.'

After caring for thousands of pets, and with pets having a shorter life-span than most humans, Heni was informed frequently of pets who had died or moved away. She'd get messages like 'Charlie passed away today.' 'Teddy crossed Rainbow Bridge.' Heni was empathetic but it took its toll. All these pets she'd bonded with, that she would no longer see again.

Clients were grateful for the photos. One was touched by a photo of their very timid cat, Coco, who came out from under the bed for Heni. Coco died from cancer shortly after and the photo was treasured.

Heni had flashbacks to pain in her childhood when she was informed that Penny, a friendly red chicken, had been killed by a fox. And that Snowy, a white cat had been run over. Snowy's owner had insisted that Snowy be raised with free access to outdoors.

The deaths didn't happen in Heni's care but she was very much affected by them. Heni tried to blank out the grief but she would be reminded of it every time a pet died. She was also reminded of one of the main reasons she quit vet nursing. All the deaths were triggering for her. Reminding her of Snowball's suffering around the time she was sexually abused.

The twins were now eight years old. Some of Heni's clients were fine with Heni taking the children to pet sitting visits after school. Heni visited some dogs without the children for safety reasons but many of the pets were very affectionate with the children.

One visit on which Heni did not take the children was to feed some security dogs for a client. The client arranged several visits while also on then off the property to make things as safe as possible for Heni when she went onto their territory. The client emphasised that things 'could not go wrong', meaning Heni could be killed. Heni was calm without fear.

Xavier seemed calm and reserved with his emotions like Heni was most of the time. Pets had a calming influence on Alexandria but Alexandria was mostly still feisty.

'The twins are like fire and ice, like your maternity ring...' said Richie '...and you'. The twins' personalities were like different aspects of Heni's personality, only Heni had shutdowns rather than the meltdowns Alexandria still had at times. Anger was an emotion that Heni was so triggered by that she suppressed it strongly.

Heni was still working on Alexandria's inflexibility which was a factor in her meltdowns. These had become less frequent with reducing her anxiety.

Richie and Xavier had gone out and Heni was alone with Alexandria. Showering had been a sore point with Alexandria ever since she was little. The agreement was that Alexandria would have a shower at least once per week, and wash in other ways daily for basic hygiene. Heni had been advised by a child psychologist to not give up on the showers.

'Alex, please go and have a shower,' directed Heni.

'In a minute,' replied Alexandria who was busy on her tablet.

Several minutes went by. Alexandria had been reminded about the upcoming shower the day before and seemed to agree to it, but now was procrastinating.

'Alex, shower,' said Heni in a more authoritative voice.

Alexandria ignored her. Without dialogue and showing no emotion, Heni took the tablet from Alexandria and locked it in a cupboard. Heni knew this was risky, but she felt Alexandria needed to have a consequence, and she was not going to nag constantly.

Alexandria started screaming. A tantrum very quickly escalated into a full meltdown. She started hitting and kicking Heni, with high pitched-screaming. More aggressively than ever before. If Heni stepped away, Alexandria pursued her. Alexandria could not hear Heni in that state.

Heni stuck one hand out with a straight arm to defend herself. A heavy curtain started coming down in Heni's mind as she was shutting down.

Alexandria fell backwards onto her bed. Heni pressed one hand on the centre of Alexandria's chest, pinning her to the bed. Alexandria's high-pitched screaming continued. Her hitting and kicking turned into aimlessly thrashing her arms and legs. Exactly like she would do when she was younger, when she used to fall on the floor.

Heni's mind was almost completely shut down, which blocked out most of the noise. She did not feel anger. She did not feel her emotions nor was she able to think. She felt some adrenaline from her own fight or flight response being activated, before it was shut down within seconds.

After an imperceivable amount of time, Alexandria went quiet and stopped thrashing her limbs. She was very still. She looked like she was waking up from a seizure, disorientated. Heni was still frozen with her hand on Alexandria's chest. She was also coming back to the present. Alexandria was in a daze, looking all around the room, making sense of where she was.

Alexandria looked at Heni's hand pinning her down. Then she glared at Heni.

'Are you trying to kill me??!!' Alexandria yelled angrily. Heni took her hand off and walked away. Her thinking started coming back.

Did I do the wrong thing? she wondered. *Did I just alpha roll my child?* She had never alpha rolled a dog before, let alone restrained a child. She saw it as a risky thing to do.

Immediately after Heni released Alexandria, Alexandria had a shower. Heni tossed Alexandria's tablet on her bed while she was in the shower. Alexandria seemed completely unfazed and resumed quietly using her tablet again.

It seemed to have have happened instinctively. She didn't speak to Alexandria about it. After that one incident, after years of physical aggression with meltdowns, Alexandria never hit or kicked Heni ever again.

Alexandria also didn't seem to be as anxious as previously. Yet she didn't seem fearful of Heni. They still had a close relationship.

A few days later, Heni asked Alexandria to shower again. She was asking for more frequent showers than once weekly. She knew it was a huge risk. Alexandria procrastinated. Again, Heni confiscated her prized object, her tablet, without saying a word and without anger.

Alexandria had another screaming meltdown. This time she stayed standing and she did not hit or kick. She kept her distance from Heni while she screamed. Heni partially shut down and just stood there very still. Shutting down helped drown out the noise. For the first time, Heni realised she had partial control over some of her shutdown states. She imagined herself 'going into robot mode'.

Alexandria also looked like she now had partial control over her meltdown states, as she didn't fall to the floor or launch into physical attack. She paced back and forth over a small area and screamed. It was almost more like a tantrum than a meltdown this time.

Sometimes the meltdowns in the past had gone on for hours, but this one seemed to last less than fifteen minutes. Then Alexandria finally went quiet. She looked strangely at Heni who was standing there very still, making no eye contact.

'Why are you just standing there?! Like a statue!' Alexandria exclaimed. She picked up a dish sponge and tossed it in Heni's direction, but it did not hit her. Then Alexandria had a shower. It was as though Alexandria would get 'stuck' in a state of emotional dysregulation, before becoming unstuck. Then, going off to do what Heni had asked of her. There was a definite decrease in intensity and duration.

Again, Heni immediately returned the tablet, putting it on Alexandria's desk while she was in the shower, rather than confiscating it for hours or until the following day. She did not dialogue with Alexandria nor get angry at her. Richie got angry very easily with Alexandria, which made things much worse. Most of the parenting was left to Heni, as Richie was usually working.

Something odd happened. After years of meltdowns over showers, after these two incidents, Alexandria started having showers on her own, daily, without being asked. No more meltdowns over showers.

Her anxiety levels seemed significantly lower. She was no longer fidgeting constantly. Heni had observed Alexandria fidgeted more when her anxiety levels were raised. Heni fidgeted herself when she was more anxious. Alexandria was still passionate in her personality yet the meltdowns fizzled out. She also started to use assertiveness skills to communicate what she wanted.

Heni was also developing her assertiveness skills. She communicated to clients that she wasn't happy with some things, even if it upset them. She had always been afraid of conflict, so she had gone out of her way to please people. But now, she had had enough.

Heni was tired of clients who didn't put their pets first. She decided that she didn't need those sorts of clients anymore. Those who left litter trays in a state of filth. Those who left the yard filled with dog poop infested with maggots. She dropped such clients, even though it was sad to say goodbye to their pets. She updated her policies requiring clients to ensure clean litter trays and yards at the beginning of service.

She also changed her policy about sharing pet care with other parties, after a new client said his mother was going to feed his cat, Harmony, on alternate days. It was obvious that no one had turned up on the second day, so she contacted the client immediately. The man initially argued with Heni and called her the weirdest person he had ever dealt with, but in the end he apologised and said he could see that Heni cared about Harmony's welfare.

The client paid the balance for Heni to visit every day. Heni decided she didn't want him as a client anymore after that though and returned the key at the end of the service.

She was more assertive than ever, very different from a younger Heni who used to be quiet as a mouse, and like a doormat with her people pleasing. As Heni walked out of Harmony's house for the final time, lightning struck the road in front of her like a blinding flash. She could smell and hear tar seal sizzling on the road.

There was a thunderstorm. Electric storms were so much more spectacular in Australia than in New Zealand. In a spring storm, Heni went to move a dog to a more sheltered area.

Most clients had their dogs outdoors in fenced yards in the warm climate with sheltered areas from the sun and storms. Whereas most clients had indoor cats, often with attached catios so their cats could go outside safely.

In an error of judgement, Heni had accepted a pet sitting assignment for a client who was more concerned with his air-conditioning unit being chewed on, than his dog, Thor, being out of a potential storm. The area for the dog was fine if the weather was reasonable. But now, as the rain was going sideways, she decided to move Thor to a more sheltered area, that had the air-conditioning unit that the client had spent a fortune on making dog-proof.

Heni moved Thor and as soon as she got back to her car, she informed the client. Heni had an argument with the client who insisted that Thor be out in the less sheltered area, where he couldn't get dry. Heni refused and told him that while Thor was in her care, her decision for his welfare overrode his, and she had confirmed with an animal welfare agency that she was liable, as Thor's caregiver.

Just then, lightning struck the client's house with a loud crash. Thor's owner insisted that the key was to be returned when he got home. He told Heni he couldn't have a pet sitter who didn't obey his orders.

During that same electric storm, a patient from a psychiatric hospital had walked out and climbed a crane on an adjacent construction site. The crane was struck by lightning and the man was killed. It was in the news and it was determined that the patient was not well enough to have been released from hospital. The hospital admitted that the man had almost certainly been experiencing psychosis.

Heni observed patterns such as locations of clients being in clusters. It seemed rather odd, but frequently, she'd be caring for several pets on the same street within a hundred metres of each other at the same time. Sometimes they'd be literally next door but they had found her independently. Sometimes people from the exact same house, when the previous client had moved away. What were the odds in a small city? She had over dozens of pets with the same name. Charlie and Molly were two of the most popular names for pets.

Heni started painting digital portraits of pets from photos she had taken. She often painted late into the night and into the early hours of the morning.

'Are you trying to avoid me?' asked Richie when Heni went to bed as Richie got up to go to work.

'No of course not.'

'We're like ships passing in the night. You're not in bed when I am.'

Heni usually needed a lot of sleep but she'd have phases when she'd be a night owl and very productive on some creative projects.

Heni started caring for a cat for a new client, Matt. Matt explained that he got cat netting for the yard, and kept his cat Lucy indoors at night, after Lucy licked a cane toad. She had frothed at the mouth. Matt had rinsed Lucy's mouth gently with the hose and then rushed her to the vet. Lucy was lucky to survive the ordeal.

'Here's a cricket bat in case you need to kill a cane toad,' said Matt. 'Bloody pests. One whack and they're dead.' Heni imagined that might be quite messy with guts. Or being squirted in the eye with poison. Or that the toad might not die straight away and suffer. Heni did not see herself using the cricket bat to kill anything.

'Usually the cane toads don't come out until night-time. The vet recommends putting them in the freezer after cooling them in in the fridge so they go to sleep as a humane method of killing them. I still feel guilty about killing them though.'

'Dunno who the idiot was that thought it was a great idea to import cane toads. Unwanted immigrants.'

Heni felt vulnerable being a New Zealand citizen living in Australia. She'd recently found out that she would get no assistance, if she were to find herself in financial hardship. The Australian Government had changed the immigration rules over the years, and she was one of many Kiwis on an unprotected visa.

She was only considered a permanent resident for some purposes, such as being able to buy a house, own a business and to pay tax. But she was not a protected permanent resident, so she was unable to apply for citizenship without Richie sponsoring her.

She didn't know much about it initially, so she started an awareness campaign on social media that attracted thousands of supporters and some protesters. Soon after starting the campaign, the social media page was stolen by someone with their own agendas. It was easy to steal as Heni never made public that she founded it, and invited collaboration from others who knew more about the issue.

'Just as well,' muttered Richie. 'Anything you do is like a bloody religion.'

Heni had learnt though, that she had no pathway to dual Australian citizenship, other than through Richie sponsoring her. If she had visited Australia as a child, she could have accessed citizenship via a loophole. Richie refused to sponsor her.

'I don't see the point in wasting a few grand on that,' he said irritated.

Heni had been feeling satisfied with life. She had built an award-winning pet sitting business, was married with two beautiful children and was living in their own home with pets. She did feel vulnerable though that Richie refused to sponsor her to gain Australian citizenship. Richie had been more irritable lately. She tried to push it out of her mind.

10. Burnt

'I can smell smoke,' said Heni. She started closing the windows and doors.

'You're imagining things,' replied Richie.

Xavier came in from outside and said 'I can smell smoke.' The smell was very strong now for Heni but still faint for the others. Heni was trying not to cough. 'It's a bushfire. I can smell the eucalyptus'. Looking through the window, she could also see a blue haze.

'I can smell things before others can and much more intensely,' said Heni.

'You should be a sniffer dog at an airport,' replied Richie. 'Or perhaps we could train you to be a drug detection dog.' Then his tone changed to irritable as he pointed to a pile of washing on a chair. 'Why is the washing not folded again?' The twins disappeared to their bedrooms.

'At least it's clean. I haven't had the energy to keep the house immaculate as well as working and looking after the kids.'

'It's not frigging good enough.' Richie started pacing. 'I'm sick of this damned house and working hard and having nothing to show for it.'

Heni transferred most of the income from Pet Purpose to Richie who insisted on doing their finances. Richie said he was putting extra on the mortgage.

'Life is more than materialistic things,' said Heni.

'We don't have enough sex. I'm tempted to cheat,' Richie blurted out while he was pacing.

'Are you cheating on me?' Heni barely whispered.

'Of course not,' snapped Richie.

'We have sex at least twice per week,' said Heni. 'That's probably more than most couples.'

'It's not enough for me. I have a stressful job and I need sex as a relief valve.'

The music video for *Wrecking Ball* was playing on the television as Heni grabbed her car keys.

'Where are you going?' demanded Richie.

'I don't know yet. Why do you have to always know exactly where I am?' said Heni, now also irritable and bordering on tears.

Heni drove to the shop and bought chocolate. When she sat back in her car, she started to cry. She felt burnt out trying to please Richie. She wanted intimacy, not just sex. While eating chocolate, she stopped crying then drove back home.

Heni struggled to get through her work over the next week, so she went back to her doctor. 'I'm really exhausted,' she said. 'Should I increase the dose of antidepressants?'

Heni gained weight with the medication increase. Her figure was now much curvier than when she had first met Richie. Richie criticised her for gaining weight. Lately, he had been criticising her more.

With the boost in energy levels, Heni had been doing some research online and she had a proposal for Richie.

'What about an open marriage?' she suggested.

'What, you're going to let me cheat?' asked Richie.

'I'm against cheating. I'm against lying and deception. What if I consented to you getting your sexual needs met elsewhere so long as you were honest about it and stayed safe.'

'I can have a girlfriend? Or one-night stands?'

'If you wanted to. Stay safe. Choose people carefully. Use condoms.'

Richie agreed. To Heni, it was either Richie cheats, they break up, or they try something different. She had only had two monogamous relationships. Considering an open marriage was radically different for her.

Richie started looking on adult websites. Heni suggested, 'Perhaps I could have some experiences too?'

'What? You want to be a slut?'

'Why is it alright for you to have sex with others but if I do I'm a slut?'

'Okay, fine but what if one of us falls in love?'

'Maybe that's a risk I'm willing to take. If the only other alternatives are you cheating or dumping me.' Deep down Heni felt lonely in her marriage. For a long time, Richie had given his attention to other women, saying they were 'just friends.' He had flirtatious banter with other women yet he was irritable with Heni. 'Treat them mean, keep them keen,' was Richie's mantra.

Heni had been very reluctant to try new things sexually. Her confidence had been knocked when Richie would make critical remarks about her body. 'You could do with a breast lift,' he said. It hurt. She knew her breasts weren't as firm and perky after breastfeeding. She hadn't been enthusiastic about trying sexy lingerie.

Richie started chatting to women online. Heni chatted to a twenty-six-year-old Irish man called Liam on social media. Richie insisted on reading all their messages. Heni felt safer talking to someone on the other side of the world because she felt it would be easier to get rid of him if necessary than if he lived locally.

Richie got jealous at times when Heni talked to Liam but then Heni reminded him that he was talking to other women. Liam said that he had a strong belief in God and that talking to a married woman intimately would be shameful to his very religious family if they knew about it. Liam told Heni that she was beautiful. It had been a long time since Richie had called her beautiful.

Richie and Heni went shopping for sexy lingerie. She allowed Richie to photograph her for the first time in her new lingerie as well as topless. She wanted to feel desirable.

Heni made up an alter ego called Desiree and role-playing as Desiree allowed her to access parts of herself she usually suppressed, such as the desire to flirt. The photos captured a side to her personality she had never really expressed before. She looked innocent, yet naughty in her face expression.

Heni shared the lingerie photos with Liam. 'Absolutely stunning,' he responded. Heni felt a bit nervous sharing the topless photos after Richie's criticisms. But she thought the topless photos of herself wearing fishnet stockings while draped on Richie's motorbike were tasteful. In some of the photos she wore a black faux leather jacket and black boots.

'Breathtaking,' was Liam's reply.

'Really? You like what you see?'

'You're a gorgeous woman inside and out.' Heni felt euphoric. Euphoria was more than happiness or joy. It felt like falling in love, only without the anxiety. Euphoria felt addictive.

'What are you high on?' asked Richie.

'Liam said I have a gorgeous body,' replied Heni, grinning and bouncing around.

'Guys will just tell you what you want to hear to get sex,' replied Richie.

The euphoria didn't last long however, as Liam would say and do things that upset Heni. He'd draw her in by being attentive with romantic words, and then he'd switch and lash out in anger at her. Heni was in tears. Liam begged Heni to move to Ireland and to marry him.

'Just get rid of that jerk if he's upsetting you,' said Richie. So Heni blocked Liam.

Heni felt closer to Richie when he was being supportive. Richie started opening up to her in ways that he never had before. 'One of my fantasies is to have a threesome,' he said.

Heni was apprehensive. 'I've never had a fantasy of a threesome. I think I'd rather have sex with someone one-on-one,' said Heni.

'Oh, come on, a threesome would be hot,' said Richie. 'Two women pleasuring me at the same time. Would you kiss a woman?' asked Richie.

'I've never considered it before. I might be curious to kiss a woman for a different sensory experience. Maybe women are more sensual?'

Richie said he was aroused by the thought of Heni and another woman kissing.

Heni admitted that she thought Mike, a new pet sitting client was attractive.

'Why don't you ask him for a threesome?' said Richie.

'I dunno, mixing sex and business might be a bad idea?'

'What's the worst that can happen? He might have to find himself a new pet sitter?'

'I'd miss Lucifer though.'

'Lucifer?'

'His cat. When I met him at the Meet and Greet he was all gooey, cuddling Lucifer, and I thought it was really attractive.'

'What does he do?'

'He's a pilot.'

'What is it with you and men in uniform?'

'Maybe because they're supposed to keep me safe and protect me?' replied Heni.

Heni felt very embarrassed, but she plucked up the courage to ask Mike if he was seeing anyone. He said that he wasn't and he agreed to a threesome.

Heni grew in confidence role-playing as Desiree. As Desiree, Heni went shopping and bought new dresses, nail polish, bolder make-up and perfume. Things she usually didn't purchase. To her, Desiree represented everything Heni usually wasn't. She was sassy, confident, sexy and naughty. Heni wondered if Desiree represented parts of herself she had suppressed.

Desiree taught Heni to use more profanity. 'Fuck,' said Heni.

'You said "fuck"!' said Richie with his jaw dropped and his eyes wide. 'You never say "fuck"! You've only ever said "shit".' Heni had hardly sworn in her life after watching Aroha wash Daniel's mouth out with soap for swearing when they were children. It hadn't stopped Daniel from swearing though.

'Fuckity fuck!' replied Heni with a cheeky glint in her eyes. 'Cunt,' said Heni, smiling. She remembered hearing children who lived on Victoria Street calling each other cunts when she was a young child.

Richie looked astonished. 'You said the C-word!'

'I have wet panties every time a plane flies over!' Heni's libido seemed to go from zero to super-charged. She had never experienced arousal that intense before. Richie and Heni went from having sex once or twice a week to four times per day. Yet she had extreme sexual frustration. She could not orgasm.

For the first time ever, Heni purchased some sex toys including a hot-pink dildo that did not look realistically like a penis. She had an extreme urge that just couldn't be relieved. Richie was asleep so Heni tried using the hot-pink dildo. Richie woke up.

'What are you doing?' Richie sat up. 'You never do that. Am I not good enough for you?'

'You were too tired and asleep. You masturbate all the time. Why can't I?'

A few days later, after Richie seemed to get over his bruised ego, they talked about it.

'I can't get release,' complained Heni.

'You mean you haven't had an orgasm?' Richie asked in disbelief. 'Ever? How do you know what one feels like?'

'I've never had an orgasm as an adult. I discovered I could orgasm as a young child by crossing my legs a certain way. It felt good. I didn't know what sex was. Family laughed at me so I stopped doing it because I felt ashamed.'

'I just thought you were really quiet at sex,' said Richie. 'How did I not notice?'

'I guess you were focused on your own pleasure?'

The following evening was the threesome with Mike. Heni had asked Mike to wear his pilot uniform which he did. He looked very handsome in his crisp white shirt, blue eyes and dark hair.

Heni wore a short red and gold flight attendant outfit without a bra and panties. She told Mike that she was going to be the pilot. She felt that acting as Desiree, she could be in charge.

Mike commented to Richie that Heni was feisty and spunky and he liked it. Heni was usually quiet and reserved but once she started accessing her alter ego, Desiree, parts of her personality came out that she'd never let out before. Parts of her that had always been on a tight leash because she'd been afraid to lose control. But now she wanted to let go.

It felt exciting sitting on Mike's lap on the couch, kissing. Mike was a very sensual kisser and Heni could have stayed there all night, kissing him. It felt taboo being married with Richie watching. She felt like things were rushed with Richie being there but she wanted to be pleasured by two men.

They went to the bedroom. Heni had recently been shopping for extra smooth red sheets and an essential oil burner and candles. She didn't usually spend money but lately she had been making purchases to enhance sensual, erotic pleasures.

Heni lay on her back on the bed, resisting the urge to make snow angel movements with her arms and legs on the softer than usual sheets.

The men both caressed Heni eagerly then they each pulled off Heni's lace trimmed stockings to reveal smooth, groomed feet. Mike started sucking on her toes. 'Yuck,' was Heni's initial thought but then she reminded herself to relax and enjoy herself and try new things. Mike had a fetish for feminine feet.

Mike and Richie were both men who liked to be in control. At one point Heni was concerned there was going to be a fist-fight as the arousal level of the men was heightened and they seemed to challenge each other with their glares.

Don't spoil it for me, Heni pleaded with Richie using her eyes. She couldn't relax and let go with the tension.

Richie got up, left the room and closed the door.

'He's jealous. Do you still want to continue?' asked Mike. Heni agreed, even though her mood was dampened. Mike got a condom. Then he was on top of Heni, with a penetrating stare into her eyes. Heni usually shied away from eye contact, but she found it hard to look away from Mike.

The door opened and Heni looked up at Richie, standing there watching. 'Are you okay?' she asked.

'Just hurry up and get it over and done with,' muttered Richie as he shut the door.

'I'm not in the mood now,' said Heni. Mike got dressed and let himself out.

Richie walked in. 'You kissed him more passionately than you kiss me! Wash him off, you slut!' he ordered. Heni started to cry. Richie seemed to soften. 'It's okay,' he said as he put his arm around Heni's shoulder.

In the night, Heni's foot stuck out from the sheets and George the cat jumped up onto the bed, brushing against Heni's toes – the exact same toes Mike had sucked. For the first time ever, a powerful whole body orgasm surged from her toes to her head and she lay there awake, breathing fast, drenched in instant wetness. She had never experienced anything like that before.

The next day, Richie was more his usual self. 'I felt jealous and sexually aroused at the same time,' said Richie. 'It was weird seeing another man with his cock in my wife's vagina. I was both incredibly turned on and wanting to rip him off and punch him at the same time.'

Heni told Richie how she had an orgasm in the night.

'You had an orgasm from the cat?' laughed Richie. 'But never with a man?' Heni looked downcast.

'I think it might be because of the sexual abuse by the babysitter when I was a child.'

Richie stopped laughing and seemed sincere when he said, 'I'm going to help you orgasm.'

Heni had figured out being in a trance-like state could help her switch over from analysing everything to being in the moment. She was hardly ever in the moment. Her mind was usually racing back into the past or into the future. If she was in the present, she was distracted by sensory issues. If Richie's stubble felt too scratchy, the room was too hot or too cold or there were smells she didn't like, she couldn't relax and allow herself to enjoy the moment.

Music helped her relax so she could go into a trance. She still had the *Yanni* instrumental CD Kent had bought her years ago. Richie hated it because it wasn't his style of music but he was willing to listen to her relaxation music this one time to pleasure Heni.

Heni wanted sensual touch, with no direct sexual touch at first. Richie massaged her back, then legs, then buttocks, then her breasts until she finally indicated she was ready for him to go down on her.

Heni went off into a trance like when she gave birth. She murmured what she was imagining. She imagined herself in a fantasy aeroplane flying to a private tropical island with lush flora.

She imagined herself swimming naked in a natural pool beneath a waterfall.

Then she imagined herself in the aeroplane ascending higher and higher, above the clouds, so high that she was in heaven. Along with her imagination, her mood was elevating into euphoria.

She started laughing while she had intense orgasms again and again, including contractions of her uterus, similar to being in labour. 'Halle-fucking-lujah!!' exclaimed Heni. 'I'm a goddess in heaven!'

Heni felt euphoria at greater heights than she'd experienced before. She'd been to Hell and now she was in Heaven. Euphoria was Heaven, not a religious Heaven but a metaphorical one.

When she had orgasms, she had an intense physical release and also an intense emotional release – sometimes laughter and sometimes crying. It felt like emotions locked deep inside from years ago were finally expressing themselves.

Then the sexual frustration started building up again rapidly, like a dam filling up again. But now that she'd learned how to orgasm, she could get temporary release.

A few days later, she had an appointment with a doctor for a script for more antidepressants. Her usual doctor wasn't available so she was assigned a different doctor.

'Your mood seems elevated,' observed the doctor.

'Because I've been having mind-blowing, incredible sex!' Heni burst out without any hint of shame. She'd never cared much for sex before and was now enlightened as to what she had been missing. Surely nearly everyone else experienced incredible sex too?

The doctor started smirking and physically put his hands on his face to straighten his mouth into a serious, expression.

'You laughed at me!' Heni called out the doctor.

'You're talking fast,' said the doctor. 'Plus you have a surge in your sex drive. I think you have bipolar disorder.' He got out of his chair and stood very close to Heni who was still sitting. Dr Paulson and her near suicide attempt flashed into her mind. She recoiled with disgust as the doctor hovered in her personal space.

'What? Bipolar disorder?' she said very fast and rather loud with dramatic almost sarcastic emphasis. 'I don't have bipolar. Lithium poisoned me. Why are you standing so close with your crotch near my face?'

The doctor went back to his chair behind his desk.

After she got her script for more antidepressants, she went straight to the reception to make a complaint about the doctor's unprofessional behaviour. She was tired of people in positions of authority abusing power. Like Dr Paulson and the teenage babysitter.

When Heni arrived home, Richie said, 'Remember Doug's wife, Vanessa, who was a witness at our wedding ceremony?'

'Yes. Never really saw her after that. Probably because we didn't really have anything in common.'

'She wants to have a threesome with us.'

'What about Doug?'

'He's cool with it.'

'Really? Isn't he your supervisor at work? As well as your friend?'

'Yeah, he's fine with it. You can ask him yourself if you want to. Vanessa is bicurious.'

'Bicurious? Is that another word for bisexual?'

'She's sexually attracted to men and she is curious to have a sexual encounter with a woman.'

'You want her to have sex with me? Don't get her hopes up about me. I don't want to touch someone else's vagina.'

'What's wrong with vaginas? I get so turned on by them.'

'I find genitalia in general unappealing. It took me a while to get used to penises. Perhaps it's that I don't like touching other people's body fluids?' said Heni screwing up her nose.

'I love pussy. The scent and taste of pussy is intoxicating.'

'No thanks.'

'Would you let her kiss you?'

'Perhaps, if that's what you really want, but I don't think I could go through with sex.'

Richie was still happy that Heni was open to trying new experiences. They had acted out some of Richie's other fantasies such as sex in a police car. Heni didn't realise before how much Richie was into taking risks before. But now she was willing to take risks too. Richie was more worried about getting caught than Heni, when it came to acting out the fantasies.

Vanessa arrived with alcohol. She looked glamorous in a short dress; her hair was now dyed intense flame red which emphasised her bright green contact lenses. She was petite and still into fitness. She looked like she'd had another boob job, going up a few cup sizes with her cleavage spilling out of her short, tight dress. A single zip ran up the whole length of the dress.

Richie seemed rather familiar with flirting with Vanessa, even though Heni had only ever seen her at Richie's work functions.

Vanessa guzzled down a few drinks quickly then stripped down to her lingerie, revealing ripped abs. She sat next to Heni who was still sipping her first drink. Vanessa said, 'I pole-dance. I would love to teach you.'

'Me? Pole dancing?' laughed Heni. 'Can you imagine me hanging upside down on a pole, Richie?'

'Yes, I can actually,' said Richie. 'It's just a variation of the gymnastics you used to do. But sexier.'

Vanessa sat down next to Heni. 'Richie said you are also curious to kiss a woman,' said Vanessa.

Heni wanted to please Richie. She felt anxious as Vanessa had been staring seductively at her all evening.

'Okay, I'll try a kiss,' she said nervously.

Vanessa went for a wide open-mouthed, wet pash. Heni remembered when she'd seen Filly pash Damion all those years ago. Heni felt repulsed and pulled away.

'I'm sorry, but it's like being slobbered on by a dog,' said Heni. Vanessa's jaw was tight and she frowned as she glared at Heni.

Vanessa grabbed Heni's breasts with both hands and squeezed hard. 'I wish I had natural breasts like you,' she said.

'Ow, that hurts,' said Heni.

'Sorry, I just wanted to know what real boobs felt like. I had to pay to be as busty as you.'

'You didn't need to be so rough.'

'How about a massage?' suggested Richie. 'Heni loves massages.'

'Okay, we can try a massage,' agreed Heni. They would only go as far as she felt comfortable with. She could speak up about when to stop. Heni had had very little to drink. She'd never been drunk because even a small amount of alcohol made her feel spacey and she was afraid of losing control.

They went to the bedroom where Richie lit candles. Raja the tiger was watching from the photo over the bed. Heni lay face down on the bed and Richie massaged her back while Vanessa started massaging her legs.

Suddenly Vanessa started making orgasmic moaning noises and straddled Heni's thighs. Heni wanted to shout, 'Get off me!' and throw Vanessa off but she couldn't move nor speak. She was frozen. Just before her mind checked out, her last thought was, '...don't want to let Richie down.'

She came to when Vanessa yelled triumphantly, 'I fucked Heni!' Vanessa was still making a lot of groaning noises and trying to insert her fingers into Heni's anus which Heni then clenched shut.

Heni was confused. *Did I just have sex with a woman? I don't remember anything?*

Dazed, she slowly sat up and saw Vanessa and Richie having noisy sex. Heni left the room. It felt awkward and strange seeing her husband have sex with another woman. Perhaps this was all a mistake?

After Vanessa left, Heni told Richie: 'I felt violated,' but they didn't discuss it further than Heni asking Richie not to have sex with her again. They argued.

After the evening with Vanessa, Heni started haemorrhaging. She had always had heavy menstruation, but now the bleeding was continuous with frequent flooding. Heni had a flooding incident at a shopping mall with Richie and she was feeling more anxious about going out in public.

She was scheduled in at short notice for a hysterectomy and internal repairs. It was confronting signing the consent for surgery form, which had a statement that the surgery may result in death. Heni had known she needed surgery for years but she had avoided it.

In the few days before the surgery, Heni was passing blood clots the size of golf balls. Her blood pressure was very low going into surgery and she was afraid she was going to die.

She was given a transfusion of two bags of packed red blood cells after she woke up, then her lungs partially collapsed, so she was unable to breathe when she lay down. Her lungs crackled like puffed rice cereal in milk.

Recovering from the surgery back at home, she'd drench the sheets with sweat like someone had thrown a bucket of water on the bed. After changing the sheets to dry sheets, she would wake up drenched again. The surgeon told her that she needed to rest for six weeks. She couldn't look after pets, do housework nor drive during that time.

After recovering from surgery, Heni gently resumed having sex. 'I want to thank your surgeon,' said Richie. 'Your vagina feels amazing. It's like before kids.'

'It's pretty much had a reconstruction. Parts no longer collapsed into it that aren't meant to be there.'

'You should have done it years ago.'

Heni had been too afraid to have surgery when she was struggling with issues such as chronic pain, fatigue and depression for much of her adult life. Doctors had diagnosed her with fibromyalgia, despite raised blood inflammation markers.

She'd felt like she was going to collapse when thyroid cysts popped out from her neck with a visible lump around the time Tripod died. She had a biopsy of the cysts. Her blood pressure had plunged more than ten units into hypotension when she went from sitting to standing. She had bruised easily.

The thyroid cysts and thyroid antibodies disappeared on a gluten-free diet. Her chronic muscle pain; joint and bone pain; teeth and gum pain; brain fog and depression; irritable bowel and dermatitis improved dramatically too. No more post-nasal drip and sinus infections.

Her blood pressure became more stable, she bruised less easily, and she lost excess weight. That was when she started Pet Purpose.

Heni asked doctors about her unusually high libido, and they did a hormone panel. All her reproductive hormones came back at high levels. 'We could try suppressing it, or otherwise just enjoy it,' said a new female doctor who Heni had met for the first time. 'Your prolactin levels are high. Have you had a head scan to check for a tumour before?'

'No.' Nothing was investigated further.

Heni contacted Mike to see if he was interested in a one-on-one meeting.

'I'd really love to but I feel a bit guilty,' Mike replied.

'Guilty? Why?'

'I have a girlfriend. I cheated on her and she doesn't know.'

'You fucking arsehole!' Heni had never called anyone that before. She was irritable and ranted at him in a very long email.

'What the fuck is wrong with you?' replied Mike. 'Are you crazy?' Mike demanded that the key be returned as he did not want a 'lunatic' to be his pet sitter. Heni felt very depressed and told Richie she didn't want to see anyone else for sex again.

Memories of the childhood sexual abuse surfaced again. Aroha and Klaus had refused to tell her the teenager's name or age or anything else. Yet Heni remembered lots of strange details. Heni thought that perhaps telling a family member of the teenager would help get closure.

Even though Heni blanked out his first name and his face, she remembered his last name and looked up his family on social media. She contacted his sister Deborah who replied and acknowledged that she remembered that night. She said that she would have been around fifteen and she was asked to baby sit but she wanted to meet up with a boy so she called in her brother Paul.

Deborah said Paul died in a car accident on Loop Road when he was twenty-one and that their mother does not speak of her dead son. Then she stopped talking before Heni could find out any more information such as Paul's age or a photograph, to try to reconcile with her memories.

The last thing Deborah said was, 'I hate that you said this about my brother. But I understand. It happened to me too. But not by my brother.'

'Why don't you just let it go?' said Richie, when Heni was trying to get closure. 'You can't charge a dead man anyway. It just remains an allegation.'

Heni impulsively got a tattoo of a cat above her ankle. The black cat looked like it was clinging to her leg, leaving scratch marks with its claws. At the same time, Richie got a tattoo of skin peeling back revealing reptile skin on the shaved muscular chest over his heart.

Heni found it hard to focus on the day-to-day running of Pet Purpose. The creative part had been setting it up but now the administrative tasks and meeting new clients exhausted her. As she was doing her Christmas bookings an email arrived from Doug.

'My wife Vanessa is having an affair with your husband. Call me.' He left a contact number. Heni's hands were shaking as she made the call.

'How long has it been going on?' she asked.

'I think it's been a few years.' The evening with Vanessa was months before. Easter weekend.

'How do you know?'

'She told me. I think she started cheating after she found out I'm infertile. She desperately wants a baby and she won't look into adoption. What Vanessa wants, Vanessa gets.'

Heni felt sick to the stomach.

When Richie got home, Heni said, 'Doug said you've been having an affair.'

'Bull dust. He was okay with it. I still want you more, my exotic bird,' said Richie as he put his hand around Heni's waist and leaned into kiss her. Heni pulled away.

'Don't touch me whenever you feel like it!' she snapped. 'You said you wouldn't see her.'

Heni's mind was struggling to focus and it was taking a lot of energy triple checking that her clients' pets were scheduled in correctly. She was exhausted.

Then she made a mistake. She visited a cat, Tilly, a day later than scheduled before she realised her error. Tilly had spare food and water so she didn't go hungry but Heni felt so guilty that she stayed three times as long when she visited. She told Richie of her mistake.

'Don't tell your client,' said Richie.

'You mean lie to them?'

'Well it's your reputation on the line. The cat was fine. No harm done. So lie.'

'But my clients trust me! I feel so bad lying.'

Then, another client informed her that their cat, Tiger, had been killed in a car accident. The client had insisted that Tiger needed her freedom so was not confined to indoors. Heni was very upset.

Ziggy had become frail over the last few months. His fur was falling out in clumps. The vet said he had cancer. When his breathing became laboured and he was having trouble standing and started losing sense of his surroundings, Heni made the decision that it was time to say goodbye.

When his ashes arrived back, Heni and the twins, who were now pre-teens, buried them.

Heni kept most of her grief about Ziggy's death to herself.

Pet Purpose was her passion, but now she felt more severely burnt out than ever before. Her brain had been previously sharp. Now she could no longer focus.

Sex had been a temporary distraction. But now she wasn't interested in sex and she didn't want to sleep in the same bed as Richie. She was now in the spare bedroom.

'I'm selling Pet Purpose,' she said wearily to Richie. 'I'm burnt out.'

'What? How much for?'

'Suzy is going to buy it for a few grand. I haven't the energy to market it to another buyer. It will change ownership in the new year.'

'Just a few grand? That business is worth more than twenty times that at least!'

'It's either that or I'm shutting it down. I'm exhausted. I'll never forgive myself if pets starve to death if I make a mistake with the scheduling. I don't trust anyone else to do it while it's my business.'

'What are you going to do?

'I don't know. Find a regular job I guess. Maybe work for Suzy after a break? I'm mentally and physically exhausted.' Heni didn't want to face the possibility that her marriage with Richie might be over.

Richie was resentful that Heni was selling her business. He had dismissed it as just a hobby at first but it had done surprisingly well financially.

Richie started being more open about his relationship with Vanessa. Heni felt like he was deliberately trying to punish her.

Heni was usually reserved with showing her emotions, but sometimes the painful emotions would rise up and overwhelm her. She'd be so distressed that she couldn't speak. Xavier asked her a question and looked at her puzzled when Heni was mute with a pained expression on her face, waving her hands around, trying to force the words. Xavier shrugged his shoulders and walked away with a baffled look on his face.

On Christmas Eve the twins were visiting Richie's mother. Heni arrived home after a long day of work and overheard Richie on the deck talking on the phone. 'It's really weird. After being desperate to keep that bloody dog alive, she's hardly cried since he's been put down. It's like she's really cold. Aww, I love you too, Ness.'

Heni felt panic then immediately shut down. That's what she did often. Shut down. So she didn't feel emotion. Eventually the anxiety would break through. From all that energy being trapped, frozen, instead of going into fight or flight. From emotion that never got to be expressed.

At times, there would be an overflow of intense, passionate emotion, typically in the form of ranting and crying that seemed very out of character for her.

'Of course I'm jealous!' she ranted. 'You always give other women more attention than me! Why did I pack up my life to come over here? After all these years you don't even know me!' she cried passionately.

'Well if you did your wifely duties then I wouldn't have to get my needs met elsewhere,' replied Richie before walking away, leaving Heni sobbing, feeling vulnerable and lonely.

11. Fully Charged and Dangerous

Heni felt exhausted as she trained Suzy in the administrative aspects of the business. She was like a firecracker, almost completely burnt out with the odd pop of energy.

On the eve of Kent's death, Heni sent the twins to stay the night with their grandmother.

Heni stood in front of Richie's enormous CD library then selected an album *Hysteria* and set it to play on a loop on the stereo. Richie had joked that pushing the 'play' button on his expensive stereo with surround sound speakers was playing an instrument.

Heni sent instructions to Richie via text message: *Kids away. Bring home full police uniform with handcuffs for a night you won't forget.* She danced around the house while getting ready. She applied black eyeliner and new red lipstick called *Reddy Now.*

Richie's motorcycle roared into the garage.

Heni as her alter ego Desiree, was standing in the doorway wearing a very short police outfit, with black, thigh-high boots. Her hair was twisted into a police officer's hat.

'Oh, sexy police officer,' cooed Richie, clearly approving. 'With "fuck me" boots. That's more like it.'

'I'm going to get lucky tonight,' said Richie, scooping Heni's waist, gawking at her cleavage and leaning in for a kiss.

'No, I'm in charge,' said Heni authoritatively, pushing him away with one hand firmly on his chest. 'I'm your superior. You do what I say.'

'Ah, I get it, playing hard to get,' replied Richie. 'You know that makes me want you more.'

'Have a shower and freshen up,' directed Heni. 'Then change into your police uniform. Without underpants.'

'I feel like I'm a box of fireworks and you like to play dangerously with matches,' said Richie. 'I like it when you take charge in the bedroom.'

Richie emerged from the en suite wearing his police uniform, smiling.

'Hand me your cuffs and key.' Heni knew it was against regulations for Richie to bring the uniform and cuffs home.

Richie was like an obedient dog and he handed the handcuffs to Heni.

'You're under arrest.' Heni cuffed one of Richie's wrists and attached the other cuff to the bed post. She slowly unbuttoned Richie's shirt and pulled it over his shoulders revealing the reptilian tattoo over his heart.

Heni unbuckled Richie's belt.

'Unzip your trousers' said Heni. She could see a bulge in the front of his trousers. Richie was nearly exploding with excitement.

Richie fumbled around with one hand and his trousers dropped to the floor. Heni kicked the trousers out of Richie's reach.

'You've been a naughty boy,' she whispered, 'and I have the key'.

Heni was being unpredictable which amplified Richie's lust.

Heni sat on the other side of the room and started dancing while performing a strip tease to *Pour Some Sugar on Me*. She took off the hat, releasing wild curls. Then she unbuckled her belt and unbuttoned her police outfit, which she tossed into Richie's face.

Underneath she was wearing a black satin corset and panties with a suspender belt clipped to the stocking. A sparkling teardrop crystal danced between her full breasts and another sparkled on the top of her matching black satin and lace panties. Brand new lingerie.

Heni fished out a key from her cleavage and waved it around. Her eyes seemed to flash with hints of violet amongst the turquoise. Her eyes truly were like polished paua shells, changing in the light and with her moods. Her eyes were extra sparkly and her skin glowed with her elevated mood.

'What are you doing?' asked Richie. He stopped smiling.

'When your nuts are full, your head is empty,' said Heni as she tossed the key in the en suite toilet.

'What the fuck are you doing?' demanded Richie, tugging at the locked cuff urgently.

'Giving you no fucks,' said Heni, as she pulled a long-sleeved mini dress in a bold print over her head, and smoothed it over her hips.

'Unlock me now so I can arrest your arse.'

'Richard. Kopf. Dick. Head.' said Heni. 'I'm sick of your lying and cheating.'

'You bitch!' yelled Richie.

Heni used the remote control to turn the music up loud to drown out Richie's yelling. She tossed his phone on the bed and she calmly walked out the door.

When Heni arrived home, there was a car in the driveway – Vanessa's car. She pulled over, turned off the lights and waited. Vanessa drove away.

Heni walked in. Richie was uncuffed and was wearing jeans with no shirt. The stereo had been turned off and the TV was now on. The sports segment was on the news, which Richie was restlessly looking at. He stood up and walked towards Heni.

'Going to finish what you started then?' he asked as he put his hand on Heni's cheek and backed her into a wall and tried to kiss her. Heni turned her face away. 'Don't touch me,' she said as she side-stepped away.

'What the hell was that about?' he demanded.

'You tell me. I saw her leave.' Heni walked into the en suite. The key was gone. 'So she stuck her hand down the toilet for you? What other favours does she do for you?'

'What are you talking about?'

'Stop lying to me. I'm not stupid. I heard you tell her you love her.'

'I wouldn't have to find another outlet if you'd do your wifely duties.'

'You cheated even when you were getting plenty of sex.'

'It wasn't cheating. You consented.'

'I did not consent for you to cheat! I did not consent to what she did to me!' Heni's voice was tight. 'Couldn't you tell I wasn't participating?!' Heni started to feel panicked. She wanted to get away. To escape.

'Get out!' yelled Richie. 'No-one fucking humiliates me like that.'

'This is my house too. I'm staying here.' Heni was barely keeping it together, trying to stand her ground.

'I don't think you understand me. Our marriage is over. I'm texting your parents right now to tell them we've separated amicably.' Richie picked up his phone and started texting.

'Amicably – another lie. How much of our marriage was a lie?'

'Our marriage was over the minute you let that pilot wanker stick his cock inside you! You forced me to have sex with others!'

'You said you were going to cheat on me. I reluctantly allowed an open marriage. You still cheated in an open marriage.'

'Fine. Our marriage was over when I said I wanted to cheat. It's been over for ages. Get out of my house.'

'I have nowhere to go. This is my house too. I'm staying in the spare room. You move out.'

Heni walked quickly to the spare room, on the way passing the television which was playing some highlights of a New Zealand vs Australia cricket match.

Richie yelled, 'I'm going to go to lawyers and get everything! The house, the cars, all the contents and custody of the kids!'

Pet Purpose

'Of course the kids come last!'

Heni shut the door. She closed her eyes and was barely able to process what had happened. Everything was spinning in her head. It was very rare for her to argue with Richie and never to that intensity.

'BAMM!!' Richie kicked the door open. He charged at Heni like a truck with no brakes, his fists shaking in Heni's face. He was towering over Heni, intimidating her with his huge size, and yelling at her close range. Heni froze; her breathing slowed as she shut down and her gaze dropped to her feet. She stood there staring. The last thought before she fully dissociated was that the man she had loved all these years was a monster.

Then she felt nothing. Heard nothing. Thought nothing. It was like going under general anaesthetic. If Richie had punched her, she probably wouldn't have felt it.

Richie picked up a hammer and smashed it into the door again and again, in a rage like an angry bull. A picture fell off the wall. Heni stood there, still frozen and unresponsive. Finally frustrated, Richie tossed the hammer aside. As Richie walked away, Heni started coming to, feeling like she was in a daze. She heard Richie yell, 'You're fucked in the head!'

Heni had felt the fear when Richie had yelled at Alexandria as a newborn. But so much more intensely. She was now afraid to be in the same house as him.

Trembling, she slowly closed the smashed door and collapsed to the floor by her digital piano. She was exhausted and numb.

Now that they were living separated under the same roof with the house up for sale, Richie yelled at Heni daily. 'Please don't yell in front of the children,' Heni asked meekly but it didn't make any difference. Most of Richie's yelling was about the sex he had felt deprived of. And his jealousy of her having had sex with the pilot, even though he had agreed to the threesome. He was jealous despite his affair with Vanessa.

143

Heni was still the primary caregiver of the children. Pet Purpose was now owned by Suzy and Heni was just trying to survive. Richie demanded half the money from the sale of Pet Purpose but Heni refused to give it to him because she had no other income. She didn't know where she would live when the house sold. She was feeling too stressed to cope with work, yet she needed a source of income until she could find a new job.

She went to a government agency to seek emergency support. She did not qualify for any emergency support payments because she was a New Zealand citizen, even though her children were Australian citizens. They told her Richie could make child support payments as the children were fully in her care. Richie started spending nights away and Heni felt terrified when he'd come back to the house.

When Heni purchased groceries, Richie went through the fridge bemoaning how she had spent 'his' money because she had bought a container of juice. Heni was hoping equity from selling the house would tide her over until she could get through the stress and find a job.

After his anger at the juice in the fridge, Richie continued to rant. 'Take your stinkin' cat with you when you leave!'

'George is the twins' cat. He needs to stay with the children.' Richie seemed to have forgotten that he bought George as a kitten for the twins after Tripod died. Richie knew that Heni loved cats and George always slept by Heni.

It was very stressful for Heni to try to stand her ground against Richie as every day he was doing everything he could to grind her down. He ignored her pleading to not argue when the children were home. He yelled when the children were in their rooms.

After dropping the children to school the following day, Heni sat in the car feeling panicked. In her mind, it was like a video was playing of a snake letting go of a mouse and the mouse was barely alive. The snake only let go of the mouse because it latched onto another snake and the two snakes were strangling each other.

Then in her mind, she saw a little bird with its wings clipped, in a cage at the top of a cliff with the door open. There were waves crashing on rocks at the bottom of the cliff. The little bird was afraid to fly. Afraid it might not be strong enough to fly and that it would crash upon the rocks.

Shaking, she drove to the lawyer's office. Richie had rejected mediation and now she was applying for legal aid.

'Heni,' said the receptionist at the lawyer's office. *I fucked Heni!* Heni was re-experiencing the trauma of the sexual assault by Vanessa over and over again. Her heart was pounding, she was sweating and her eyes were darting rapidly from side to side. She felt extremely distressed. She felt disorientated and the room seemed to spin. It was like a panic attack together with flashbacks re-experiencing the trauma. Only the extent of her distress was not visible to onlookers.

'Please fill out this form.' Heni was unable to write her name. To see her name, hear her name or even to think her name was extremely distressing. Her name had become a trauma trigger.

'Please don't say my name,' Heni asked the lawyer. She had fifteen minutes of time with no charge. The lawyer said she could represent Heni and would take a fee from the property settlement.

'You cannot take the children out of the country without Richard's written consent,' said the lawyer. 'Not even for a holiday. If you do so, he could have you charged with child abduction under the Hague Convention. I cannot stress how important this is. Penalties include jail.'

'Here is a support line for domestic violence,' continued the lawyer. 'I strongly recommend taking out a restraining order against Richard.'

145

'But he hasn't actually hit me.' Heni minimised it just like she did with the sexual assault.

'Intimidating you, verbal abuse, financial abuse, being controlling and making you feel unsafe counts as domestic violence. Domestic violence does not always involve hitting,' replied the lawyer.

When Heni arrived back to the house of stone that had previously been her family home, she saw an azure kingfisher sitting on the fence. Heni had previously rescued a young azure kingfisher that had smacked into a glass window and was still and cold as though it were dead. It revived in Heni's hands and she rehabilitated and released it.

Heni looked in the filing cabinet for her passport. She found her passport but noticed the children's passports were missing. She could see no other way to avoid the trigger of her name but to change her name. Her mind was racing and she couldn't think of a new name. The scrapbook with the Larry the Letterbox Lizard story was in the file where the passports were usually kept. *Larry...Larissa.* Larrisa was born.

Larissa ditched Heni's middle name Victoria, because it was the same name as the street where the baby sitter, Paul had lived. Larissa decided not to have a middle name. Larissa ditched the surname Hertz, because it rhymed with 'hurts'. Her mind was unable to focus to think of a new name.

Then she saw an advertising brochure on the table with the rear end of an aeroplane. *Take Flight. Be Free.* She glanced out the window and saw the azure kingfisher fly away.

It took a lot of effort to focus to complete the documentation to legally change her name to Larissa Flight. A New Zealand name change certificate had the option of plain paper, a beach or a forest. Larissa chose a forest.

'Where are the children's passports?' Larissa asked in a text to Richard. She was extremely anxious about communicating with him but she needed to know.

'I have no idea what you are talking about.'

Larissa felt extremely vulnerable as she went to the court to have the documents signed to apply for her name change certificate. She also filled out an application for the protection order. She wanted Richard to stop yelling at her and intimidating her. She was terrified of him now and it was very difficult for her to speak to him about anything.

Richard was furious about the application for the protection order. He accused Larissa of trying to stop him from seeing the children. He told her he would fight to get full custody of the children.

Larissa felt exhausted but she was determined to try to stay in the house until it was sold. She didn't know where she and children would live. She told the children she might not have any choice but to return to New Zealand. She asked them whether they would prefer to live with her or their father.

'I'd rather live with you, Mum,' said Alexandria. 'You understand me better than Dad.'

'Me too, but I want to stay in Australia,' added Xavier. 'It's the only place I know.'

'Our friends are here,' said Alexandria. It had been hard for Alexandria and now she had friends after a rough start at school.

The costs of living independently exceeded the child support payments. Larissa was feeling more and more panicked as the court hearing date loomed. She directed the stress energy into detail-cleaning the house, preparing it for sale.

She confided in a new online friend who lived a few hours away. Todd was a solo dad with a son who was the same age as the twins. Todd visited and the children got on well together. After the children went to bed, Todd held Larissa in his arms. Larissa offered sex to him.

'No, you're too vulnerable,' Todd said. 'I get the feeling you need to please men with sex. You don't need to do that with me.'

'Thank you for not having sex with me,' said Larissa.

'You're welcome. I want to show you that some men are different.' Todd held Larissa in his arms until she fell asleep.

Todd, Larissa and the children were swimming in the pool together when Richard turned up to replace the broken door. Richard shook Todd's hand but it was obvious to Larissa in Richard's voice and body language that he was jealous of Todd. Larissa got out of the pool and took down a large family photo of herself, Richie and the twins and put it in a wardrobe. They were no longer a family.

When Todd left, Larissa's anxiety increased and she felt unsafe. Four days before the court hearing, she started having severe migraines. She'd had migraines ever since she was a teenager, usually pre-menstrually. But never this severe. She was unable to sleep.

Aroha rang. 'I'm coming over.'

Larissa was pacing while panicking and not thinking straight. 'Don't come over!' She was in a state of fight or flight.

'I've already booked the ticket.'

'No! Don't you come over or I'll take out a restraining order on you! I won't open the door!' Larissa was losing control. She felt unsafe.

The migraines continued all day and all night, with severe nausea. She was terrified that the judge would rule that Richard's behaviour wasn't 'bad enough' for domestic violence and dismiss it. It was a massive trigger for her – the fear of being dismissed.

It was like history was repeating itself. Richard and Vanessa now reminded her of The Monster. The Monster who had sexually abused her as a child. The judge was her parents, dismissing it as 'not that bad' when she told them her secret that she felt so ashamed of. The secret she had kept for years.

The day before the court hearing, Richard collected the twins for the day. It was the first time in weeks that Larissa had had a break from the children. She had been barely holding it together but now she was unravelling. She stood in the shower with her eyes closed, trying not to think about court.

Then she was aware her heart was racing and pounding hard as she went into a state of full panic. Feeling faint, she collapsed in the shower, sitting on the tiles. She kicked the door open, gasping for air. She tried to stand up but collapsed again. Her body surged into hyperarousal state of fight or flight then plunged into to a shutdown state. She could feel the rapid changes in her blood pressure and heart rate as she went from panic to immobilisation.

Naked, she crawled to her phone. She tried to call emergency services but she couldn't speak. She hung up and struggling to focus, she sent a barely coherent message to Todd full of spelling mistakes because of her inability to focus.

She pulled a sheet off her bed because getting dressed was too difficult. She fought to crawl to the door to unlock it. The ambulance arrived and she still couldn't speak. She wrote a note in scrawly handwriting, 'Call Todd', and handed her phone to an ambulance officer. He called Todd who explained she had been under a lot of stress with a marriage breakup. He said he was on his way.

It took a huge amount of mental and physical effort to get dressed. In a disorientated state, she took her phone and keys and nothing else.

On the way to the hospital, the ambulance officer took her blood pressure, using an automatic machine. Usually her blood pressure was low to normal on the many occasions she'd had her blood pressure measured before. This time, the cuff felt painful instead of the usual firm pressure. It felt like the machine was squeezing, tighter than a python, crushing her arm.

She started to speak for the first time to the ambulance officers. In huge distress, she cried out, 'It's hurting! Take it off!'

'It's just a blood pressure cuff,' the ambulance officer said, dismissively. 'Your blood pressure is high.'

At the hospital, Larissa felt distressed that she had to give her current legal name as it was such a huge trigger. There were no rooms available for hours, so she was put in an unused waiting room with a couch and a coffee table. She was on her knees on the couch, rolled up into a ball rocking back and forth under a blanket, crying. She felt like she was going to die. She thought she either must have a brain tumour or be having a stroke for her mind and body to feel so distressed.

Then she was transferred to a room with painted, grey brick walls and no windows. A room with just a mattress on the floor and two chairs. She was still waiting to be seen by a doctor.

Suzy arrived. Larissa didn't really have any local friends other than Suzy. 'I'll go back to the house and get some clothes and toiletries for you,' Suzy said.

While Suzy was gone, Larissa asked for paper and wrote 'Final instructions' in a scrawling mess because she genuinely believed her brain was about to explode and she was going to die. Pages and pages of large scribbles, rambling incoherently about her wishes for the children. Her distressed handwriting was nearly illegible and very different to her usually beautiful handwriting.

When Suzy arrived back with toiletries, a woman with red hair arrived and starting asking lots of questions. Larissa felt agitated. 'Get out! Go away!' she yelled at the woman. Larissa had never shouted at anyone before. The woman left the room.

A psychiatrist, walked in at the commotion. He used a very gentle, quiet voice. 'I'm doctor Floyd, I can see you are distressed.

Would you like me to give you something to help calm things down?' Suzy nodded that it would be a good idea. Dr Floyd gave Larissa a pill to swallow.

Todd arrived and Larissa put her head on his lap. She felt safer with him. 'Just relax there and a room will be ready for you soon,' said Dr Floyd in a soothing voice.

Todd gave Larissa a packet of chips as she'd had nothing to eat. 'You're eating the chips in slow motion,' observed Todd, as Larissa's hand went very slowly to take a chip from the chip packet and then in slow motion to her mouth as the tranquilliser took effect.

There were no spaces available in the psychiatric hospital so Larissa was at first transferred to a bed in the mainstream hospital. Todd and Suzy went home. Larissa had insisted that Richard not be told where she was but someone had to tell him so he could make arrangements with the children. Larissa was in no state to care for the children. She was unable to care for herself.

The lights were dimmed and curtains were drawn and a young nurse was sitting in a chair next to her bed.

'Do you have to stay there all night?' asked Larissa.

'Yes.'

'Am I on suicide watch?'

'Yes.'

'I smell bad. I got all sweaty when I was upset and I don't like how I smell. Do you have some wipes or something?'

The nurse handed Larissa some wipes.

'Thank you,' said Larissa. The extreme distress had caused her body to release a strange smell that she didn't like at all.

'Do you mind watching me?'

'Not at all.'

'I feel awful. I yelled at someone before.'

'The other nurses didn't want to look after you. I find you okay.'

151

Larissa was drugged to fall asleep. When she woke up, a nurse asked, 'What is that bruising on your arm?' There was bruising with red dots.

'That was from the blood pressure cuff.'

'Wow, I haven't seen that happen before. There is a room available for you in the mental health unit.'

Suzy popped in to see Larissa just before she was transferred. 'I'm sorry, but my husband won't allow me to see you again.'

'Why not?'

'It freaks him out. He doesn't actually want me to see you again at all, ever.'

'Because I'm going into a psychiatric hospital?'

'Yes. I'm really sorry. I need to keep him happy. I'll do you proud with looking after Pet Purpose clients.'

Then Suzy left. Larissa had no-one else to confide in apart from Todd. She felt very, very alone.

12. Nut House

An older nurse, Edith, who had red and blonde streaks through her hair showed Larissa around the psychiatric hospital.

'There are rules. You get up at 7am, make your bed and line up for medication. You will also line up for medication at 8pm. No women are allowed in the men's sleeping area and no men are allowed in the women's sleeping area. No plastic bags, mirrors, razors or belts are allowed. If you need to use a razor, you will need to request it from a nurse and return it immediately after your shower.'

They walked into a dingy room with grey concrete walls without pictures. There was a mattress on a built-in wooden base and a wardrobe that could be locked with a padlock. The room had a shower and toilet.

'You're lucky. You have your own room for now,' said Edith. A piece of shiny metal was attached to the wall as a mirror without glass. 'Guards will check all through the night that you stay in your bed.' Edith kept talking as they walked back to the corridor past the nurses' station which was behind clear security windows and locked doors.

'You do your own laundry. You'll have to ask for a portion of laundry detergent and to be let into the laundry area. Ask for permission to be let into the music room if you want to listen to music. As you are a voluntary patient, you may ask for permission to leave the premises for a few hours daily between allocated hours. We'll need to unlock the security doors for you to come and go. There are no phones and no computers. If you want to use the pay phone, you will need to put your name down on the board for a time slot. If you need more toilet paper, ask for it. If you don't make your meal requests in advance and turn up for meals, you won't get food. Did you have any questions, Heni?'

'My name is Larissa.'

'I will call you Heni as it is your legal name.'

'Please don't call me that! It upsets me! My name is Larissa.' Larissa suddenly became very distressed. She was panicking, looking for somewhere to escape.

'Larissa is not your legal name, so I will call you Heni,' said Edith in an authoritarian tone of voice.

'Then I can't stay here!' She didn't know where else she could go. She didn't have the strength to go back to the house. She was panicking at the thought of being homeless on the street. It felt too emotionally and physically unsafe.

Dr Floyd walked past, wearing a light pink shirt with grey trousers. Very quietly in his gentle voice he told Edith, 'Larissa may be called by whatever name she feels comfortable with.' He smiled at Larissa. Larissa felt some relief. Edith's expression was sour but she and the other staff complied with Dr Floyd's directive.

Larissa was advised the domestic violence protection order hearing was dismissed because she hadn't turned up to court. Larissa had been fearful it would be dismissed anyway. Who would believe a patient in a psychiatric unit over a police officer?

Aroha and Klaus arrived. As soon as Larissa saw them, she became very distressed and cried out, 'Tell them to go away!' She felt unsafe. Her parents felt hurt but a mental health advocate supported Aroha and Klaus. Klaus cried after seeing Larissa as he barely recognised her in her state of extreme distress.

For a few days Larissa had her own room, then she was moved into a shared room with another patient. Every few days or weeks she would share her room with someone new.

One woman she shared a room with took her anger out on the steel-lined door, kicking it and cursing at it. The same woman also needed to use the toilet briefly over a dozen times every hour, so Larissa had to frequently request toilet paper. Larissa forgot her name and also other names. She had difficulty recalling names at the best of times but now her recall for names and words was severely impaired. Larissa wrote names and descriptions of people down in a little purple notebook she carried with her because otherwise, she could not remember.

Larissa was taken off antidepressants and started on a new concoction of medications, including a mood stabiliser.

To pass the time, she coloured in mandalas and other outlines printed on pieces of paper in the art room using the felt pens and crayons. The art room was the only place with colour. Larissa asked if she could attach her pictures to the wall above her bed and she was given permission to do so.

'Have you been diagnosed yet?' asked a woman who was sitting next to Larissa while they coloured in.

'They haven't told me anything. My diagnosis for years has been treatment-resistant depression and anxiety.'

'My diagnosis is bipolar disorder.'

'How does that affect you?'

'I turned into a different person. I lied, I cheated, I stole. I cheated on my husband with a police officer. My husband said he would forgive me if I got help.'

'The police officer wasn't named Richie by any chance?'

'No, why?'

At lunch, Larissa carried her tray and sat next to a man with long hair.

'What are you in here for?' he asked.

'I had a breakdown but I don't know yet.'

'I have bipolar with psychosis.'

'How did you end up in here?'

'I believed I was Jesus and rode down the main street naked on a donkey.'

'Really?'

'Yep. I still can't believe they tasered Jesus!'

Larissa walked to town and went shopping when she was released for up to two hours daily. She had no income yet bought items she would normally not buy, including a purple off-the shoulder ballgown with a sequinned bodice and a flowing skirt on sale. She didn't know why she bought it. She bought tiger-print pyjamas.

She also went to the library and used a computer. She poured out her angst on a private page on social media. She felt like she had practically no friends in 'real life' yet some people she had never met expressed support of her.

Some 'friends' betrayed her. They contacted Richard who contacted the hospital.

'You've been disparaging the hospital on social media,' scolded Edith. 'Saying it's a hellhole.'

'That's because it is a hellhole.'

'You don't have to stay here if you're going to be ungrateful. How are you getting access to he internet after we confiscated your phone?' Larissa refused to tell her. As long as they kept letting her out because she was a voluntary patient, then she could walk to the library and use a computer to access the internet. She had nowhere else to vent her distress.

There were no counsellors in the hospital. Larissa felt guilty for not confessing how she was getting access to the internet, but it was a matter of survival. She needed someone to hear her distress. If someone would listen, even one person, it was reason to stay alive.

Larissa wrote in her notebook things she need to do such as purchase earplugs because the patient next to her snored. She wrote that she wanted to get a quote for a tattoo. She wanted to get two butterflies on her wrist representing the children.

She spent hours in the mental health clinic designing the tattoo, although she didn't actually get it done as she wasn't happy with the design because she was unable to do her artwork as neatly as usual.

Her design ideas came out messy which frustrated her, although she could painstakingly colour in the mandalas.

Larissa bought a necklace with two birds sitting on a branch in a circle, representing her children being free as wild birds. Free like she longed to be.

A letter arrived from Richard's lawyer. It said that there was no equity in the house after all the debt from various loans was applied against the assets, not including superannuation. Larissa wasn't able to focus to process the figures. How did they only have the same amount of equity in the house as the original deposit? After more than twelve years of paying a mortgage and with an increase of property values?

The lawyer concluded that Larissa should take on half the debt and that Richard should keep the house and his superannuation which was more than Larissa's. It was too confusing as she couldn't think clearly to try to make sense of it. How could she have gone into the marriage with savings but come out with so much debt?

Larissa managed to make an appointment with the bank. She asked about the mortgage account. Had there been withdrawals against the mortgage? The bank manager looked up a few of the transactions. There was twenty thousand dollars transferred to another account which was closed a few days later. Another transaction of ten thousand dollars. Another of thirty thousand dollars.

'Who authorised those?'

'We have both your signatures.'

'I have no memory of signing those.' Larissa's head was spinning. How many others were there? Did she sign them and forget? But why would they go to accounts that were closed shortly after? Accounts she had no knowledge of. It was too overwhelming to deal with.

The only big expense Larissa was aware of was installing the swimming pool. But Richard had insisted on handling all the finances, so she didn't know the details.

Each day, she carefully applied make-up in the poorly reflective metal mirrors. Even though she didn't usually wear make-up. Sometimes she wore the purple ballgown with her new sparkly golden strappy heels around the hospital even though she didn't usually wear high heels.

Larissa bought vivid purple hair dye called *Ultraviolet*. She knew the nurses would not allow her to have it. Except perhaps Vince. He was one of the few nurses who was kind to her. 'I'm not supposed to,' he said, looking around to see if anyone was watching. 'Quickly, go and do it and then give me the rubbish to dispose of.'

Larissa dyed her hair then smuggled the used packaging back to nurse Vince without his colleagues knowing.

Three weeks after being admitted to hospital, Larissa bought an instant scratchy ticket and won fifty dollars. Back at the hospital, she opened an envelope from New Zealand with her new name change certificate.

She immediately applied for a passport in her new name. Finding someone to be a witness would prove to be difficult as she didn't have any local 'real life' friends who had known her for the required time-frame after Suzy had ended the friendship.

Larissa found an old friend, Jo, from years back via online contacts who drove from the next city to sign the forms to change her passport into her new legal name.

Larissa asked Bernice if she would bring the children to see her but Richard wouldn't allow it.

She had spent less than ten minutes with each of the two psychiatrists. She watched Dr Floyd inject a patient in the buttocks. Dr Floyd had moved swiftly after the male patient was wrestled to the floor and restrained by two male nurses for physical aggression. The patient went limp and was carted away to isolation.

Other patients had talked about isolation. One patient said, 'You don't want to go there – if you think it's a shithole here, it's worse in isolation.' There was also talk of electroconvulsive therapy. The patients said amongst themselves, 'It's to help them forget.'

Another patient, Carol, said she was surprised Larissa hadn't been carted off to isolation after arguing with a nurse who wouldn't let her go to the music room, which was a small, dark room with a stereo. Larissa was anxious and agitated and felt that the nurse had been condescending and had punished her unfairly.

Larissa noticed that Carol was using a laptop on her bed. 'Why do you get to use a laptop when no one else is allowed?'

'I've been here for four years. It's one of my privileges, just like you being allowed to leave the hospital is one of your privileges. I use the laptop to run a business. I build websites.'

'You mean you haven't stepped foot outside this place for four years?'

'Correct.'

'Why? Don't you want your freedom?'

'Because I won't tell them what they want to hear. Being right is more important to me than being free.'

'What do they want to hear?'

'It's none of your goddamn business! Plus you keep interrupting me! You're the rudest person I've ever met!'

Larissa was confused. Carol seemed very articulate and then she would suddenly become irritated. Larissa didn't know what Carol had been diagnosed with. Carol asked for Larissa to be moved away to a different room. The nurses moved Larissa immediately.

One of the psychiatrists, Dr Roberts, called Larissa in for a meeting. He had an abrupt tone. 'We have decided on a diagnosis. Your diagnosis is bipolar disorder.'

'Bipolar disorder? What makes you diagnose that?'

'Your rapid speech for a start.'

'You're diagnosing me with bipolar because I speak fast?' Larissa asked incredulously. 'I always speak fast!'

'It's based on our observations and your responsiveness to the medications.'

'I've hardly seen you! How can you observe me?'

'The nurses have been observing you.'

'But the patients here with bipolar said they do things like lie and cheat and steal and believe they're Jesus and are naked in the street! That's not me! People tell me I'm too honest!'

'Your first mistake is to compare yourself to other patients with a similar diagnosis. Your second mistake is to believe anything a patient in a psychiatric facility tells you.'

'These medications don't even make me feel any good! I'm getting fatter and I can't remember anything!' Larissa had gained weight rapidly. Her feet had been swollen painfully for the first few weeks on the new medications.

Dr Floyd had a kinder manner. He said, 'One can feel very energised and productive with the highs. Feel amazing and invincible. We'd all like to feel like that. But what goes up must come down.' Yet neither psychiatrist explained any more what bipolar actually was. Larissa was very much in the dark.

In the final week of Larissa's stay, Edith said, 'We've decided that you are well enough now to leave.'

Larissa certainly did not feel well. She felt drugged up and scared. 'I have nowhere to go. The social worker said the homeless shelters are full.'

'We're not a homeless shelter,' replied Edith coldly. 'You will be discharged in three days.' The thought of being homeless terrified Larissa. She would not be able to feel physically and emotionally safe. When she walked back from the library, she saw a woman curled up in a garden bed. That could be her in a few days time.

A storm was brewing. She stopped to look at the crane above the hospital. Larissa imagined herself climbing that crane. The nurses thought she was 'fine' because she was no longer arguing with them. She felt medicated into submission. Larissa stood very still in the rain in the electric storm, staring at the crane.

Then she walked slowly back to be let back into the hospital, her clothing drenched.

Her new passport had arrived. Larissa Flight. With an even more terrible looking photo than most passport photos.

The hospital informed Larissa that Aroha was flying to Australia to take Larissa back to New Zealand. Larissa didn't want to leave her children but her fight had gone. She was in a state of learned helplessness and no longer speaking up for herself. Other people were making decisions for her.

Todd had visited a few times while Larissa was in hospital. He'd stroke her hair gently. She had also talked on the phone to him each week. Todd said that if she needed, he would pick her up and take her to his home so that she wasn't homeless. Larissa knew that wasn't a good option with no income and having only known Todd for a few months.

Larissa was sitting on her bed. Nurse Gina walked in with Mia, who looked remarkably similar to Filly.

'I'm not sharing a room with that slut!' yelled Mia. They walked out and Gina returned on her own.

'I'm sorry about that. It's her condition,' said Gina.

The following day at lunch, Mia apologised. 'I'm sorry for saying those things,' she said. 'I didn't really mean it.'

Aroha arrived back in Australia.

Larissa wanted to hear the bellbirds in a picnic area one last time, so Aroha took her out of the hospital for a few hours. The bellbirds made enchanting tinkering sounds high in the trees and there was a little creek nearby which Larissa watched for several minutes. The delicate and magical sound of the bellbirds was a contrast from other birds in Australia, which were often loud and screechy.

Aroha arranged for the children to see Larissa briefly in a park. She hadn't seen them for two months and she didn't know when she would see them again. Richard waited at a distance, watching.

'Why is he hovering around? Why won't he let me see my kids?' Larissa asked Aroha anxiously.

Aroha stopped at a shop on the way back to the hospital to buy a snack. Aroha's phone was in the car and beeped.

Larissa glanced at the phone and saw her name was mentioned, so she picked up the phone to read the message. It was from Richard.

Aroha got back into the car.

'You both think I'm going to kill my children?!' she said, tossing the phone at Aroha.

'We didn't know what you were doing to do. You weren't supposed to read that.'

'If I was going to kill someone, I would kill myself! Never my children! You're both treating me like a criminal! Take me back to that hellhole! I'd rather be there than with you right now!'

'I'm sorry.'

Larissa was distressed and banging on the mental health unit's doors. 'Let me in!' She didn't want to go back to New Zealand if her own mother thought she would kill her children. She didn't feel emotionally safe.

Several hours later when Larissa was calmer, she talked to Todd one last time on the phone. Just after she hung up, the phone rang and Larissa answered it, just as Mia walked around the corner.

'You slut! You stole my boyfriend!' Mia charged at Larissa with her fist pulled back ready to strike. As her fist collided with Larissa's jaw, Larissa hardly felt pain as she was already collapsing. It was like a dream in slow motion. She curled up into a ball, sobbing.

Her ear was bleeding. One of her new gold butterfly earrings had cut her ear with the impact. She hadn't even tried to defend herself despite having learned self-defence previously.

Two of the male nurses pounced on Mia who was taken away. 'Are you going to press charges?' the nurses asked. Larissa didn't want to go to the police station. She didn't trust the police anymore. As the nurses checked her ear, they told her that they had already observed that Mia had targeted Larissa and one of the female nurses.

The following morning Aroha arrived to pick Larissa up with a letter for her doctor in New Zealand and enough medications for a week. Dr Floyd quietly said, 'It would be better if you didn't press charges. You would have the stress of dealing with the court. Mia would get off any charges anyway as she is unwell. Go start afresh in New Zealand.'

Aroha had made arrangements for Larissa to go back to the house for one hour to collect her things. Larissa had transferred the ownership of her car to Richard's name, thinking it would make it easier but not realising that it now counted fully as Richard's asset without her receiving payment in return. The pet personalised number plates she had requested in exchange for signing over the car were sitting on the bench.

Larissa didn't recognise the inside of the house. Nearly all the furnishings including the couch and curtains had been replaced. There was a sign up saying, 'Our Home' and another saying 'Growing Family'. Underneath was a photo of Vanessa showing off an engagement ring. Vanessa had changed her hairstyle and colour to be similar to Larissa's. Another photo was of Richie cuddling Vanessa's pregnant belly from behind. A new nursery was set up. Larissa was choked up.

To her surprise, there were still a few photos up in the house that she had chosen. The photo of Raja the tiger was still above the bed, and a photo of a little black and blue bird, a superb fairywren was also still on the wall.

Larissa had chosen the photo of the bird when Richard had chosen a photo of a green python during their last holiday together after Richard had announced he was tempted to cheat. She took the photo of the tiger and the little bird from the wall to take with her.

Larissa packed a suitcase. Most of Larissa's things were dumped in the garage in cardboard boxes. The dolphin stained glass ornament was still hanging in a window in the garage. It was blowing in the wind and the edge of the tail of one dolphin was damaged from repeatedly hitting the door frame. She left it behind along with the colourful 'exotic' crystal bird Richie had given her as a wedding present.

She packed a few sex toys including the hot-pink dildo that didn't much resemble a penis but had helped give her release. She left the vibrators behind. The vibrators had annoyed her, especially the very expensive one that Richard had bought because he liked the idea of operating a remote control attached to it. Larissa had called them annoying mechanical mosquitoes.

She packed her make-up including the red lipstick called *Reddy Now* and a perfume called *Sensual Goddess*.

She went through the filing cabinet and took her qualifications and medical records that had come over from New Zealand years before. She took her laptop and the camera with the lens scratched after being struck by a snake. She took some of the photos of the children but left most of them behind for the twins.

She was still wearing her *Fire and Ice* maternity ring. From her jewellery, she kept the ruby heart engagement ring and left the emerald snake wedding band behind.

The house was eerily quiet. Larissa hadn't seen George at all while packing her suitcases. She noticed his litter tray was gone from the bathroom. She looked out the window and saw the cat netting outdoors had been removed.

A text message arrived. It was from Richard

'Vanessa is waiting. Your time is up.'

Larissa's heart was racing seeing the text but she replied. 'Where's George?'

'He's gone.'

'Gone where?'

'Put him down.'

'Why?'

'Vanessa doesn't like cats.'

'You killed him?! You monsters!'

Blinded by tears, Larissa pulled the suitcase to the rental car. Vanessa was sitting in her car wearing sunglasses and ignoring Larissa. Larissa had the fleeting thought of picking up a rock and throwing it at the windscreen and yelling 'Murderer!' but she did not act on that impulse. Her body was too lethargic and her mind was dissociating.

Aroha and Larissa went to a motel. Larissa was quiet and withdrawn.

Aroha repacked the suitcases. 'What's with all this kinky stuff?' asked Aroha, referring to Larissa's lingerie. The sexy lingerie had made her feel empowered as Desiree. She was too tired to think but she had decided in her exhausted state to keep it. No rational thinking had been involved with anything she packed.

'Don't open that one,' said Larissa when Aroha picked up the pillowslip with the sex toys.

Larissa fell into an exhausted sleep that was so deep it was like she was in a coma.

Suddenly, she flung her arms out in a defensive panic and cried out, 'Don't hit me!'

'It's okay. It's just me putting a blanket over you,' Aroha said gently.

Larissa reorientated herself in a heavily sedated state, confused at first about where she was and what had happened.

It's Mum. I'm at the hotel. I'm safe.

Then she fell back into a drugged-up sleep.

She felt numb as she boarded a plane. It was a grey, cold day when the plane landed in New Zealand.

13. Denial

Back in New Zealand, Larissa slept a lot. Twice as much as usual. She was chronically exhausted. Aroha said she'd heard Larissa snore. Larissa didn't usually snore.

'You're lazy,' said Klaus. 'You need to get out of bed and do some housework and get a job.' Klaus didn't understand what depression was like. Being judged as lazy made Larissa feel worse.

Going to the supermarket was a frightening experience. She felt panicked. Previously she had felt anxious at times when there were lots of people. Now she was having panic attacks because the noises in the supermarket such as beeping and people talking sounded exaggerated and all jumbled together.

Wearing earplugs helped block out the noise but Larissa avoided places like the supermarket as much as possible. She mostly stayed in her room, isolating herself.

An email arrived from Richard's lawyer. It stated that Richard wouldn't grant permission for the children to visit until Larissa had signed legal documents about property. Legal aid had fallen through as Larissa had left Australia.

The remaining money she had left went on lawyer's fees to have the document read and amendments made. The lawyer changed the wording from Richard having 'sole parental responsibility' of the children to 'joint parental responsibility'.

Larissa was in no frame of mind to try to negotiate anything regarding the property but she didn't want to take the children's home away from them, even though she was doubtful they would ever inherit it. Richard kept making excuses that he could not pay Larissa anything in exchange for keeping the house and assets.

Larissa was confused and depressed and signed over the house without receiving any payment. Richard kept the house, all the household assets, the cars, all his superannuation and the debt.

The twins visited in the winter. Alexandria seemed fine but Xavier seemed unsettled. He retreated to the bedroom which was unlike his usual self. Alexandria wanted to go to see snow for the first time on Mount Whakapono.

'Do you want to go see the snow tomorrow, Xavier?' asked Larissa.

For the first time ever, Xavier exploded. 'I hate you! I hate you for leaving us!' he yelled. Larissa went to her room, quiet and in pain which she internalised.

Mt Whakapono had a small eruption of ash that evening so Larissa was unable to take the children to the mountain which was now closed. The following day, Larissa sat down with Xavier to have a little chat.

'You're allowed to feel upset. Words can hurt though, said Larissa.' Xavier nodded. Larissa continued gently, 'I want you to understand that I had no choice but to come back to New Zealand. It hurts me too that we are apart. I didn't abandon you and Alexandria.'

'I know you didn't, Mum. I just wish it wasn't like this.'

'I love you.'

'I love you too.' They hugged.

Xavier had always been so close to his mother and he was finding it hard to adjust. He was more subdued than usual, whereas Alexandria was upbeat and chatty.

The twins had brought with them the dolphin stained glass ornament and the 'exotic' crystal bird. As soon as she saw them, Larissa felt like throwing them away but she kept her emotions to herself and quietly put them in the back of a wardrobe, thinking perhaps she could sell them if she could find the energy.

She was glad to see Xavier and Alexandria again but she was chronically fatigued. She was depressed and the medications didn't help her to feel better.

A week later, the twins flew back to Australia. They both procrastinated getting ready to go to the airport. It was like they didn't want to leave. Larissa didn't want for them to leave either. Saying goodbye was so very hard.

Larissa had an appointment with Dr Eric Wright, a psychiatrist, and Angelina, a mental health nurse. Larissa was obviously still depressed and it was a struggle to get out of bed.

'You can call me Eric,' said the psychiatrist in a Canadian accent. He had a tattoo of a red maple leaf on his hand and he was wearing jeans and a baseball jacket, which was different to the other psychiatrists who had worn formal attire.

'I don't think I have bipolar,' said Larissa.

'The letter from Australia says that you have been diagnosed with bipolar affective disorder.

'They haven't told me much about it. I don't think I have it. My emotions are not up and down like a yo-yo. Most of the time I don't even know what my emotions are.'

'Bipolar disorder is a mood disorder with episodes of mania and depression. Mood is different from emotions.'

'They've called it 'treatment-resistant depression' for two decades as they could never fix it. Do you think I have bipolar? Could they be wrong? I'm not like other people in the hospital who said they had bipolar.'

'I haven't seen you in mania with my own eyes,' said Eric. 'All I've seen so far is depression. We don't prescribe antidepressants on their own with a bipolar diagnosis as it can trigger mania. We treat according to what it looks like to us on the outside no matter what the label. I think you need more time to adjust to the medications.'

'I hate these medications. I can smell them in my room when I wake up in the morning. They make me feel like a zombie. I'm the fattest I've ever been. I wake up with pins and needles in my hands and fingers, gasping for breath.'

'Medications can have side effects but you are highly likely to relapse with mania if you do not take the medications.'

'I don't believe I have bipolar. The two psychiatrists in Australia hardly saw me. I think they've misdiagnosed me.'

Angelica gently asked Larissa. 'What is it about bipolar that makes you reject this diagnosis?'

Larissa started to cry. 'I'm not an awful person. There's all this stigma – it's been bad enough with suffering from depression and anxiety all these years – being told I'm possessed by the devil and other crap. I don't want to have something else on top of all that. I don't want to take medications that make me fat and make me smell weird and make me feel drugged up to the eyeballs. I've felt like a guinea pig for all these meds over the years.'

'You're a consumer,' said Eric. 'I cannot force you to take the medications. However I strongly advise it. I've seen medications help many, many people.'

'I feel like my emotions are stuck in the mud. The meds stop me feeling. It's like they're suppressing my emotions and the problems aren't dealt with. I want to try coming off the medications to see if I feel better.'

Eric and Angelica discussed a care plan for Larissa to wean off the medications. Eric also recommended that Larissa get into a routine of getting up the same time each day and start looking for work – 'any old job' to start with. Starting with just a few hours per week and gradually building up.

Angelica pointed out it was important for Larissa to get physically moving, even if she didn't feel like it. Going for walks daily would help with the blood flow around her brain, help increase her low blood pressure and help improve her overall physical and mental fitness and resilience.

Larissa felt both better and worse coming off the medications. Her emotions were thawing and her grief would nearly sweep her away at times. The excess weight started falling off on its own and within a few months Larissa went from being overweight to being slim like she was before she had ever started on psychotropic medications.

After coming off the medications, the heavy sedation effect was no longer there but Larissa felt constant low to moderate level anxiety and hypervigilance. She went for a walk most days – it was easier to get up and to walk now without the sedation.

She lay down on a yoga mat. Her brain had been constantly busy and her anxiety had been building. She felt fatigued yet her brain felt wired. She decided to do some progressive muscle relaxation and deep breathing exercises to help her anxiety. She used a foam roller to knead out tension in her upper back and a rubber ball to knead out painful knots in her shoulder blades and buttocks.

Then she lay on her back on her mat in the darkness, imagining the tension floating away from her muscles, starting with her feet and moving up to her head. She started to fall into a state of relaxation as she focused on her breathing becoming deep and slow, with emphasis on the exhale. When she had tried this exercise before, it had been refreshing.

But this time an overwhelming loneliness ached at the core of her being. She missed her twins, separated by a chasm of deep blue sea. She felt like she was tumbling in the sea, being pulled under by strong tows and undercurrents of grief, loss, heartbreak, politics and the legal system.

Tears welled up and then she started to sob, her whole body heaving. She rolled onto her side and curled up into a ball and the pain she felt psychologically was worse than the worst physical pain she had ever experienced. *Why do I have to suffer this much pain?*

Larissa turned on the light and rushed to the wardrobe and frantically pulled the belt off the soft, fluffy purple dressing gown that Aroha had recently given her. She ran outside where, in the moonlight, she stared at a hook attached to the eaves of the house. She just wanted the pain to end. She fought with every fibre of her being not to hang herself on that hook.

Somewhere amongst all the extreme distress, a small voice within told her that suicide would hurt her children and parents. Sobbing and feeling ashamed, she walked back to her room, curled up on her bed and fell into a troubled sleep.

Larissa shut down emotions to the extreme and the medications had enabled her to suppress even more strongly. She wanted to face her fears of experiencing intense emotions. Yet she was unprepared for how painful her grief was. She'd lost everything – her marriage, her pets, business, house, car, piano and her ability to think clearly. Most importantly of all, she was separated from her beloved children.

Larissa started a job as a part-time housekeeper at a hotel for the minimum wage. It was physically demanding work under time pressure but she didn't have to think much. It was difficult for her to try to remember how many soaps or rolls of toilet paper or how the towels were folded for each room.

At first, her muscles burned in pain and she was extremely exhausted but pushed through. She was generally quiet and withdrawn, but sometimes she'd joke around and make her co-workers laugh.

Several of the housekeepers were solo mothers and most of them were trying to quit smoking. One turned up with a black eye hidden by makeup. 'It's nothing,' she said as she turned away from the light.

Gossip got around fast. 'Her partner bashes her up,' said one of the other housekeepers.

Larissa wondered how much they knew about her. She hadn't told them much. One time she had a tearful outburst, telling them that she hadn't seen her children for months, after one of the housekeepers complained her ex didn't take the children one weekend. The other housekeepers looked startled yet didn't say anything. Larissa was embarrassed but she went back to work and didn't talk about it.

The housekeepers worked in pairs and turned on the music channel on the big screen TV or stereo while working. Larissa hadn't listened to music for a long time. She'd avoided music in her depression but it did help her to get through the physically demanding work with less pain. She found herself starting to listen to music again.

She saved up and bought an old yellow car which she named 'Lemon' after it needed rust repairs when a cracked windscreen was replaced. Aroha had said, 'Did you buy a lemon?' So that's what Larissa named her, as a joke. Larissa gave Lemon a cut and polish which brought back some of her vibrant yellow.

Lemon gave her some more independence. She drove Lemon to different places in nature to go walking. She was becoming moderately fit with both housekeeping and walking.

She started listening to music when she went for her walks. It seemed to help with release of pain with minimal distress. When she was listening to *Arlandria* as she walked by the river, she started feeling intense emotions that felt like a mixture of anger and sadness. Hot tears streamed down her face. It felt like a release.

Anger was an emotion she struggled with and she suppressed it so extremely that she rarely allowed herself to feel mild irritation. She had never experienced rage before. Her depression was worse when she had unexpressed emotions. She'd shut down and feel nothing instead. Often her depression wasn't sadness but rather a numbness. Existing but not living.

Listening to music was the start of accessing the shutdown emotions.

Sometimes a song would be annoying going through her head – an earworm. So she listened to it. Then, again on a continuous loop. If she was feeling energised, she improvised dance or walked briskly to it. Or if she was very fatigued, she'd lie down or sit and gently rock while listening to the music. Sometimes tears would flow but it wasn't excruciatingly painful as the music eased her pain with the release.

Music was the main way she coped off medications for nearly a year. Plus walking in nature, frequently stopping to take photographs. She took thousands of photographs. She especially liked taking photographs of birds, free in nature.

She felt better off the medications. The anxiety was there though as so much was still unresolved.

She desperately missed her twins. She thought of them every day. Anxious hyperarousal energy had been building up inside. She decided that she would go skiing on Mount Whakapono.

'Are you sure you don't want me to come with you?' asked Aroha.

'I'll go by myself,' said Larissa. She wanted to prove to herself that she could be independent.

Larissa drove to Mt Whakapono with Lemon. *I'll be fine. I'm going to have fun today*, she told herself. The mountain air was crisp and fresh and as she went up on the lift she could see Kakariki Island like a mystical mountain shrouded in distant clouds over the ocean.

The mountain felt like a magical place even though it could also be dangerous. Skiers had been killed by avalanches and blizzards on the slopes before. Conditions could change so quickly but the forecast was for more sunshine with no wind.

She exited the ski lift. Her hired skis and boots felt comfortable. She skied down the slope and went up on the chair lift again.

Larissa was sitting next to a young boy and his father on the chair lift. It amazed her how fearless young children were on skis. She didn't learn to ski until she was an adult. Kent had talked about having children and teaching them to ski, snowboard and kayak. She pushed aside any emotion with the memories. She didn't want to cry.

She was here to have fun and to prove to herself that she could go alone.

This time she decided to take a steeper run with some rock hazards as well as cliffs. Very soon in, Larissa noticed that the snow on this run was icier on top, not powdery. She felt apprehensive and looked down rather than ahead.

At that moment her ski lodged in an icy crevice. Her bindings didn't release and her ski stayed firmly wedged between a vise of ice. Her body crumpled down on her trapped boot and her leg twisted beneath her with most of the torque between her ankle and knee.

She almost cried but held it all in. Like she did with all of her pain. She had to get out of the way of other skiers. A young man stopped and extended his gloved hand. 'Are you okay? Do want some help getting up?'

'Thanks,' she said and stood up. There was a burning pain from her knee down to her ankle. She figured she could get to the bottom of the mountain on her own and get it checked out. She didn't want to create a lot of drama getting rescued. She thought it would be embarrassing to waste everyone's time getting taken down the slope in an emergency sled for a sprained ankle and sprained knee.

When she had sprained her ankle playing netball at school, her ankle was strapped and she continued to play. Block out the pain. That's what she had learned to do since she was a young child, even though she was sensitive.

She could no longer distribute her weight correctly to ski. It hurt and she had practically no control over her left ski. She fell again. Hard on her tailbone on the ice.

Stubbornly, she tried to ski down the mountain with a sprained knee, sprained ankle and injured tailbone. She also strained her chest and shoulder trying to push herself up on one pole. The strain burned through her chest.

She had practically no control now with her injuries. She tried unsuccessfully to stop as she accelerated towards a snow wall which she collided with and sprained both wrists.

Feeling humiliated, she was taken down the rest of the mountain on a rescue sled. The doctor at the mountain clinic was concerned that she may have completely ruptured a ligament in her knee – he said it was the same ligament that rugby players often tear. She was unable to drive Lemon home.

Aroha and Klaus came to collect Larissa and Lemon. Her parents were always rescuing her. Larissa felt so bad about that.

The pain inflamed nerves connecting her hip and knee and ankle so she was unable to sleep.

'I hate it that you have to wipe my bum for me!' Larissa said after her mother helped her hobble to the toilet. 'It's humiliating!'

'It's what family does,' said Aroha. 'I hope you'll look after me the same if I need it.'

Aroha helped Larissa limp to the bathroom for a shower.

'Sorry Mum,' Larissa said. 'Thank you for helping me. It's just that I hate that you have to deal with my shit when I should be able to deal with it myself.'

'Why did you insist on going skiing by yourself anyway?'

'It would have been my thirteenth wedding anniversary. I was trying to distract myself.'

'Oh, hon, I'm sorry. I should have remembered that.'

'Some way to distract myself, huh? The physical pain actually hurts less than the psychological pain.'

'I know you've bottled a lot of that up.'

'My emotions are stuck like in ice. I'm scared that if I start crying I won't be able to stop.'

'You need to let it out.'

The physiotherapist, Luke, opened and closed his mouth like a goldfish when he saw the dark bruising down the whole length of Larissa's leg. 'Wow. Oh, wow,' he managed eventually.

'I still can't sleep at night,' said Larissa at another appointment. 'I'm in pain all down the length from my tailbone across to my hip to my ankle – it feels like nerve pain – constant, gnawing pain that allows me no rest. Ice calms it slightly. Heat makes it worse.'

Initially the treatment was focussed on her wrists, knee and ankle but as that eased slightly, the nagging pain in her buttocks, hip, tailbone, shoulder and chest became more prominent. The dial on one set of pain had been turned down slightly and now the pain was turned up more in other body parts. It had been there all along, just more noticeable now. It had been weeks now without sleeping and Larissa was exhausted.

Luke suggested trying acupuncture to quieten the nerve pain. Larissa was initially sceptical but was surprised that the spasms released from her tailbone through to her hip less than half an hour after treatment. Larissa felt a bit embarrassed having needles stuck into her buttocks close to her tailbone but Luke was professional about it.

Luke's empathy and attentiveness and the nature of a therapist-patient trust relationship resulted in Larissa feeling romantically attracted. She didn't tell him as she didn't want the treatments to stop. Neither did she want her physiotherapist to take advantage of her vulnerability.

In between acupuncture sessions, Larissa had massage therapy with Amanda. Amanda was also very professional. It was painful having deep massage of the injured areas but there was definite improvement after each session. The bruising came to the surface.

'There's a dark bruise larger than a deck of cards on your buttock,' Amanda said. Luke commented on the bruise too.

'Sometimes bruises are locked deep within. Bruises are like pockets of bleeding that are sometimes trapped. Until they come to the surface where they can be cleared out, they can be very painful and cause more problems,' Luke explained.

'I feel like that with meds. I've been on antidepressants most of my adult life and it makes me seem calm on the surface but I know the pain is trapped deep inside. I felt like a zombie with changing to other meds, like my emotions are suppressed. They said I have bipolar but I don't believe I do.' Larissa said. 'I think it's trauma'.

Both Luke and Amanda listened without judgement. Both the acupuncture and massage involved draping and getting near to intimate body parts and Larissa was able to relax more and more each session which then helped her injured tissues to heal.

Non-sexual therapeutic massage by a trustworthy woman helped Larissa after the sexual assault. Amanda draped Larissa so she didn't feel exposed when treating the injured tissue around Larissa's breasts and shoulder.

'The injured tissue is similar to the scar tissue with women who have had breast surgery,' said Amanda.

'Ow,' said Larissa, trying to breathe out slowly as Amanda used firm pressure to clear out toxins accumulated above and around Larissa's ankle. When the massage finished, she inspected her ankle in which she felt a massive improvement. 'It looks way less puffier,' said Larissa. 'It hurt though, like burning pain when you were working on it but it feels improved already.'

'Strains are less painful initially than sprains but they can take longer to heal.'

Luke encouraged Larissa to walk, including on slightly uneven surfaces, despite the discomfort. Just like Eric encouraged her to work a few hours per week to start with.

Larissa started doing contract work for a virtual assistant agency working from her bedroom. Her tailbone ached from sitting and her wrist and shoulder burned when she used the computer mouse. The work was flexible and she would get paid according to how much work she took on. It was hard to focus on the administrative computer work but she managed to build up to more than ten hours per week.

For months, Liam, the Irish man she had talked to online, had tried to contact her with numerous fake profiles on social media with the same sexually explicit message. She had blocked him many times and it was very upsetting to her that he kept harassing her.

Then she received a blackmail threat. Liam threatened to post intimate photos of Larissa online unless she talked to him. Larissa was triggered into a depression.

Exhausted and depressed, Larissa asked for advice about cybercrimes. She was instructed to not give into his sextortion demands and to continue blocking all his fake profiles.

'I will not stand by and see a friend be treated so badly,' said Tom who lived in England. 'Do you want me to confront him?' Tom had been very concerned about Larissa's mental health.

Larissa consented.

Tom contacted Liam.

'We don't like people who blackmail women. Perhaps the people you work with would like to see what you get up to? Plus your devoutly religious family?'

'Who are you?'

'If you post photos of your targeted victim online, your blackmail threats will go viral too. Smoke some weed and think about it.' Liam smoked marijuana which was a secret from his family as they would not approve.

'Oh, you're threatening me? I was in love with Heni. I just wanted her to talk to me.'

'She's not interested in talking to you. I have a copy of your threats. You have your instructions. Leave her alone. Do not contact her again.'

'I don't believe I've blackmailed her but if she believes I have, please pass on my sincere apologies to her.'

'If you try to contact her again or carry out your threats, I will ruin your fucking worthless life. I hope you understand. Have a nice day.'

Immediately, the harassment stopped. Larissa remembered when Alexandria had been ground down by bullying in the playground and she had intervened.

After Tom stood up for her, she felt grateful that she had some friends who looked out for her, even though her friends were online friends and she very rarely met up with 'real life' friends. Some people had said that online friends weren't 'real' friends but they were real to her. They helped her not feel so lonely. They helped her to feel heard.

Larissa talked to the twins on the phone. 'Lucky got out of her enclosure and we don't know how she got out,' said Xavier. 'She's vanished.'

14. Earthquake

Daniel's wife Hayley, adopted an energetic older puppy Halo, but she was ready to surrender him back to the shelter after a few weeks as she felt so frustrated. Daniel asked Larissa if she could help out with training Halo. Larissa was still struggling with depression, but she agreed because she wanted for Halo to stay in his new family.

Larissa asked if she could video the training so she could watch it back. She had been mentored by Suzy in how to improve her dog training skills.

When Larissa arrived to meet Halo for the first time, he was excitable and was eager for Larissa's attention. He was black, with large paws and a gold heart shape on his chest. He looked very similar to Zoey when she was the same age.

Halo was jumping up at first and trying different things to get Larissa's attention. Larissa stayed calm and walked away so Halo missed when jumping up. She pretended to ignore him while she chatted to Hayley. As soon as Halo offered what Larissa considered to be an acceptable behaviour, such as sitting or lying down rather than jumping up or zooming around the room, Larissa gave Halo attention with a look, a friendly voice and sometimes a touch to the side of his neck. Halo very quickly settled and started offering more of the desirable behaviours.

'That's amazing,' said Hayley. 'I get so frustrated with him, but you've calmed him in just a few minutes.'

'Halo is like most dogs and wants attention. He's also a fast learner. He's offering a sit position more as I give him more attention for it. We can teach him the word 'sit' and a hand signal to go with it. He can't jump up if he's asked to sit when greeting people. We could also use food but since he's enjoying the reward of attention and affectionate touch so much, we don't really need it here. Some people become reliant on food so that it's more like a bribe.'

Very quickly, Halo was sitting on command. Larissa explained that in her opinion, 'sit' and 'come' were two of the most important commands for basic manners. A solid 'sit' could stop him from crossing a road or stop him from jumping up, which could injure a frail person.

Larissa also explained to Hayley that dogs pick up on frustration easily. She suggested that Hayley take herself for time out if she needs it, if she feels herself getting frustrated. Larissa had the view that anger was detrimental to a bond with a dog. Suzy used mostly rewards with training although she also used some aversives including leash corrections but she had emphasised that anger had no place in dog training.

Larissa had struggled with the use of corrections after witnessing excessive force being used with Ziggy. It was something she avoided other than a change in tone of voice or spatial pressure, which was changing her body position and posture. She preferred techniques that minimised the use of aversives. Suzy believed that a few split-second corrections applied effectively helped a dog to learn and was less stressful for both the handler and the dog in the long term than either avoidance or ineffective nagging corrections.

Larissa taught Hayley how to practise with Halo basic commands such as 'sit', 'down', 'come' and 'bed', using techniques with positive reinforcement. She also taught Halo how to progressively relax and he became a lot calmer.

'I want to teach him what "leave" means,' said Larissa. '"Leave" is really useful for out walking because you can tell him not to eat poop or rubbish for example. I also use "leave" to have dogs take their eyeballs off something, like a cat or a dog and pay attention to me instead.'

Larissa started teaching Halo 'leave' with her fist closed around a food treat which at first he nuzzled at. When he left it alone, she said 'leave.' Then she rewarded him. Then they progressed to a toy with

Halo unable to reach it because he was on a leash. They practised with various distractions at home.

Halo was now calm with basic manners at home but when Hayley tried to walk Halo off the property he was lunging at humans and dogs. Larissa hadn't had a chance to teach Halo loose leash walking at home yet.

Hayley called Larissa. She had walked to a park with Halo but was having difficulty with Halo's lunging. Larissa drove to meet them in the large park.

'It looks to me that Halo is leash reactive. He is friendly and wants to greet people and dogs but he's frustrated being on a leash. Yet he's not trained yet to be off-leash safely. Let's walk over there to get further away from distractions,' said Larissa. Halo was no longer lunging well away from people and dogs but he kept looking off to the distance distracted by various sounds.

Larissa put a martingale collar on Halo. Larissa explained how the triangle of chain makes an aversive sound if a correction needs to be given and the collar gives more even pressure around the neck than a flat collar for better communication via leash pressure. She showed Hayley how to fit it to the correct size so that it had a limited tightening effect compared to a full chain slip collar that had been used to train Zoey and Ziggy.

'I try to avoid using corrections, but are you okay if I correct Halo if I think it's appropriate?'

'Yes, I trust you,' said Hayley who started filming the training session.

Larissa started with a method of stopping and waiting for Halo to loosen the lead before rewarding and continuing, frequently changing direction. It was a method requiring patience.

A man with another dog started walking within the invisible bubble Larissa had made, yet still at a distance. Halo stopped to stare then started lunging and barking.

Larissa gave a firm leash correction by zipping the leash towards Halo to loosen it then towards herself quickly as a pop then release. Halo stopped lunging and barking and sniffed the grass. But then he caught sight of the dog and started to stare again.

Larissa tried to block his view by standing in front of him. That had worked for dogs who tended to freeze and shut down – they would come out of a freeze state with the trigger blocked from view. Then Larissa would help the dog focus on her and jog past the trigger, with the dog gaining confidence getting past triggers.

Halo stepped past her and was fixated, staring again. He didn't lunge or bark though after his first correction. He also wasn't interested in a treat. Larissa knew his arousal was building again with the fixated stare which would soon result in more lunging.

'Leave,' said Larissa in an authoritative tone. Halo ignored the command so Larissa gave Halo another firm, split-second leash correction. Halo stopped staring and seemed to be processing the correction by sniffing around for several seconds. Then for the first time since they were in the park, he started to focus. He looked at Larissa and took a food treat.

From that point on, Halo was attentive to Larissa and responded to gentle pressure. Larissa started training Halo to walk beside her on a loose leash. She used gentle pressure on the leash to indicate to him when she was turning. She explained to Hayley that it was as though she were leading Halo with a rubber band kept loose.

Now and again she would let Halo sniff at things briefly. When Larissa said 'leave', Halo immediately stopped what he was doing and moved back towards Larissa who rewarded him with a food treat or affectionate touch and praise in a cheerful tone of voice. Then then they resumed walking.

Hayley finished filming the session. 'Wow, it's incredible, the difference,' she said. 'Although I was a bit scared with the corrections. I don't think I could have done them.'

'I don't like doing it but it's better to give one or two firmer initial corrections than lots of nagging ones. It's important to have no fear or anger. Now all I need is a feather touch. Look how much closer we are to triggers.' Halo seemed a lot more relaxed and confident. 'The key is to feel calm and confident yourself. Your dog will feel less anxious if they feel they can trust you to handle situations.'

Larissa offered to give Hayley and Halo a ride home. Her car was in the carpark which had several people and dogs around. Trying to get to the car would risk Halo going over threshold and lunging again.

As they got closer, Larissa could see Halo's body starting to tense up. Larissa knew it was a risk. Just as they got to the car, Halo started lunging frantically towards the other dogs. He couldn't hear the 'leave' command anymore and it was pointless trying to correct him. Larissa opened the door to the back seat and quickly bundled Halo into the car. Hayley got into the passenger seat. Halo was in a state of hypervigilance and panting. He started to calm down as they drove away.

'I'm so sorry. I made a mistake there', said Larissa. 'I knew that so many people and dogs that close would be too much for him. It will set him back slightly with the progress we've made but we'll have to pick up where we left off. It's a bit like a child getting tired with too much going on and having a meltdown in the supermarket. One can't give up going to the supermarket because their child has meltdowns. Just start off by going at quieter times of day. A lot of people won't walk their dogs because they are reactive and their dogs stay anxious. They never learn how to manage their triggers and anxiety with avoidance.'

Larissa dropped Hayley and Halo off. Halo's nose marks were on the window and his paw prints were on the back seat of Lemon.

Hayley tried walking Halo again in the park. She tried to keep her distance from triggers and Halo was responding well to the 'leave' command. But Hayley didn't yet feel confident reading subtle changes with Halo's body language.

'How about we set up a session with some stooge dogs?' suggested Larissa. 'Then we can control the environment to practise.'

'Where do we get stooge dogs?' asked Hayley.

'Good question,' replied Larissa. In Australia, Larissa had had access to several socialised dogs with good leash skills. But back in New Zealand, she didn't know anyone with suitable dogs.

Larissa's speech had gotten faster and she felt bolder. She walked around parks and by the lake, seeking out people with well-behaved dogs. She asked strangers if they would like to volunteer with their dog to help a puppy practise being around other dogs on a leash. All they had to do was to turn up and enter the property with their dog on a leash and pretend to mind their own business. To her surprise, several people agreed.

Klaus and Aroha went on holiday and left Larissa to look after Rosebud, the cat. Larissa did the training with Halo which she called Halo's therapy. Halo was soon confident being close to other dogs on a leash. Some of the dog owners allowed some off-leash play as a reward.

Larissa watched back the videos of training Halo over the past few months. She noticed that her posture had changed from having hunched over shoulders and talking with a quiet, timid voice to standing straighter and taller and speaking more confidently, even though she spoke rather fast, enthusiastically and a lot more than usual.

Her jeans were baggy as she had lost all the excess weight after stopping the bipolar medications. She had felt more anxious internally lately, even though she and Halo had a calming effect on each other.

In the first video when she was feeling vulnerable and masking her depression, she accidentally called Halo, 'Zoey'. Larissa had used her posture, body language and touch to train Halo to 'come' like she had done with Zoey. She'd lowered her height and extended her hands and Halo came running. Then she added the command 'come.' He loved affectionate touch as a reward, just like Zoey had.

Larissa watched the videos over and over on a continuous loop. Like her brain had been like lately. Usually in analytical thinking mode to stop her from feeling that awful pain of grief that would overwhelm her whenever she tried to relax. Quiet meditation exercises did not bring Larissa peace. Anytime her mind relaxed, she'd be overwhelmed with pain and terror.

It was strange watching herself on the videos as though from the outside looking in, noticing her body language and speech patterns. As though she were observing someone else.

As she watched the videos back, she started to feel strange. A restless energy started to build within her. She tried doing martial arts style self-defence kicks as exercise to try to discharge the energy but it kept building. She felt like she was going to self-combust. It was now late at night. Larissa went back to watching the videos of herself training Halo.

'I keep saying 'correction,'' she whispered to herself. Even though she disliked corrections, it had helped Halo. She remembered when she had restrained Alexandria. Larissa wondered if there had been something therapeutic in the way she had restrained Alexandria by letting her thrash out the fight energy. There would have been moderate pressure on her chest and upper back.

Larissa had had a huge sense of physical and emotional release when Amanda, her massage therapist, had pressed firmly on her upper back when she was lying on her front. She wondered if she could mimic that pressure. Amy, the physiotherapist, had said that the parasympathetic nervous system that helps the body to calm ran through the thoracic spine, where Amanda had applied pressure.

Correction. Correction.

Larissa started to go into a trance. Her vision was dizzy as she closed her laptop. *Was that an earthquake?* She felt a trembling that reminded her of the earthquake that had shaken the house a few weeks earlier. The earthquake had made her door swing open and closed as the floor had swayed beneath her.

You are Larissa.

You are in a trance yet your body has an extreme level of energy which you were unable to discharge by exercising vigorously. Your mind is exhausted but your body cannot rest. You lie on a relaxation mat on the floor to try to do some relaxation exercises. You pull a heavy blanket over you and drag a heavy book onto your chest to apply pressure.

Within seconds of the book going on your chest, you become aware of your heart pounding. You focus on the sensation of your beating heart. It reminds you of the sound of a baby's heartbeat in the womb. You feel calm yet supercharged. You feel another tremor. Another earthquake? Or is it you?

You get up in the darkness and lie on your back on your bed. You pull the heavy book back onto your chest and again feel your heart beating hard and fast. You focus your mind onto your feet. You are visualising your feet and how they feel.

Your feet begin to tremble. The earthquake was really you all along. You feel calm, breathe slowly and let it go. Your feet start to twitch and jerk. It feels strange but doesn't hurt. You lie there almost in a dream, a trance. Your feet and lower legs are convulsing.

A name comes into your head like is someone speaking it. It is not your own voice but an unfamiliar voice. A woman's voice. The voice says, 'Heni'. You do not feel distressed. Previously when someone said 'Heni' you became extremely anxious and distressed. You panicked and tried to get away. Even to think your former name or see it made you feel very anxious. But now you are in a trance you do not feel distressed to hear your former name.

You whisper 'Heni…Heni'. You feel relief. The convulsions spread up your body in a wave like a full body orgasm, only jerky and involving the muscles and surface of the skin rippling quickly up and down. As the muscles on your head start to convulse, the unknown voice says 'correction'.

The muscles of your scalp and face ripple like waves for an undetermined time. Images briefly flash into your mind. Of Ziggy with the harsh trainer. Of being hit and scolded by Mrs Castle on the first day of school. Of restraining Alexandria. The images flash so briefly they are not re-traumatising. It is more like observing with detachment as an outsider.

The waves of convulsions feel very strange but you stay in the trance and focus on the bizarre sensations. The muscles of your scalp oscillate.

Your head starts thrashing from side to side. *I'm going to die,* pops into your head briefly, with fear. The surgeries where you feared you were going to die flash briefly. Ava flashes into your mind. Outwardly, you look like you have having a seizure, like Ava did. Like Zoey. In the trance, you have an altered state of consciousness and you are aware. You do not lose control of your bladder.

If I die, then I die – a brief thought. You are no longer afraid to die. You are at peace.

Your body is convulsing but it does not hurt. Your muscles ripple up and down in waves with the strangest sensations. You do not analyse, just observe.

'Voice' is the next word said by the unfamiliar voice. Your facial muscles tremble as your jaw opens and closes rapidly so your teeth chatter. You sense you will have a voice. You *need* to have a voice. A voice you did not have because you were too afraid. Too afraid since you were a young child and told to keep a secret.

The convulsions sweep down your hands and your hands raise into the air as though they are jerkily playing the piano, side to side, together and apart, your fingers wiggling. You felt disapproval associated with playing the piano.

You don't analyse this experience. You just observe what you see and hear and feel. Now and again you feel sensations of chills and pressure. You push the book off your chest but you feel pressure on your chest like it is still there. Firm pressure like from a hand.

The convulsions seem to discharge the overwhelming energy. As though the trauma were stored in your nervous system and muscles, not localised to your brain. It feels like a release.

You are now still and feel calm. You glance at your alarm clock. More than an hour has gone by. Then you fall into a deep sleep.

You wake up several hours later. You say your former name out loud. 'Heni. Heni. Heni.' You write your former name on a piece of paper. You cry with relief as you no longer feel distress and panic hearing or seeing Heni. The flashbacks are no longer intense.

You make a snack but are trembling – your right arm is jerking and your teeth are chattering. You feel hot and cold. You feel the energy building up again like water in a dam needing release. You feel the need to let it go again.

This time you play your *Yanni* instrumental CD. You lay back on your bed on your back. You feel warm so do not cover yourself with a blanket this time. You put the heavy book back on your chest and feel the pressure and your heart pounding. Your feet start to tremble so you toss the book aside and it still feels like pressure of the book is on your chest. You are back into a trance and focussing on the bizarre sensations in your body.

You feel firm pressure on your upper arms as though someone is holding you down. 'Control' is the word you hear, spoken by the voice. Your body convulses but not as vigorously as before. The whole time you feel pressure on your arms like you are being pinned to the bed. Sensations of pressure and of hot and cold move around your body. There are tingling sensations in your hands.

Finally the sensation of pressure on your upper arms lifts and you are aware the CD has stopped. More than an hour has gone by if the length of the CD was a measure of time. Then you fall back into a deep sleep for hours.

You feel the energy build up again but not as extremely as the first time. The energy of each seizure-like episode is less than the previous one.

You lie on your side on the bed, half-asleep. The convulsions are now localised. *Skiing accident* flashes through your mind briefly, more like your own thought, than the unfamiliar voice. Only the specific parts of your body you injured in the skiing accident are trembling now. Convulsions sweep from your ankle to your knee, to your hip and across your buttocks to your tailbone. They seem to last several minutes.

Your right arm trembles the most. You can access it when fully alert between the episodes by raising your arm to a point of tension. Then a tremor starts in your arm, with involuntary jerking. You feel tingling in your hand.

When you come out of the trances, you feel calmer and know it can't be epilepsy like Ava and Zoey had. If you tried to hold it back, then you would tremor. But when you let it go your body seemed to know what to do. You've just allowed yourself to feel safe enough in your room to let it go. You vocalise at times, making sounds that aren't words. You do not feel distressed. You feel calm and refreshed after you wake up from a deep sleep.

Larissa had four full body seizures within forty-eight hours, mostly sleeping in between. Each episode was less vigorous with more pauses and more localised jerking. The only body part that continued to tremble was her right arm, which lasted about a week.

Larissa had split-second flashbacks of the sexual abuse when her right arm trembled. She had held Paul's erect penis with her right hand when he had unzipped his jeans after a hug to read a story.

Her right wrist and shoulder had also been sore when she used the computer mouse a lot for work after the skiing accident. Also, she remembered how Ava's right arm had had a tremor after her accident. Brain surgery did not correct it. She remembered also that it was Kat's right arm that had been amputated.

Klaus and Aroha returned home and the first thing Larissa said to them enthusiastically was, 'Heni. I can say Heni.' Klaus and Aroha were so pleased with the dramatic change in Heni. There was no trace of the depression. Larissa was interacting more instead of isolating herself.

Larissa booked a massage with Amanda.

'You look so well,' Amanda said. 'Like a huge load has been lifted off your shoulders.'

Larissa couldn't completely relax as she chatted through the whole massage. She now felt energised. She felt so different now than when she'd been depressed. Apart from some constant low-level anxiety, she felt better than she had in a long time.

15. Tiger Awakens

Larissa tried to do some progressive muscle relaxation exercises in the dark on her mat under a heavy blanket. The wind was causing the closed door to her bedroom to make thumping noises. Despite the annoying distraction, she tried to focus on each muscle group in her body, melting into her mat like a relaxed cat. She was managing to ignore the noise.

Then suddenly, when she was almost asleep, she heard *thump, thump, thump* and was filled with sudden terror as if a monster was trying to get into her room. Her right arm convulsed violently and then she passed out. When she woke up, her room was quiet. She felt rested and realised that she had been asleep for hours.

Larissa was finding it hard to focus on the virtual assistant contract work as she felt anxious. Anxiety which would not be noticed by most people on the surface. Her income and bank balance had depleted with the reduced workload. She had stopped receiving any government assistance with the part-time work. Lately her income had been much lower than government assistance, yet she stubbornly refused to apply for financial assistance again as she was determined not to ask for help.

Despite her bank account diminishing and needing to use her savings to pay for food and board, Larissa went shopping. She purchased items she didn't usually purchase, such as nail polish and lingerie. Usually she had bare nails and wore plain underwear. She chose a bottle of *Onyx Panther* nail polish and a lacy burgundy camisole with matching panties.

She was aware that the manager of the store was watching her. It was obvious that he was the manager because he was dressed differently to the rest of the staff. He wore a formal blue shirt with trousers whereas the other staff were in uniforms. He walked very confidently. She had seen him once before. He'd walked up to

Larissa, smiled and asked if he could assist her. Larissa instantly thought he was attractive but she tried to escape out of embarrassment and she could not look at him.

But today was different. She felt confident. She was aware from her peripheral vision that the manager had looked up from talking to a customer and was staring at her. Usually she didn't like people to notice her but this time she felt confident. She glanced at the manager and then looked away half-smirking. It felt like a game of cat and mouse. Previously, she had been the mouse, but now she was the cat. She felt in control.

Larissa took her time looking at lipsticks, then she took her purchases to the counter. The manager hustled to the counter to serve her. 'Nate – Store Manager' was on his name tag.

'Someone looks like they are in for some fun,' said Nate as he packaged Larissa's purchases including the *Euphoric Seduction* perfume.

'I make my own fun,' said Larissa, making only fleeting eye contact with Nate's intense deep blue eyes.

Nate was grinning. Larissa smiled back; her skin looked youthful and radiant.

'I bet that's a smile that gets you into and out of trouble,' said Nate.

'Wouldn't you like to find out?' Larissa replied with an alluring smile and tossing her hair casually. It was fun to flirt sometimes.

'What are you doing for lunch?' asked Nate.

Larissa spontaneously agreed to a lunch date with Nate. She liked his confidence.

Over lunch, the chemistry between them felt magnetic. She had only experienced that feeling previously when she had met Richie. Nate revealed that before he went into retail management, he used to be in the army.

'So you are trained in how to kill people efficiently,' said Larissa matter-of-factly.

'You could say that.'

If Larissa tried to sustain eye contact, she felt dizzy like she was going to pass out, so she forced herself to look away.

'Are you okay?' Nate asked, squeezing her hand.

'Blood sugar a bit low, I think,' Larissa replied, trying her best to mask that she had almost blacked out. Larissa had been having blackouts lately, since around the time she'd the cluster of seizures. She knew it was her blood pressure plunging but she didn't want to reveal that vulnerability.

Nate touching her hand felt electrifying. Larissa was breathing fast and shallow. She felt enticed by danger.

'I'm so attracted to you,' said Nate. 'I find you fascinating and *exotic*.'

'What do you mean by exotic?'

'You have a glow about you that most other women don't have – big compliment. Your colouring is striking too. You look like a supermodel. Are you Italian?'

'No, I'm not but I get asked that all the time.'

They finished lunch and got into Nate's light truck. Nate drove to a remote bay of the lake. They talked for a while.

Nate squeezed Larissa's hand again. Larissa brought Nate's hand up to her cheek with her eyes closed.

Then she said softly, 'May I kiss you?'

'Yes,' Nate replied. 'She kissed his hand and then his lips. She was immersed in a passionate, sensual kiss.

Nate kissed down Larissa's neck, then started biting.

'No,' she said firmly. 'No hickies.' She didn't want bruises on her neck. Aroha would surely notice. Aroha noticed everything.

Nate followed Larissa's command and they resumed kissing passionately while their hands explored each other. Larissa brushed her lips over Nate's ear.

'What do you want?' Nate asked softly.

'What do you think?' Larissa murmured back.

'You want me?' he asked.

'Yes.'

There was an element of danger about Nate but she was drawn in. Nate drove along the lakefront and chose a hotel called *Endeavour*.

'Still okay to do this?' he asked.

'Yes,' said Larissa.

Their clothes came off quickly. 'You have a great body,' Nate said. 'Fantastic breasts.' A contrast from the criticism from Richie.

Nate had a toned, athletic body with defined muscles all over but not excessively bulky. When he wasn't at work, he was training as an endurance athlete in triathlon. Nate wasn't into much foreplay. He was goal-driven and just wanted to fuck. And fuck. And fuck. To her surprise, Larissa had a surge of energy and kept up with a very fit athlete.

Then Larissa felt a seizure coming on. It had been a few weeks since she'd had the seizures. She felt very vulnerable.

'I think I'm going to have a seizure but I'm aware,' she said quietly. 'Just hold me and not freak out?'

'Okay,' Nate said and held Larissa's shoulders as they lay on their sides facing each other. Unlike the other seizures, this time the jerking was mainly around her groin but at times the jerking went down to her feet and up to her head. She was vulnerable but Nate showed no emotional reaction. When the seizure eased and Larissa came out of her altered state of consciousness, she was alert and responsive again.

Nate put his hand on Larissa's tummy. Larissa felt an orgasm sweep through her body.

'Everything feels more connected now,' she said. Her doctor hadn't been too concerned about the seizures because she had felt better afterwards and they had reduced in intensity.

They resumed having sex. More aggressive sex. Nate started biting at her neck again. 'No,' she said and pushed him over so she was on top.

Nate was on his back and started scratching Larissa's back with his fingernails. 'No, I don't like that,' Larissa said assertively.

Nate flipped Larissa onto her back again and started fucking her hard. 'Scratch me,' he said. 'Hard.' Larissa knew there was a fine line between pleasure and pain. She had experienced a euphoric trance giving birth. Nate had said he'd liked the endurance training in the army. He continued it with triathlon. He liked the endorphin highs.

Larissa started scratching Nate's back, lightly at first then harder. He liked it. He fucked harder. It almost hurt. Then Larissa scratched frantically like a trapped cat, like her inner tiger was coming out. 'Yeoww!' she screeched as she slipped into a trance and scratched his back like a wild animal. She had never done that before. Then she started laughing hysterically while Nate showed no emotion on his face, other than perhaps mild amusement.

Nate finally seemed satisfied. They talked some more. Nate revealed he was divorced and hadn't had any relationships since because he was so busy with work and training for triathlon events.

Nate said, 'You and I are alike.' Larissa was going to ask how so but then Nate started making claims that seemed unlikely. He said his best friend was a multi-millionaire and that he was going to pay over two-hundred thousand dollars to train Nate to be his personal pilot for his private jet.

Bullshit! Thought Larissa but just said coolly, 'that's interesting'. She was put off that Nate seemed so full of himself. Full of his own bullshit. The confidence was an act.

Nate showed no emotions apart from their initial flirting game, and apart from the hysterical laughing episode, Larissa had hidden her emotions from Nate too. She told herself that she would not fall in love with his man. 'I don't see myself in a monogamous relationship any time soon,' said Larissa. 'I don't see myself getting married again.'

Nate nodded then stood up. 'Shower?' he said.

As they showered together, Larissa stroked his strong arms. She was attracted to strong arms in men. Arms that could protect her. Or harm her. Was he dangerous?

'I'd like to see you again,' said Nate.

'Okay,' Larissa replied calmly. Then, stroking his biceps, she looked him directly in the eye and said, 'but it would devastate me if you turned out to be a monster.' Nate had been very intense with his gaze but broke eye contact and turned around and finished showering.

'What was most memorable for you?' asked Larissa in a text after they parted ways.

'The touch of your soft, smooth skin.'

Larissa's family had noticed an extra glow about her. They commented on how beautiful she looked. She felt euphoric for a few days. Before the post-sex depression and irritability started setting in.

Various emotions came up – conflicted emotions. Despite not wanting to be in a relationship, she'd pictured the possibility of being with Nate. Could she fall in love with him? She was afraid to fall in love. Intense emotions started coming to the surface so she stuffed them all back down again.

After a few days, Larissa was feeling irritable and wasn't sure if Nate was playing some stupid game not replying to the few messages she'd sent.

With the crash into depression came physical pain. She went for a walk by the lake and instead of one hour at a brisk pace, it took three hours to limp home after her hips painfully seized up. She felt lethargic, fatigued, and as if a heavy weight was crushing her.

She messaged Nate: 'Am I just another notch on your belt?'

Nate replied: 'Crazy women are sexiest. Like you.'

'Fuck you!' Larissa replied. Larissa felt irritable but she still did not fully feel the emotion of anger. Anger was the emotion that scared her the most out of all intense emotions.

She took a calcite egg she'd recently bought, inserted it into her vagina and then fell asleep. She'd read that a stone egg could massage out trapped emotions in her yoni, her sacred space. She didn't know if it was true or not but she decided to try it. She didn't know if the egg was the right size or even if it was a yoni egg. Perhaps though, it was safer than meeting a stranger for sex?

An hour later she woke up with an extreme arousal energy that needed release. She listened to *Addicted to You* on a loop and went into a trance-like state as she vigorously massaged with her hot-pink dildo. Various emotions were released along with the egg as she orgasmed intensely again and again. Then she showered and felt refreshed, alive, pain free and able to move freely again.

The relief didn't last long. Soon the energy built up again but not as extremely as before. It was like when she'd had the seizures – it was like water in a dam building up and then releasing but each time was less extreme. Only this time it was intense sexual energy.

A few days later, Larissa was listening to music and was starting to feel stronger. Listening to a song that was on her mind on repeat helped ease her anxiety as she released stuck emotions.

She listened to *Stronger* then *So What* on repeat. She opened an official envelope from Australia. It was the divorce certificate. Larissa laughed out loud because it seemed to fit the songs she had listened to.

She felt happier getting her divorce certificate than signing her marriage certificate. She felt more than happy. She felt euphoric. She felt free. She had married Richie as Heni Hertz then divorced him as Larissa Flight. Neither of the official documents had her name as Kopf. She realised she had never been his property.

She went for a drive by the lake. She got out and walked up to a big tree with a huge branch outstretched over the cliff, overlooking the lake. She climbed onto the branch and took a selfie in front of a chain fence with a warning sign of a person falling off a cliff.

The dolphin stained glass ornament was hanging in her bedroom window. It had been there for the past week. She had wanted to try and reframe it as not being her and Richie, but instead, the emotional intimacy she desired. She had glued a glass bead back on for one of the dolphin's eyes as it had fallen off during transit. Now, both Larissa and the dolphin could see clearly.

She knew what she wanted to do with the ornament. She had created it. Now she could destroy it. She knew Aroha still didn't approve of stained glass hangings anyway.

'What would be best to smash this ornament up?' she asked Klaus.

'Why do you want to do that?' replied Klaus. 'Why don't you just sell it or give it away?'

Larissa thought it might be like burning painful writings. Part of a process of letting go. It was time to let go of any attachments to Richie. He had broken her heart. She could express that by breaking something symbolic, something that had symbolised their love.

Klaus got some wooden batons to lie it on and some safety glasses and instructed her to smash it between some newspapers using a hammer. He told her to leave what was left on his workbench and he'd dispose of it. Larissa had flashbacks looking at the hammer. But she wanted to overcome that fear.

Larissa put on some music that fitted her mood. Music put her in a meditative trance and helped drown out the sound of the hammer. Larissa had been having panic attacks at the sound of hammers since she had left Australia.

A woman had asked her if she was okay as she'd stopped to take slow deep breaths when she'd heard hammers at construction site when she'd had gone to town recently. She was pale and felt faint as she experienced flashbacks. She grounded herself by closing her eyes and focused on slowing her breathing as she pressed her upper back against the wall. Making long, humming noises helped slow her breathing and take her out of the panic in her head and chest.

She'd also had panic attacks in the supermarkets – it was mainly from all the crossed noises which jumbled together like fighting voices. Again, she'd grounded herself by closing her eyes and humming while she experienced the flashbacks of angry, arguing voices from her past. A woman had stopped to see if she was okay, saying she looked like she was in a trance and was concerned that perhaps she had diabetes.

Larissa decided to film herself destroying the stained glass ornament so she could watch later to see what it looked like from a different perspective. She placed the batons on the workbench, then sandwiched the ornament between newspapers. She felt calm yet energised as she listened to *Is She With You?* which was a soundtrack associated with *Wonder Woman*. She picked up the hammer. Then, harder than she'd ever hit before, she whacked it down, BAMMM!

She lifted the newspaper to look and the dolphins were cracked right between them. Just like her marriage was fractured. Then she remembered to put the safety googles on. Forgetting safety first. Then she hit again, very hard, BAMMM!   BAMMM!! Over and over, periodically checking to see how the glass was all cracking. It had been well put together so it took a lot of blows to shatter all the glass. Then she picked it up and tugged and twisted the metal apart. She wanted to disintegrate it as much as possible.

While she was hammering, she felt calm but with some adrenaline. She hit the ornament over seventy times. From above her head, she brought the hammer down hard and fast, with the kind of force that Richie had used with the hammer to smash the door. But without Richie's emotions of rage. Larissa was calm emotionally yet energised.

Smashing the ornament felt strangely therapeutic.

Later Aroha asked, 'Did it feel good?'

'Yes it did.' It had felt empowering.

'I think you scared your father when he saw all the little pieces.'

'I did it calmly.'

'I think that's what scared him most. How calm you were.'

'I'm not violent.'

'I know you're not.'

After gaining so much satisfaction from destroying the stained glass ornament she had created, Larissa wanted to destroy more symbolic objects.

She went to town and walked into a sports store. The store only had Australian branded cricket bats. Larissa purchased a cricket bat with a logo of a laughing kookaburra on it.

Larissa gathered together objects that felt symbolic to her at the time and that she thought would smash well. The objects included vases, bowls, glasses and light bulbs. Three classic style light bulbs, for each of the times she had been told it was too dangerous for girls to change light bulbs. Even though Klaus had shown her how when she was a young girl.

She took the colourful crystal bird Richie had given her as a wedding present out of the wardrobe.

'Dad, can you show me how to use the sledgehammer?' she asked Klaus.

'What are you going to do now?' Klaus asked.

'I want to smash some more stuff up.'

'What are you going to smash up this time?'

'Vases, crockery, light bulbs, things like that. Can I use your garage?'

Klaus sighed. At least Larissa was doing something rather than staying in bed depressed. 'You can do it only if you sweep up every little bit of glass.' The garage had to look as immaculate as it was before without a speck of glass.

'Cool.'

Klaus showed Larissa how to use the sledgehammer. Aroha was looking on. 'It's the same as using the axe,' she said. Larissa hadn't used the axe before either.

'There's plenty of wood you can chop up while you're at it,' said Klaus.

'Have you got any danger tape?' asked Larissa. Klaus looked puzzled but got a roll of white tape that had 'DANGER KEEP OUT' in red letters.

Larissa also gathered together a cup that said *Best Friends*, a green apple, drinking glasses with painted apples on them and glass mason jars. She carried a heavy wooden tree round sliced with axe marks from the woodshed to use as a base for the sledgehammer. Klaus provided some safety googles – there was likely to be a lot of flying glass and crockery. She placed the cup on top of some stacked saw horses and a bowl on the wooden tree base.

When she was ready with her equipment which also included a hammer and the cricket bat, she dressed up in new red and black lingerie and sprayed herself with the *Euphoric Seduction* and *Sensual Goddess* perfumes. She applied the *Reddy Now* lipstick.

Larissa put on the stretch mini dress she had worn only one night in Australia. Her figure was slimmer in the dress, after weight loss since stopping the medications. Elongated curves, like when she'd first met Richie. She pulled on the black knee high leather boots with platform heels, also worn only once before. 'Fuck me boots,' Richie had called them.

Then, just before she started smashing stuff, she wrote *CAN* on a piece of paper with a sketch of a butterfly, some music notes, a pet paw print, a flower and a light bulb lit up. She drew an apostrophe followed by the letter *T* on another piece of paper and taped them to a plywood door in the garage. Then she set up some danger tape like a construction area. Or in her case a destruction area.

Then she filmed herself to watch later. It had been interesting filming herself to see what she looked like compared to how she felt on the inside. Plus it was a form of creative expression. She had always been very introverted so doing a video diary was daring for her. She uploaded the videos online as a vlog. She found it therapeutic to do creative things rather than just talking to Angelica the mental health nurse.

Again, she was listening to *Is She With You?* Music helped her go into a trance so she didn't analyse but instead used her intuition.

She threw the first light bulb fast which hit the letter *T* on the paper. Glass shattered everywhere. It sounded fantastic shattering through the music. Then she remembered to put the safety googles on. She threw the other two light bulbs hitting the *T* accuracy with force. The *T* fell off leaving the word *CAN* – *no T in Can't*. Broken glass shimmered like diamonds all over the concrete floor of the garage.

Then Larissa picked up glasses and vases and smashed them onto the concrete floor in time to the music. They shattered pleasingly, with pieces flying high into the air. Then she picked up the rare exotic bird crystal ornament, lifted it above her head with both hands then brought it down quickly and forcefully. It smashed euphorically, with pieces flying above her head. Larissa looked calm yet intense and very much in control.

Then she picked up the cricket bat, swung it hard and smashed the *Best Friends* cup. Broken pieces bounced off the wooden doors and shattered further.

She selected the sledgehammer and lifted it to rest on her shoulder, waiting for an explosive piece of music. Then she struck an upturned bowl which was resting on the round of wood. Just like with the seizures, symbolic images flashed through her mind but she was not distressed. She was not overwhelmed with emotion. She did not feel angry. She felt empowered. She was processing.

She smashed more bowls with the sledgehammer. Just one blow and they were in many pieces. Just like her heart. Men had hurt her but she wasn't going to let them hurt her now. She was going to be in control of the situation. She was definitely not ready to fall in love again.

Larissa placed the apple on the saw horse. She brushed her hand along a selection of tools and chose the hammer. She was no longer afraid of the hammer – no longer having panic attacks. She picked up the hammer and brought it down hard like when she smashed the stained glass ornament. She missed and hit the wooden saw horse. For the first time, she felt frustrated with annoyance.

She put the hammer down and picked up the cricket bat. She put the apple back on the saw horse. She took a swing like with the cup, but missed. Frustration again but she would not give up.

Leaving the apple on the ground, she raised the bat above her head and brought it down with a single blow, smashing the apple apart. Success. In her mind flashed how she had been unfairly punished at school. Also the pet sitting client who used a cricket bat to kill cane toads.

She ripped down the danger tape. She'd often been told things were 'too dangerous' and that she couldn't do things 'because she was a girl.' She'd faced her fears many times in her life. She remembered how she was the only person who had helped a stranger when two powerful dogs were in a fight, intent on killing each other.

She'd felt then what she felt now – calm with some adrenaline. She'd told the other woman what to do. The woman had stopped screaming and took instructions. The dogs came apart when they each took a hind leg and destabilised the dogs. It was risky but it worked and the two dogs full of puncture wounds looked dazed from hyperarousal energy.

She was fearless. She'd already experienced the full spectrum of physical and psychological pain. She'd been close to death more than once. The only thing she hadn't experienced for a long time was a full spectrum of intense emotions. Anger was missing.

She picked up the camera, showed what was smashed and then turned the camera onto herself standing by the word *CAN*. She didn't say anything but she flexed her bicep and had an intense look on her face of determination layered on top of the pain she'd been through yet did not fully show.

She had been able to express anger despite not being able to feel it, as well as the determination and perseverance that pushed through despite all odds. To keep surviving. To keep challenging herself. Even when losing nearly everything.

She still had her life. She was determined to stay alive. Determined to live. She could live without Richie and she was breaking ties with him. The only connection she had now to him was the twins. Her beautiful twins whom she rarely saw. The pain of separation from her children was still so raw.

The destructive exercise was strangely therapeutic. After smashing the symbolic objects, she spent a very long time listening to music, sweeping slowly in zig-zag patterns like mowing the lawn, to get every little bit of glass and crockery. Even the clean-up process to music was a meditation in action.

Larissa watched the video of herself back several times. It was strange looking from the outside. The relative calmness on the outside was very different to the intense energy she had felt on the inside.

Energy started building again. Anxious energy. To help relieve the anxiety temporarily and discharge some of the energy, Larissa danced in her room while listening to music. Listening to *Roar*, she held the photo of Raja the tiger in her arms before hanging it back on the wall and then she danced, imagining her voice being heard.

Then suddenly, she went into a hyperarousal state of fight or flight. She launched into martial arts style blocks, strikes and kicks. Then, she imagined she was a tiger, fighting off invisible attackers swiping at the air with her fingers curled like claws.

Breathing heavily from the intense workout, she changed the song to *Feel*. She felt intensity, yet couldn't fully feel emotion. She suddenly felt faint, so dropped to the floor with her forehead touching the carpet until she revived. Then she danced to *Stronger*.

Creative dancing and improvised movement using her imagination helped her discharge some of the extreme energy. It also helped her process some of the trauma as the music accessed emotion she was unable to feel.

A few days later, Larissa had an appointment with her doctor. She felt anxious about her sexual encounter with Nate.

'I want to have an STI test. I had sex with a stranger. I feel so stupid because we didn't use a condom. I'm relieved I can't get pregnant now though...but I'm paranoid about catching something... I feel so stupid....got caught up in the passion of it... felt like I couldn't resist him once we touched.... couldn't think rationally...' Larissa was talking fast, as if she had something very urgent to say and not enough time to say it.

Doctor Keyes was reassuring and she ordered a test. 'I won't judge you,' she said. 'How has your anxiety been lately?'

'It's still there all the time but I do feel better off the meds. I feel very anxious about this though.'

'Do you still feel in control of things?'

'Yes, I feel better than I did when I was on those meds. Apart from the anxiety. I've lost all the weight I put on with the meds. I don't think I'm bipolar? Do you think I'm bipolar?'

'You seem to have pressure of speech – talking faster and more urgently which could indicate mania. But that could be anxiety too.'

'I can slow down my speech if I want to.' Larissa demonstrated how she could deliberately and consciously speak slower if she chose to. But it took all of her effort to try to focus on slowing her speech.

'If you feel in control of it, then there's no need to medicate. You've been off meds for nearly a year. If you have bipolar, you would likely have had a relapse of mania by now. You've got the number for the mental health crisis team if you feel like you're losing control?'

'Yes, I have it on my phone somewhere.'

'Is it okay if I call your mother to give her the crisis number too? Our conversations will be private but I just want for you to be safe and have her look out for you.'

Larissa agreed.

Larissa liked Dr Keyes. She was never condescending and Larissa felt heard without being dismissed or judged.

16. Mania Mouse

Larissa drove to the swimming pool where Ava used to train. As she braked at an intersection, she felt the sensation of her car skidding slightly, on loose gravel, as a truck hurtled past in front of her. It was like she was in a dream.

It was a bright, sunny winter's day, so Larissa went to the outdoor pool, wearing her sunglasses. Instead of swimming laps, she wanted to relax her muscles in the warmer pool. Her joints had been aching lately and she had felt more anxious. In the pool, she danced and did martial arts style kicks under the water to the music blaring over the loudspeaker.

Then she went into a trance, staring at the colourful ripples of light on the bottom of the pool. As she danced, rainbows seemed to radiate out of her shadow. She felt like a goddess radiating love and she was euphoric.

Going into trances and zoning out like staring at rainbows and moving to music helped ease her anxiety. She went to the pool edge and blew bubbles, just like when she was a child. She let herself sink to the bottom of the pool. There were different sensations – the sounds under the water and the bubbles tickling her skin. When she blew bubbles, she could see flashing lights behind her eyes. It was hypnotic and relaxing.

Larissa felt a blackout coming on as she suddenly felt faint. Dr Keyes had said she was still allowed to drive short distances but if the blackouts became more frequent and the warning time shortened, she wouldn't be allowed to drive anymore. Larissa was getting the blackouts more often, sometimes accompanied with jerking.

Larissa clung to the edge of the pool with her fingertips and closed her eyes and pressed her forehead to the tiles. Her mouth dipped under the water and her legs were jerking while she was in her trance-like state. Flashing into her mind was a fear of drowning and not being able to surface. There were brief flashbacks of nearly drowning in the accident with Kent, even though she had blanked most of it out.

After several minutes, the trance eased and she came back to the present. She glanced over at the lifeguards and all three of them were laughing and chatting.

She got out of the pool and stood in front of the lifeguards, dripping wet. 'I nearly blacked out in the pool. Would you have noticed if I had quietly slipped under and drowned?' she asked assertively.

'Of course we would've,' a lifeguard replied.

'If you have a medical condition, you should wear a medic bracelet,' added another lifeguard.

'As though a bracelet would stop me drowning!'

Larissa walked off, irritated, to shower and change. She sang to try to stay present. She still felt faint so bought a juice and small packet of salty chips to try to raise her blood pressure.

'You should have been looking out for me!' she muttered out loud as she put her foot hard on the accelerator. 'Can't trust anyone to look out for me!'

She sped to places where she had done her driver's licence exam years ago.

'I can still drive!' said Larissa as she swiftly did hill starts on the steep hills by the cemetery. 'I can reverse!' she said, backing into a driveway by the basketball courts where Paul used to play.

Underneath the irritability, Larissa was fearful she would not be able to drive anymore. Driving, even short distances, gave her some sense of freedom. Under the fear was trauma from the past, too painful to acknowledge.

Larissa drove to the outskirts of town. She turned her music up and sped down Loop Rood, energised by a hyperarousal energy that she'd been experiencing more frequently lately, taking the bend fast where she knew Paul had died. 'I can drive,' she said out loud in a determined voice. 'I will keep my licence,' as she sped, breaking the speed limit and driving like a racing car driver.

Then she drove back into town feeling calmer and went shopping for boots. Earlier that morning she'd had an appointment with Angelica, her mental health nurse. Angelica had been providing counselling services while Larissa was on a waiting list to see a psychologist.

'On a scale of one to ten, how well do you feel?' Angelica had asked.

'A seven,' Larissa had replied.

'What would it take to move from a seven to an eight?'

'I'd like some creature comforts. I want financial independence to be able to enjoy some nice things. I need some winter boots.' Larissa was frustrated at her low income.

The assistant measured Larissa's feet and brought out a pair of blue suede ankle boots which fit well and were comfortable.

'I like them. How much are they?'

'Ninety-nine dollars. They're on sale for half-price.' As the assistant put the boots in their box, Larissa noticed for the first time that the boots were called *Creature Comforts*. She remembered her conversation with Angelica that morning. A coincidence?

Larissa felt restless and decided to go back to the pool at night. She was the only person in the pool on a foggy night. The warm water helped her to relax. The fog looked mysterious as the steam rose from the surface of the water.

As she drove home, a black cat appeared in the dense fog. Larissa braked heavily to avoid hitting the cat. The cat leapt off into the darkness.

The next day, Daniel called to say that his new apprentice, Maxine had died.

'She died in a car accident on her own last night, driving along Loop Road. They think she might have been texting and she flipped her car. No-one knows why she was out there.'

The accident had been around the time Larissa had braked to avoid hitting the black cat in the fog. She'd been driving along Loop Road only hours before the fatality. She'd had no apparent reason to be there either. Maxine died on the same bend that Paul had died at many years before.

Larissa had an uneasy feeling that the accident was more than a coincidence and that she had somehow caused it. That she was responsible for killing Maxine.

The following day Larissa went shopping. She saw a little teardrop prism and remembered how Ava had had one in her bedroom. She purchased the prism and hung it on the hook in her bedroom window in the place where the stained glass ornament had been.

'Where are those rainbows coming from?' asked Aroha looking at the patches of intense colour all over the walls and carpet.

'From my teardrop prism,' said Larissa happily.

'They go all the way across the hall to the toilet.'

'I can turn shit into rainbows.'

'Well, you used to eat crayons and poop rainbows when you were a toddler.'

Usually Larissa wasn't interested in shopping but over the past several weeks she had still been making purchases she normally wouldn't make. She was drawn to a silver ring with little, green glass leaves. It was like a symbol of healing to her so she bought it. She thought of Ziggy's ashes buried under a tree.

She tried on a black onyx ring. The salesperson said it represented protection and absorbed negative energies. Larissa didn't know if she believed in that but she liked it anyway and put it on the third finger of her left hand.

Larissa hadn't cleaned Lemon since she'd dropped Halo off from the park. It still had Halo's muddy paw marks on the seats and his nose marks on the windows. Larissa stopped in to see Halo. Halo did zoomies in excitement for a few minutes but didn't jump up as Larissa had trained him not to. Halo calmed quickly with Larissa's touch and voice.

Larissa took a selfie with Halo. Halo stuck his wet nose in Larissa's ear. Larissa laughed then started to cry. A gentle, healing release.

She felt like Halo had been an angel sent to help keep her alive as she had struggled with suicidal thoughts the night before she'd met him for the first time. Helping Halo had given her a sense of meaning and purpose.

Angelina had told Larissa that she was a 'rescuer' – Larissa tried to 'save' animals. When she was a child, Larissa had tried to save a baby bird that had fallen out of a nest.

After visiting Halo, Larissa went shopping again.

Aroha had said never to buy herself a Maori bone or jade carving for herself because of *tapu* – sacred spirits. She didn't know if she believed in spirits and curses or not anymore.

Instead, she bought herself a tiger's eye pendant which was carved in an infinity twist design on a black cord. She read that the infinity design represented love and friendship. She figured it would be safe as it was not bone or jade and not made of traditional Maori carving materials.

She also bought a matching tiger's eye pendant for each of her twins who were due to visit soon. She wrote the twins a card each, explaining what the tiger's eye pendants meant and how she felt protective of them like a tiger.

Larissa chose a little angel prism similar to the teardrop but with little blue wings. She hung it from Lemon's rear-view mirror.

When she arrived home, she felt ready to wash Halo's 'angel' kisses off Lemon. She realised that she hadn't washed her car because it reminded her of Halo, which made her feel protected when she had started to have so many blackouts.

After vacuuming the dried, muddy paw prints from the car seats, she parked Lemon on the lawn and the late afternoon sun shone through the angel dangling from the mirror. She felt gratitude as she slowly washed Lemon. She was thankful to have met Halo, who had helped give her a sense of purpose and to stay alive when she had been very depressed. She didn't need Halo to protect her now. She felt protected by the little angel prism.

She went inside to get her camera and took photos of the late sun shining through her little guardian angel. Then she opened a new computer mouse intending to try and do some work. She was still avoiding work because it made her feel anxious.

It was ever since they had punished her with no work for a month after she had reminded the agency she was a contractor not an employee. This was when they had tried to pressure her with more work than she was able to cope with.

She decided to destroy the faulty computer mouse which had given her so much pain from her wrist to her chest after the skiing accident.

She took the Australian cricket bat and the faulty computer mouse, and went to the backyard and placed the mouse onto an old tree stump in a garden. BAMM! The cricket bat came down and the battery flew out of the mouse and disappeared into the weeds of the garden. BAMMM!! BAMMM!! BAMMM!!

Larissa felt adrenaline and started to feel angry. She hadn't felt anger before when she had destroyed objects. She started swearing at the mouse. 'Fuck you!' she muttered over and over.

'Is it dead yet?' asked Aroha, poking her head out the window.

Larissa gathered up the bits of mouse – bits of circuit-boards and plastic and put them on a table and took a photo. She couldn't find the battery.

She felt energised, feeling angry for the first time like she'd never felt before. She got into Lemon and sped away, deliberately breaking the speed limit. She stopped in front of *Endeavour*. 'Fuck you!' she said, pacing back and forth, agitated, in front of the hotel.

Then she stood in the freezing cold lake in bare feet as the waves, which were rough like the sea washed over her. She took photos of her feet then felt calmer, very briefly.

Then, energised again, she drove to various places around town to where people had hurt her by telling her she was demon possessed or hungover when she had never been drunk. 'Fuck you!!' she yelled as she raised the middle finger of her left hand wearing the black onyx ring, which was now assigned her 'fuck you' finger.

She yelled 'Fuck you!' hundreds of times as she drove angrily around – the closest to rage she had ever experienced. She felt like she was still just in control of it and felt an exhilarating energy, like riding a wild horse with not enough experience.

She drove past the cemetery. Larissa hated cemeteries. The gate was still open so she drove inside. With tyres squealing, she sped through the main road of the cemetery yelling 'Fuck you! Even though I don't believe in you anymore! Fuck you for letting innocent babies die and children suffer! What kind of sick joke is that?!'

She parked Lemon outside the cemetery and got out. She walked to an older part of the cemetery that had a garden memorial for very young children. She felt overwhelmed with grief as she clutched her abdomen with intense emotion flooding over her. She felt a strong conviction that she had miscarried when with Kent. She felt the grief of losing a child, even though it was never confirmed with certainty that she had been pregnant.

Then she got back into her car and drove around, again breaking the speed limit. She drove past police cars and raised her finger with the black onyx ring, where they couldn't see. She dared them to pull her over, driving a little above the speed limit, then when they were out of sight, she floored the accelerator, driving faster than she ever had before. 'Fuck police officers!' 'Fuck Australia!' she yelled.

Finally, she parked by another part of the lake and felt calmer. The lake was still rough like the sea and the waves were crashing onto the shore. She took some photos of the setting sun and the light through the angel. 'Xoe,' she said quietly. 'Xoe means life.' She named the little angel, her angel, Xoe, in memory of Zoey and Ava, two angels she felt were watching over her. Usually Larissa didn't pay any attention to spiritual symbols like angels but currently she felt very spiritual.

She got out of her car and the lake sounded almost like the ocean with the waves crashing onto the shore. She took photos of the lake. She felt calmer and drove home as it was getting dark. When she looked through her photos, there were vibrant green orbs. Her rational brain would say they were probably lens flare effects, especially because some of the photos were taken directly into the Sun. But now she was starting to believe in angels and orbs and healing energies.

Aroha and Klaus were worried when Larissa arrived home after dark. They knew she had been having blackouts and were fretting.

'I'm fine,' Larissa said. 'You don't need to keep tabs on me.'

Larissa went to her room and looked up what orb colours symbolise. She read that green means healing and nature.

She went onto social media and typed a public status, 'I felt so alive today. Psychiatrists say I have bipolar but they can stick their meds up their arses!' Lately she had been posting prolifically on social media, entertaining some people and offending others. Her judgement was impaired, she lacked a filter and she was impulsive.

Even though she had hardly watched television, she flicked through and saw a talent show was on. Larissa was captivated by the voice of a singer performing a song she had heard years before by another artist. *The Power of Love.* The surface of Larissa's skin rippled with pleasure in response to the music which also stirred her emotionally.

The next morning, there was a parcel at her door. The packing slip said: 'Personal massage stone'. So much for the discreet packaging that was advertised. Larissa tore open the bubble wrap and opened a box inside. There it was – glossy, dark green jade egg. 'You're beautiful,' Larissa said as she held the smooth, polished stone in her hand. It was as beautiful as the photograph on the website promoting the egg as an authentic nephrite jade yoni egg called 'Queen'.

Larissa had experienced emotional and physical release with an inexpensive calcite egg but she was concerned that the egg might be toxic, as it was not an authentic yoni egg. Larissa was currently curious about the claimed healing benefits of yoni eggs and other gemstones.

Larissa went for a walk by the lake with her Queen egg in her pocket, warmed by her hand.

Listening to *The Power of Love*, she took her egg and baptised it in the lake. She didn't know if she believed in God or not anymore. Religion grated on her. Larissa had decided years before that she wanted to live a life with simple values rather than being anxious she was breaking prescribed rules of religion. Her core values included integrity, honesty, authenticity and mutual respect.

It felt like a deeply spiritual experience as the water washed over the egg in her hand. Like the water was washing away anything negative associated with the egg and preparing it for good. Tears flowed as the water washed over the stone, bringing her to life. Larissa named her Diana.

Larissa felt light as she walked with Diana in her pocket. Diana seemed to warm her hand and her whole body on a sunny winter's day.

Larissa listened to *Friend of a Wounded Heart*. As she listened to the music, emotions started to flow. Emotions that had been frozen like the deep ice on Mount Whakapono. She picked up weathered rocks and threw them into the lake. Intense anger erupted.

'You weren't there for me!' she yelled. 'You didn't look after me! Fuck you!' as the stones splashed and disappeared beneath the surface. People walking past turned their heads. When Larissa ran out of rocks, she grabbed handfuls of pebbles and tossed them into the lake too. She was temporarily calmer after a huge release of emotion.

At home, the hyperarousal energy built back up. Diana the yoni egg helped her release the intense sexual and emotional hyperarousal energy. Tension causing temporary pain in her hips and tailbone area would also be released.

The following day, Larissa walked barefoot through a fresh pile of sand dumped at a playground in a park. She used to play with Kat and Daniel in a sandpit as a child.

Then she sat on a swing, scuffing her feet. She remembered when Kat had told Heni to ask Jesus into her heart when they played on Heni's swing. She started swinging as high as she could go. She remembered she would swing with Ava as high as they could go before leaping off and flying into the air. She missed her friends.

She listened to *Friend of a Wounded Heart* again and this time sang along, while swinging high. She didn't feel angry at Jesus anymore. Could Jesus be real? Or did Jesus used to be her imaginary friend?

Then Larissa started listening to *Gone Away*. She got into her car and accelerated quickly out of the park, singing along to the music passionately, remembering her departed friends. She glanced in the rear view mirror and saw flashing lights. She laughed as she had been daring police officers to pull her over a few days earlier.

Instead of feeling irritated at the police officer, she decided to be pleasant. Larissa was still wearing her sunglasses as she wound down Lemon's window. A handsome police officer was standing at the door.

Larissa was smiling. 'Officer,' she said, while unable to suppress her laughter.

The police officer smiled back. 'Going a bit quick there,' he said.

'Blowing out the cobwebs,' Larissa replied with a broad grin, still trying to stifle laughter.

'That's what the open road's for,' the police officer replied, chuckling.

Been using the open road for that too, Larissa thought. The officer took her licence and went back to the police car. Larissa looked in the rear vision mirror and could see both police officers laughing.

Then she glanced at herself in the mirror and realised she was still wearing sunglasses. She took them off, and her reflection reminded her she was wearing no makeup. She looked like a beautiful scruff with her glowing complexion, wearing a tatty woollen jacket, zipped right up to her throat.

She decided she was going to flirt her way out of any tickets. To Larissa, flirting wasn't about makeup, false eyelashes, high heels, perfectly groomed hair and cleavage on display. It was about confidence. She felt confident. She felt sexy. She felt desirable.

She didn't have much money left in the bank after investing in Diana. She hadn't been able to stop impulse buying things she didn't really need.

The police officer walked around Lemon checking her registration and warrant of fitness. He came back to the window.

I know you want me. Larissa tried to influence the police officer with her thoughts and alluring glances. *When your balls are full, your head is empty. Forget to give me a fine.*

'Your warrant of fitness has expired,' said the officer. 'Expired three months ago.'

'What? Three months? Really? I'm sure I asked for one when I got a service.' Larissa was puzzled.

Damn it! How did I forget to do that? Her smiles and laughter subsided. 'How much is that going to cost me?' she asked.

'It's a fine of two hundred dollars.'

'I honestly thought I had a warrant.' Larissa put her elbow on the windowsill with her hand framing her face. Her trimmed nails were painted with glossy black *Onyx Panther*. Her hair tumbled with perfectly imperfect waves. Her face without makeup had a youthful natural glow. She looked at the officer with pleading eyes.

For the first time she gazed at his chocolate eyes which reminded her of the eyes of a friendly Labrador puppy. 'Is there anything I can do? That's a lot of money to me.'

The police officer shifted his weight back and forth. Larissa noticed he was wearing a wedding ring. 'Tell you what, I can write this ticket so you can have an exemption if you get your warrant within two weeks.'

'You mean I can get off and not pay the fine?'

'I still have to write you a ticket but yes you won't need to pay the fine when you provide evidence that you have a warrant. I've been burnt before.' He smiled.

Haven't we all, darling? Larissa felt like saying but refrained. Only just. It was so tempting to blurt it out.

She beamed at the officer. 'Thank you so much.'

He smiled back. 'The ticket will arrive in the mail but get that warrant straight away, won't you now.' He raised his eyebrows briefly as she handed Larissa's licence back. He was flirting too. She knew it.

'I will.' As she drove off, she started laughing again. She knew she could get off and she did! Flirting was like a fun game. She was confident Lemon would pass her warrant.

Larissa booked Lemon in for her warrant of fitness and decided to keep herself busy in town while waiting. She had no particular plans other than buying more nail polish – even though she normally never wore it because she hated the fumes from both applying the nail polish and then the solvents to remove it later.

After dropping Lemon off, Larissa walked to the other end of town and was captivated by the colours on the nail polish stand. Larissa was usually irritated by advertising but now she found it inspiring. Phrases such as 'Be natural,' and 'Beautiful you'. She wanted to be told she was beautiful, even by a sign in a department store. It felt like it was speaking directly to her, like a special, personalised message. The names of the nail polishes were symbolic to her as well as the colours.

She was drawn to a shimmery bluish lilac colour called *Magnetic*. Recently she was starting to believe in things she didn't usually believe in, such as her ability to communicate via energetic thoughts. She was starting to believe that everything in the universe was connected and that she had the ability to draw positive energy to herself like a magnet. So she felt that was the nail polish for her.

She wanted to wear *Magnetic* straight away. She bought a bottle of nail polish remover and some cotton pads.

She passed a restaurant where she'd had the date with Nate. The same restaurant she'd been to with Kent years ago where she hadn't been sure if she'd miscarried. It had been renamed *Ignite*.

Larissa sat at a big stone table outdoors and ordered lamb rack with vegetables. The waitress asked her if she'd like some wine. She normally didn't drink alcohol. She decided on a glass of Rosé. The wine arrived first and after two sips she was high, listening to *Danger Zone*. She sat at the table and removed the black nail polish, then painted her nails with *Magnetic*.

Admiring her nails, she stood up to dry them in the sun. She swished her hands back and forth to pass the air over her nails quickly. Then she started dancing to *Dangerous*. She turned around and two women in the restaurant were laughing at her. She smiled and kept dancing. She told herself they were laughing with her, not at her and if they were laughing at her they were jealous because they didn't feel as free as she did.

A van pulled up and tooted at her. Two people in the front seat started imitating her dancing then drove off. Larissa danced back to the large, elevated stone table. Elevated, like her mood. High on music, a new nail polish colour, a few sips of wine and a whiff of nail polish remover fumes in the open air.

She polished off the meal and drank less than half the glass of wine.

Then she walked through a park where she used to play as a child, towards the library. She still had some time before picking up Lemon, so she decided to look around the library.

Now she was listening to *Is She With You?* the instrumental music she had listened to during her smashing ceremony. She felt like she was in a strange dream as the automatic doors opened to the library.

The first word she saw was on a sign: 'Romance'. Her head was swirling and she felt light headed so sat down in a red chair. Then she managed to stand again and stumble around the library.

Dozens of words and images jumped out at her – things she had seen before – it was like she could see in advance. Words and images and colours leapt out at her while everything else rushed by like a blur. She ran her fingers along the book spines. Everything that jumped out, she had seen before and was connected somehow. It felt like a surreal and spiritual experience.

The word 'feel' jumped out at her. She touched it. She wanted to feel, to not be numb. Lately she was starting to feel intense emotion.

She stumbled to the children's section and sat on a big cushion underneath a painting of a dragon. She listened to *Feel,* a song she had recently filmed herself dancing to in her room, wanting to feel emotions she had shut down. Instead, she felt intense energy. In the library, she rocked back and forth to the music, in her own little world.

Then she stood up and started grabbing children's books until her arms were full – any titles or pictures that jumped out at her. When her arms were full, she put the books on the ground and gathered more books. A young man, a librarian, brought her a trolley. After adding over fifty or so books she realised she couldn't take the books with her as her car was at the mechanic's at the other end of town.

'Sorry,' she mumbled to the librarian who would have to put them all away again.

She walked back to the garage feeling confident that Lemon would pass her Warrant of Fitness.

'I'm sorry but your car has failed its warrant,' said the manager. The rules have been tightened up and some things we let go through before we can't let through now.'

Larissa was worried. This was going to cost extra money. Her confidence evaporated. 'What's wrong with her?' she asked, feeling fragile.

'The windscreen needs replacing as there is a chip in the field of vision and there is a buildup of residue that needs to be removed from the headlights. Both issues impair vision and are safety issues. There is also a small spot of rust that needs addressing at the next warrant.'

Larissa started to cry. 'How much is that going to cost me?' she quavered.

The service manager explained the costs to her. Lemon would need to stay in. 'It's the effects of age, pollution and some knocks. Just getting older that's all. She still runs really well.'

Like me, affected by age, pollution, knocks of life, Larissa thought. Even though she was in her forties, she was often mistaken for being in her early thirties. She looked youthful on the outside but she had been deeply affected inside by circumstances outside her control.

She was in a daze as a young mechanic dropped her home. It would be several months before Larissa would drive again.

17. Magnetic

Larrisa went for a walk in a forest without listening to music. The air was cool and there was a fog when she breathed out. She hummed and felt tingling vibrations all the way to her fingertips. The vibrations were stronger when she made lower pitched humming noises. The vibrations made her feel like she was connected to nature with a heightened state of awareness.

She told Aroha excitedly that all the energy in the universe was connected and transforming from one form into another.

'What do you believe in? You must believe in God,' said Aroha.

'I don't believe in God anymore,' said Larissa.

'Surely you believe in something with all your energy and universe talk?'

'I believe in *Wonder Woman*,' replied Larissa.

'Yeah right,' Aroha scoffed.

Larissa had recently seen the *Wonder Woman* movie, sitting at the back of the cinema covered with her plush purple blanket. She felt intense emotion with the visuals and sounds especially when she re-enacted the fight movements. She felt so empowered that afterwards, she danced through the supermarket listening to the song *Running Away.*

She felt upbeat and euphoric and didn't care if anyone thought she was silly for dancing in the supermarket. Then, after watching the movie again, she walked confidently through the supermarket without music and without having a panic attack. She was conquering all her fears.

In her room, she went into a trance, imagining she was *Wonder Woman*, deflecting harmful energies away from her with the cuffs she imagined were on her wrists. She visualised the negative energies of hurtful words others had said reflecting right back at them.

Now, she was starting to believe that Diana, the yoni egg, had given her superpowers such as reading people's minds and seeing the future. Diana allowed her to discharge the hyperarousal energy when it built up. The energy felt exhilarating. She had incredibly intense orgasms that would temporarily calm her.

When she had a bath, she'd hum and feel the vibrations go all the way to her toes. It was a novel sensation. Humming long, low notes helped calm her when she felt anxious. After an extended bath, she climbed into the shower to rinse her hair.

She felt her blood pressure plunge, so she shut the water off, sat down and kicked the shower door open for fresh air. She was having flashbacks of being taking to hospital by ambulance when she'd had her breakdown in Australia.

With her eyes closed, she pressed her upper back to the wall and started humming to try to relieve the feelings of distress. The long humming sounds also helped regulate her breathing. When she felt panicked, her voice got higher in pitch and she started gasping for breath, but then she brought it back down deliberately with humming low, long sounds.

She also visualised her diaphragm area to get herself outside of her head while she slowed down her breathing. This enabled her to get through the panic attack brought on by re-experiencing flashbacks from traumatic experiences. The episode passed and she got up feeling liberated. She could manage panic attacks on her own.

When she emerged from the bathroom, Klaus said, 'Kuini has been taken to hospital via ambulance.'

'What happened?'

'She collapsed in the shower and is in a diabetic coma.'

Larissa felt deep down that Kuini wouldn't make it through the night. She felt uneasy that somehow she had caused Kuini to go to hospital. That somehow it was her fault, even though that wasn't

226

rational. 'I don't think she's going to make it,' she said quietly to Aroha and Klaus before she went to bed.

She couldn't sleep. She hadn't been sleeping lately. In the middle of the night, Larissa felt intensely anxious because she felt certain Kuini was dying. She listened to music and tried to sing quietly along. She sang along to *You're My Best Friend* and felt emotions much more intensely than usual.

The phone rang early in the morning. Aroha answered. It was Lindsay. Kuini had passed away.

Larissa heard Aroha and Klaus talking. 'She knew. She was singing. She always said let someone know you care when they're still alive because when they're gone it's too late.'

When she emerged from her room, Aroha and Klaus were standing in the kitchen waiting.

'Kuini died. You knew though, didn't you? You were singing before the phone rang.'

'I thought I was singing quietly.'

'You were singing loud. And flat.'

'I had my headphones on. I felt overwhelmed with emotions. I felt like I absorbed her emotions and her pain.'

'Well, you don't need to do that,' said Aroha curtly. 'Next time you sing flat in the night, we'll know someone has died.'

'Did she die peacefully?' Larissa asked Aroha.

'Yes she did.'

Arrangements were being made to bring Kuini back home. Extended family were on their way.

Klaus said, 'Kuini said a few days ago there was something special about you. She said you've become more confident and standing taller lately and that you have a special gift.'

'Her family said you can see her when she comes home before the funeral,' added Aroha. Aroha had been to a lot of funerals. They were very significant occasions to her. Larissa avoided funerals. She had never been to one since Kat's funeral.

Larissa didn't want to see Kuini in a coffin. She was afraid but she pushed those feelings aside.

That night, Larissa was using her computer and the song *Over the Rainbow* came on without her choosing it. She felt emotional and watched the music video which showed sprinkling of ashes into the sea.

In the morning she put on her new, blue suede boots, her tiger's eye infinity pendant, her silver ring, her maternity ring and her black onyx ring. She put Diana the jade egg in her pocket to give her strength.

'Hurry up, Larissa. Lindsay needs to go meet family soon. You've been given this opportunity.' Aroha and Klaus had both already seen Kuini and said she looked like she was sleeping.

Larissa was in a daze. She grabbed a flat tin of moisturiser and put it in her pocket. She had recently purchased it, remembering opening one like it in the bathroom when she was a young child. She had been sniffing it lately to ease her anxiety. It had a distinctive fragrance. Larissa also remembered that Kent had used it after shaving.

'Take off your shoes,' said Aroha. Larissa only knew a little of Maori protocol. She'd been on a Marae a few times. She wanted to keep her boots on as they made her feel protected and stronger, but she removed them as instructed and left them on the doorstep.

Lindsay greeted her. He was clearly grieving but he welcomed Larissa and Aroha in.

'I'm scared,' Larissa said.

'It's okay, there's nothing to be afraid of,' said Lindsay.

'If it's okay, I'll listen to my music with my earbuds.'

'Yes, that's okay. She's just this way.' Larissa turned and saw a coffin in a room, draped with a traditional Maori cloak.

Aroha said, 'You can go up and see her.'

Larissa felt like her feet were lead but shuffled closer. At first she didn't see Kuini lying there but her childhood friend, Kat. Then she saw Ava. Then Kent. All her best friends who had died many years before were lying in the coffin. She started to wail out loud.

'It's okay, let it out,' said Aroha.

Larissa was now beside the coffin. Kuini was lying there peacefully. There were some photos of her in her youth. She looked just like her daughter, Kat, in the faded black and white photos.

'Is it okay if I touch her?' asked Larissa. She had been afraid to touch a dead body but she wanted to overcome that fear. She had practically no recollection of Kent's death, even though he had been attached to her when he drowned.

'Yes, you may,' said Lindsay.

Larissa gently touched Kuini's cheek. It felt hard like a river stone – rough yet smooth, without warmth but not chilled either.

Larissa pulled the tin of moisturiser out of her pocket. 'Can I put some on her cheek?' she asked.

'No, don't put anything on her,' said Aroha.

'Can I open it near her face?' asked Larissa.

'Yes, that's okay,' said Lindsay.

Larissa opened the tin then waved it around Kuini's face, like some strange ritual so the fragrance was in the air. Then she closed the tin and put it back in her pocket.

Lindsay seemed touched, watching the video with the song *Over the Rainbow* on Kuini's tablet. Larissa and Aroha went to the doorstep and put their shoes back on.

'Wash your hands when you get back home,' instructed Aroha. Larissa thought perhaps it was Maori protocol, but she wanted to wash the death off her hands anyway. Larissa washed her hands more often than most people. Lately she had been washing even more frequently as she felt contaminated.

Larissa slipped the moisturiser tin back into her little box of treasures, in which there was now a cola pen in a test-tube container, an invisible ink book and the magnetic nail polish. The box was the cardboard box from her new suede boots.

She'd had a box of treasures in her childhood – a tea tin. The treasures of her childhood included a dried leaf, a few favourite marbles and a feather.

Recently, she'd found a big white feather by the lake and had taken it home, feeling inspired that she was going to write songs. The last time she had written a song was when she'd won second prize in a song writing competition with a mental health theme. It was the first time she had written a song since Kent died. She had been presented with a trophy and a small monetary prize at an awards ceremony in Australia. She had felt disappointed to have come second. Silver, not gold. She didn't like silver as it tarnished easily.

Klaus and Aroha decided to go to town for afternoon tea. Larissa went too. She wanted to go to the shop and buy a yellow, lemon-fizz scented pen she'd seen when she'd bought the cola pen in a plastic test-tube container. Yellow was her sunshine colour. Yellow was the colour of her car, Lemon, who was still at the mechanics. Yellow was the colour of the crayon she'd scribbled with messily, to colour in the baby chick on her first day at school. Like the yellow chicks she'd seen hatch at Kuini's house when she was a child. New life. Larissa didn't want to think about death and funerals.

At the café, she ordered camomile tea, mainly for the colour but also because Aroha said it might be relaxing. The tea looked clear and bright yellow against the white cup. The last time she'd had camomile tea was the day Tripod died.

Larissa started listening to *I Can See Clearly Now*. She had picked it out that morning. Listening to it over and over in a continuous loop eased her anxiety and made her feel happy and temporarily forget about death. The lyrics mentioned a rainbow and sunshine after the rain. She was tired from lack of sleep but she felt euphoric and danced around, listening to the song. People in the street smiled. She smiled back as she danced. Aroha and Klaus stopped to chat to a friend.

There was a cubby house in the street. She crawled inside. It was small, like the tree house Klaus had built young Daniel and Heni from recycled materials.

Larissa sat in the cubby house listening to music and rocking. She doodled in her bright yellow school exercise book with the new lemon-scented pen.

Over the past month, since she had the seizures, she had been making a video diary, a vlog, as she was feeling better.

'Did you put a video online of yourself dancing in lingerie?' Aroha had asked Larissa the week before.

'Yes, it's an expressive dance video. It's not porn.'

'What if your kids see it?'

'What's the difference between wearing lingerie and swimwear at the beach? Who told you anyway?'

'Richie.'

In the video, she did a sensual, improvised dance, pretending to apply lipstick and spritzing herself with perfume. Her hair was still wet after a shower. The video was improvised with only a few props gathered just before recording.

She'd danced wrapped in a soft, purple blanket, then undressed to her lingerie, pausing at the cat tattoo when she'd removed a ski sock that represented a stocking. She'd fallen from the chair when an invisible force seemed to hit her.

In the video, her eyes looked vacant. She was not really there. She was in a dissociated trance.

Larissa had also posted videos showing the destruction of symbolic objects on social media. It had felt therapeutic. She never mentioned Richard's name even though she knew he was always watching.

Larissa wasn't sleeping through the night. Her anxiety levels were high and she was constantly hypervigilant. She tried to nap on her bed with her door slightly ajar. She was lying on her back and nearly asleep, when Aroha put some cutlery in the drawer in the kitchen, which was down the hall. The sound was extremely amplified so that it sounded like a car crash up close. Larissa's nerves were jarred so much that her whole body leapt suddenly and she couldn't relax.

She went to the kitchen talking very fast. 'Mum have I been in a car crash?'

'Yes, as a baby. The car was written off but you weren't hurt. I was screaming but you were quiet. You landed under the front seat, unhurt. You won't even remember it.'

'My nervous system remembers it!'

'Stop being dramatic, Larissa!'

Larissa kept having visions of dying with Lemon. She knew there was something about car crashes. More than Snowball's accident.

She asked Klaus, 'Is it true that a child died, drowning in the creek that runs through Victoria Street when I was little?' It was something the other children in school said had happened when Heni first started school.

'Yes, it is true. Also a child died right in front of our house. A little girl.'

Larissa started to remember something she had blanked out that had happened before Kat died.

'Kat's cousin? A crash with a truck? Daniel and I were watching you chop wood in the back yard when we heard a massive crash.'

'It was a car overtaking Lindsay's logging truck. He had taken Kat and her cousin for a ride in his truck. Missy was so excited she ran across the road to tell her parents. Lindsay could never drive trucks again after that. Then Kat got cancer. Lindsay started drinking heavily after Kat died.'

Larissa could remember bits and pieces. She remembered Daniel had been there. She remembered Klaus had dropped the axe and said 'Don't come to the road'. She remembered she had heard the ambulance. Yet she had blanked out the memory for years. Larissa couldn't remember if she had looked out the window. Bits and pieces of hazy memories. Like her brain was trying to protect her from the horror.

She had never used an axe before but she went to the woodshed and cut up several pieces of wood while listening to *Under Pressure*.

In a video she filmed for her vlog, Larissa used the axe to destroy the fishnet stockings stretched across a block of wood. She had found the fishnet stockings in a shoebox in the wardrobe. She was listening to *Defy You* and looking relatively calm on the outside, she quietly said, 'Fuck you,' each time the axe struck.

Then she destroyed the lingerie she'd bought the day of her sexual encounter with Nate. She stretched the lacy camisole between her hand and a metal stake in the garden and stabbed it with a big kitchen knife. The camera she was wearing around her neck picked up the sound of her heavy breathing, from the hyperarousal.

In the final video, taken by the woodshed after seeing Kuini, she was looking exhausted yet babbled away, saying she felt euphoric. She was jumbling up her sentences, reversing the order of words and missing words out altogether.

She prattled on about how purple used to be her favourite colour but now yellow was her favourite colour. That yellow was the opposite of purple. She held up a packet of yellow, lemon-scented soap that she had bought. Soap she remembered from her childhood. She pretended to use the lemon-fizz pen test-tube as a microphone.

A few weeks earlier, Larissa had seen a specialist at the hospital about an ongoing issue she had with her muscles not being able to relax to go to the toilet. Larissa had broken down at the specialist's, anxious that she might need more surgery, which had been traumatic. She'd become very distressed, crying and shaking. The specialist gave her a bear hug said 'I feel confident that we don't need anything as aggressive as surgery. I'll refer you to a physiotherapist.'

'I've started using a yoni egg,' said Larissa to the physiotherapist, Amy. 'It's been helping me achieve emotional and physical release with orgasms.'

'In your case, I would not advise wearing the yoni egg around the house and only for short periods of time,' said Amy.

'Why is that?'

'You already have a strong pelvic floor and the muscles of the pelvic floor for the vagina and the anus interlock, so further strengthening the vaginal muscles with a yoni egg will make your problem worse. We need to retrain those muscles to let go. So only use the yoni egg for short periods of time, occasionally, and don't walk around wearing it.'

'Is it common with trauma to have trouble letting go?'

'Yes, it is. Often women have a similar issue with the vagina after trauma. The muscles of the vagina may clamp painfully.'

'I've had that occasionally but most of the issues have been with trying to poop with muscles that don't want to relax. It's been chronic since my marriage breakup.'

'Your problem is more psychological rather than physical and may improve with therapy. Using a step to raise your knees so you are in the correct position can help. Singing can help you with diaphragm breathing which can help you relax your muscles. Sing on the toilet. Some studies have demonstrate that emotions affect the pelvic floor area.'

Larissa continued to use Diana during short naps before experiencing a physical and emotional release of the hyperarousal energy that built up. Then Diana would be expelled forcefully and

Larissa would use the hot-pink dildo to finish off to get the full intense physical and emotional release which included intense orgasms. It felt therapeutic. She could get the release on her own without a man. It seemed less complicated and less risky.

Larissa was back in her room soon after seeing Kuini lifeless. Larissa reached for Diana then fell into a deep sleep. A sleep crash after weeks of poor sleep.

A few hours later, in the early hours of the morning, Larissa stirred. Her brain was fuzzy and she felt disorientated. She remembered Kuini.

I need to pee, she thought as she stumbled to the toilet. As soon as she sat down, she heard a loud clattering noise, like a crash. *What the heck was that?*

Her brain jolted awake.

Diana! Diana must have crashed! Larissa stood up and looked in the porcelain bowl. There under the water, was Diana. She had to rescue her. Next, Larissa was making a decision which disinfectant to use so soak Diana. Green pine or purple lavender. Larissa chose lavender. Diana only suffered minor injuries – just a few tiny dings. She was tough – she was jade, the stone of queens.

Larissa lay a freshly disinfected Diana to rest in the shoebox of treasures next to the tin of moisturiser and the lemon and cola pens. To help ease her anxiety, she listened to music in the early hours of the morning as she lay in bed.

The song from when Kuini died was going through her head. As Larissa listened to *Bohemian Rhapsody* again, she tried dancing to ease her anxiety. There was only the light of her digital music player in the darkness. Suddenly, she felt terrified that a sinister presence had entered her bedroom, like a demon.

During her childhood and teenage years, she was very heavily immersed in a church that was preoccupied with demons. On one occasion, adults from the church swarmed around a very distressed young Heni to cast out demons they believed she was possessed by. This was because she was anxious and crying, after being made to have forced eye contact with a grown man, while singing *Jesus Loves Me*. On other occasions, members of the church had insisted that Heni needed 'deliverance' from demons and had tried to cast them out.

But now Larissa was afraid. She felt sure the demon must have been attracted to her *Magnetic* nail polish, then absorbed into the moisturiser she had put back with her treasures. It might have sounded odd, but it wasn't too different from the indoctrination she had grown up with, that demons can possess people and inhabit objects. She crawled back into bed.

She sat up in bed covering herself in her purple blanket and feeling afraid of the dark. Or rather what she felt was in the darkness. 'Go!' she said, clutching her tiger's eye pendant while sitting under the photo of Raja, the tiger. 'Raja is protecting me,' she told herself. It was very hard for her to speak as she was so terrified.

She turned on the light and got up and threw the tin of moisturiser into the outside bin and hoped that it hadn't contaminated her other treasures. She was very concerned about contamination now. She ran another bath, added drops of lavender and tried to decontaminate herself by fully immersing herself under the water. She was so anxious that an itchy rash started breaking out on her face. She attributed it to an evil spirit trying to attack her. Aroha and Klaus had very strong beliefs that curses and demons and eternal damnation in Hell were real.

Larissa had practically no sleep. She anxiously told Aroha what had happened the following day.

'You've opened the door to it with your prisms and rainbows,' said Aroha. 'You've always been attracted to things of the darkness – crystals, rainbows, stained glass.'

Previously Larissa had told Aroha that was a load of rubbish but now she was vulnerable and suggestible and wondered if Aroha was right. Her interest in geology when she was a child had resulted in a collection of different coloured rocks. She had turned them into pet rocks by adding googly eyes.

'Open up your curtains and windows wide and let the sun and fresh air in,' said Aroha. 'I should have told you to leave that tin in the coffin. Aroha started chanting prayers to cast out evil spirits. Nothing dramatic happened but Larissa felt bad that Aroha was upset.

Larissa took the prism down from the window. It was just a piece of clear crystal that refracted white light into pretty colours. That was all, surely? Rainbows reminded her of friendship. Larissa also loved colour. Larissa was anxious about upsetting Aroha and possibly inviting demons into the family home via rainbows and glittery nail polish.

Larissa hadn't had any restful sleep for over a week and her anxiety was becoming harder to manage. She was also not thinking rationally. Now she felt anxious that Diana was contaminated by being exposed to death and by falling into the toilet. She removed the *Magnetic* nail polish, believing that with the prism taken down from the window, and by not wearing the nail polish, she would no longer be attracting evil spirits.

Larissa spent a lot of time typing into her computer. She felt like she just had to get everything on her mind out, as Aroha and Klaus were annoyed by her constant talking and endless questions, especially questions about the past, trying to match up their recollections with hers.

She couldn't write fast enough for her mind to keep up but she could type fast. She typed long posts on social media with loose links and associations and metaphor that others would have trouble following. Sometimes she'd feel frustrated after typing for hours, and before she could post what she had written, the computer came up with the word 'crashing' then shut down.

In her bed again at night, she felt terror again. Like the evil presence was in her room again. She couldn't see it but sensed it. She felt like she was being watched. By someone in her room who was not supposed to be there. She was too terrified to go to sleep.

The terror continued during daytime too. She kept having visions of dying with Lemon, her car. Her family couldn't remember which pet chicken it was that had died when she'd asked but now she felt certain it was Lemon. She bombarded her family with questions to confirm her memories. Talking fast and annoying her family with endless questions and chatter.

'You're talking on loops,' said Aroha, exasperated. 'You keep repeating yourself.'

'We're old. We don't remember all the details,' said Klaus, frustrated.

Larissa was constantly pacing back and forth. She was speaking fast and urgently yet no one was listening. Or they were tired of listening and couldn't understand her. She felt distressed inside.

'You already told me that!' said Aroha, expressing annoyance. 'Snap out of it!'

'Correct me! Correct me!' pleaded Larissa. 'Thump me and it might help me to snap out of it!'

'No.' So Larissa pleaded with Klaus. Klaus looked like he was barely able to contain frustration but walked away. 'You're sick and need help,' he muttered.

'No I don't. I'm not sick. Correct me!' Larissa slapped her wrists like the teacher had done on her first day of school. Over and over, she slapped her wrist hard while she was clearly distressed. It was the same as when she'd accidentally nicked her leg with a razor and it bled but did not hurt, after an initial sting that only lasted a few seconds. Just the same as when she tore during childbirth. No more painful than a bikini wax which numbed in seconds.

Aroha stood there with a disapproving frown as she watched Larissa slap herself on the wrists over and over. Larissa was trying to communicate the distress she felt but it was not getting through. Her distress was not heard.

At times there had been arguments, even though arguing was usually very upsetting for Larissa. But instead of her usual avoidance mode, Larissa felt defiant.

'You will respect me if you live under this roof,' said Klaus sternly.

'No, I believe in mutual respect.'

'No, you must respect your elders,' said Aroha.

'Respect goes both ways,' replied Larissa.

'If you don't abide by the rules of this house, you can pack your bags and get out,' said Klaus.

'That's right, disown me then,' said Larissa, feistily.

'You're being manipulative. You're being a bitch,' said Aroha.

Larissa did not call her parents names. She walked away and picked up a purple pen. She wrote barely legibly, several loosely associated words from her memories, past and recent. 'Truck...crash...axe...111...ambulance...breakdown...abuse...purple curtains...Snowball. Then she picked up a red pen and scribbled out her trauma, pain, rage and shame on top of the purple; covering and disguising, so that not even she could make out what she had written. In the huge wave of hyperarousal energy, she downloaded onto a page which ended up looking like an original, multilayered, doodle with patterns.

Only a few words could be seen around the edges with less overlap. 'Can't afford a dog....all rescues no one wants...pets no one wants...no one wants me.'

The hyperarousal eased temporarily, but it would soon be like a huge wave of energy and intense emotion, again and again. Creative expression was mainly how Larissa was managing the energy but now it was becoming too big and out of her control.

In the early hours of the morning, unable to sleep, Larissa's mind racing, somehow it all made sense, even though she struggled to communicate what was going through her mind – the multiple connections all at once.

Diana the yoni egg crashing into the toilet. Visions of Lemon the car crashing. The computer crashing. Lemon the chicken dying. Remembering hearing the crash of Missy being killed in front of their house. Kat dying. Snowball being killed. The skydive accident.

Crashing. Larissa was crashing. She knew what it felt like to fall from a height and it was happening again.

She felt scared and overwhelmed. She felt scared of how she would cope when Aroha and Klaus died. She was unable to hold a job. With difficulty focussing, she struggled to type an email to the manager of the virtual assistant contracting company. 'Sorry to let you down. Can't continue. Having breakdown.'

She woke Klaus and Aroha up in the early hours of the morning. 'I'm scared you're going to die soon like Kuini. I'm having another breakdown.'

Aroha called the mental health crisis line. They said that Larissa could either be admitted to hospital immediately or she could wait to hear back from the psychiatrist in the morning. Dr Eric Wright had the flu but he would see Larissa if she came immediately as he needed to recuperate at home.

Aroha took Larissa, who was wearing her cow-jumped-over-the-moon printed pyjamas and purple dressing gown, to see Eric. Larissa was clutching a purple blanket and a soft toy which looked like a dinosaur and a frilled dragon lizard.

She'd given one just the same to each of the twins before she'd left Australia. This was the toy she had clutched while crying herself to sleep when in a psychiatric ward. Angelica also made herself available at the appointment.

'I can see you're very unwell,' said Eric.

Larissa nodded.

'You know you're unwell? And you asked for help?' said Eric incredulously. He looked at Angelica amazed. Angelica looked back at Eric, also astounded.

'Something's not right,' Larissa mumbled, barely able to get her words out. She was at a point now where she was so exhausted that it was a major effort to speak any coherent words at all as her mind was so confused.

'That's really incredible that you were able to ask for help. I feel very confident the diagnosis of bipolar disorder is correct. You're in mania. I strongly advise you go back on medication,' said Eric.

Larissa looked to Angelica with a questioning face expression. She didn't trust psychiatrists anymore. Aroha was opposed to medications. She didn't know who to trust. She had been seeing Angelica weekly for non-trauma counselling.

Angelica said, 'I did notice pressure of speech when I saw you last week. Yes I agree with Eric's diagnosis.'

'Most people in mania don't realise they're in mania. How did you know?' asked Eric.

'The crashing...can see outside myself looking in.' It was too complicated to explain right then, all the complex web of links including being 'warned' by Diana crashing and her computer crashing and her visions of Lemon crashing. Also from watching her video diary she was able to see herself from a different perspective. Her brain was now too confused and exhausted to try to construct coherent sentences.

'First thing we need to do is sedate you so you can get some sleep,' said Eric.

'You look like you haven't slept in days,' added Angelica. 'Probably no decent sleep for weeks.'

'Sleeping pills?' mumbled Larissa groggily.

'You're going to need something a lot stronger than sleeping pills. Your thinking and speech are very disorganised.' Eric started writing a prescription and talking about doses.

'Can't remember...numbers...dose,' Larissa mumbled as she waved her hand frustrated. Larissa couldn't even remember what day of the week it was. She was utterly exhausted and confused.

Eric explained to Aroha the doses of an antipsychotic medication that was very sedating. Larissa would have to trust Aroha to follow the instructions even though Aroha felt conflicted about psychiatric medication with her religious beliefs.

Eric said that if Aroha could administer the medication to allow Larissa to sleep, then she might not need to go to hospital. Eric also prescribed a tranquiliser to use sparingly if Larissa was extremely panicked.

The medication sedated quickly at first. Within minutes, Larissa was very wobbly on her feet and unable to stand up. Aroha changed the sheets on her bed and Larissa went into a deep sleep as soon as her head hit the pillow. When she finally awoke, she was unable to get her words out or get up. She was given another dose and slept further.

Finally, when she woke up, she managed to stammer with great effort, 'Scrambled eggs'. She'd always hated eggs on their own ever since Lemon was killed but now she wanted scrambled eggs.

'To go with your scrambled brain,' said Aroha.

Larissa staggered to the toilet to pee like a very drunk person while Aroha cooked eggs.

After another dose of the medication, Larissa went back into a deep sleep. She was sedated around the clock for several days. After a while, the medication took a bit longer to have an effect yet it was unpredictable when she would fall asleep. It was like Larissa now had an on-off switch – either awake for a short time with a busy mind then knocked out in just minutes.

Larissa swallowed a pill and was sitting on the end of the bed sipping camomile tea. She was looking at childhood photos. As she stared at a school class photo, she blacked out when she saw Ollie.

She felt herself falling backwards but she couldn't do anything about it. It was like being in a dream where she was falling in slow motion. Her head and shoulder hit a small cabinet and the camomile tea went flying and splashed up the wall and curtains. Aroha scolded her for not getting into bed straight after taking her medication.

Lemon was ready to be picked up from the mechanic's but Larissa was still anxious that her visions of Lemon crashing would come true. She wasn't allowed to drive, being under such heavy sedation. It was also not safe to drive in mania as she was unable to focus. While she was sleeping, Klaus and Aroha brought Lemon home.

18. Killing the Tiger

After several days of mostly sleeping, Larissa started to feel energised between medication doses. She woke up to lucid dreams. Usually, she couldn't remember her dreams. Now the dreams seemed to be a hybrid of things from the past combined with recent memories. All in new, metaphorical ways.

In one vivid dream she reached out to embrace purple curtains after her fingers were touching her plush purple blanket that was draped over her headboard. In her dream-like state, she interpreted the soft, furry blanket as cat fur and thought that Snowball was alive and with her again. She reached out to grab purple curtains that weren't there, then fell back onto her bed, which was when she fully woke up and realised it was a dream.

She could smell roses, even though there were no roses in her room. Then, she heard scratching at her window. Rosebud the cat was scratching at Larissa's window wanting to come in, just like Snowball had years ago. Rosebud had never done that before. Larissa got out of bed and opened the window to let Rosebud in, then opened her door.

Instead of going through the door, Rosebud stayed and was smooching and chatting with affectionate little meows. She had never done that with Larissa before either. Rosebud was a selectively affectionate cat who only wanted cuddes from Klaus. Larissa started to cry. She felt like Snowball and Kent were visiting her via Rosebud. It was a strangely spiritual and intensely emotional experience. 'Thank you for being a messenger,' said Larissa.

After Rosebud finally left the room, the tune to *Kiss from a Rose* was going through Larissa's mind. She looked the song up as she couldn't remember all the words. As she listened to it, she wasn't sure if the lyrics said 'grey' or 'grave.'

At that exact same moment, she heard a howling sound which spooked her. She looked out her window and saw a misty grey tomcat prowling. Larissa had never seen this cat before but it was the exact same colour as the dead grey cat Daniel had dropped onto a dusty footpath outside Paul's house many years before.

The cat stopped howling, snapped his head around, then stared directly at Larissa with his emerald green eyes. Larissa felt panic. *It says grave,* she thought. *Daniel is going to die!* Recently, she had started believing that cats and music were sending her messages.

Now she anxious that Daniel was going to die next. She went to tell Aroha.

'What's that tomcat doing hanging around?' asked Aroha.

'The grey one?'

'Yes, never seen it before. It's probably trying to harass Rosebud.'

'I'm scared Daniel's going to die next.'

'Daniel's not going to die anytime soon.'

The song *Daniel* name came onto the radio. Larissa became even more anxious. She was clutching at her tiger's eye pendant and rubbing it anxiously.

'What does your pendant mean?' asked Aroha.

'It represents being strong like a tiger. Raja the tiger gives me strength.'

Aroha picked up a best-selling Bible reference book and flicked through the pages. 'It says here that tigers are evil,' she asserted. 'They're vicious. Tigers are not of our culture anyway.'

Larissa didn't see how tigers could be evil. She remembered how she'd petted Dewi at a tiger sanctuary and she had sensed her strength and poise. Larissa had recently read about a tiger spirit animal having stripes, representing a contrast between doubt and conviction. A tiger spirit animal was a protector of cubs.

Lately Larissa had been feeling spiritual. She felt like she was believing in something that made sense to her but Aroha didn't approve of any forms of spirituality other than Christianity.

Larissa went back to her room. She had been feisty lately – arguing with Aroha instead of just walking away. Especially about religious themes. It had been painful to be told she was possessed by demons when she was anxious, depressed and distressed. Larissa felt deep down that she didn't need demons cast out of her. She just wanted to be accepted and loved.

Larissa took the framed photo of Raja off the wall and looked at him. The sinister presence had left when she'd sat under Raja, clutching her tiger's eye pendant. A tiny part of her wondered if the evil presence was a complete figment of her imagination with all the recent stress and past trauma. Yet it had felt real and she had been very scared. Sometimes, she was so scared, she was unable to speak.

Larissa's usual rational and analytical thinking was not currently operating. Instead, she was going by her intuition. She was seeing symbolism everywhere and she was interpreting it differently while she was vulnerable.

Raja looked strong and majestic in the photograph, swimming in water. He'd been watching over her bed for years. He had quietly watched when Larissa had been sexually assaulted by Vanessa. Larissa started to cry. 'You weren't there! You didn't look out for me!' That's how she felt about Jesus too. Why did Jesus let bad things happen to her? Especially when she had believed as a young child? Then, after so much pain, she'd lost her faith.

Christians had been judgemental and gossiped behind her back. She didn't want to go back to church or read the Bible again. She refused to discuss religion with Aroha and Klaus. Some Christians told her that she must never have been a 'true' Christian or else she would have not stopped believing. She was told that she would be 'tortured in Hell forever' with specific details about how she would be tortured. She felt she had already been tortured for years, so she no longer feared the doctrine of Hell.

Now Larissa was torn between conviction and doubt. She wondered if Aroha was right. Had she invited evil spirits into the home? Did the crystals have power?

When she was sedated at bedtime, she stared at photos on her laptop. Photos of a holiday with the twins. Alexandria and Xavier were standing next to one of the largest amethyst geodes in the world. It towered above them. It had looked so dazzling with sparkles of deep purple gemstones but now, in the photo, there seemed to be an eye in it. It seemed to resemble a distorted embryo in a crushed eggshell. Like the dead chick in the egg she had cracked open as a child.

Larissa started at it in horror and saw ugliness instead of beauty. She became convinced that the little angel prism, Xoe, was not a protector but an angel of death.

She felt convinced that she was on a mission from God to destroy the angel of death before sunset.

Larissa had been starting to express an interest in Maori spirituality. She asked Aroha what she knew but Aroha claimed she hadn't listened growing up. Larissa pressed her for information, especially after Aroha had insisted that her pendant could come with supernatural curses from the maker of the ornament.

'How do you get rid of the curses in Maori culture?' asked Larissa.

'*Noa* it.'

'Naw it?'

'*Noa* – N-O-A by submerging the item in clean water.'

Larissa had recently been submerging herself with baths, trying to remove the 'contamination' of death after seeing Kuini. She had done little rituals with water and pink Himalayan salt to try to 'decontaminate' items. She had asked Aroha to baptise her in the lake on a cold winter's day but Aroha said to wait until the weather was warmer. Aroha said that submerging in clean water was required to remove supernatural forces associated with objects. Usually with a *karakia*, a prayer. Nothing else like salt was needed.

Larissa removed all her jewellery to 'noa' it in a cup of water with Diana, the jade egg. Diana had already been originally 'baptised' but now she was going to be again. Noa and water baptism seemed rather similar to Larissa. She put water in the bathtub and submerged items such as the car number plates, her hot-pink dildo and her tiger pyjamas, all from Australia.

She currently believed that items from Australia had been contaminated by a port bottle with a picture of a 'possessed' cat on it that had been retained as an ornament. The port bottle had come from a winery that was previously a morgue and it had been left at the house in Australia. The bottle had been a joke memento. Now Larissa was starting to believe that spirits of dead people had attached themselves to the port bottle and then contaminated everything in the house. She also thought it had poisoned Richie against her, causing the death of her marriage.

Larissa explained very quickly to Klaus how she believed the curses from the port bottle came from all the spirits of the dead people at the morgue before it had been converted to a winery. 'Curses most certainly are real,' agreed Klaus. Both Klaus and Aroha believed in curses and reinforced these ideas that Larissa had grown up with.

Larissa had a restless, agitated energy. She was moving around fast, talking fast, and sweating excessively while still in her pyjamas and dressing gown. There was friction with Aroha and Klaus. There were frequent arguments. Larissa was remembering things from the past. How she'd been hurt.

'Don't dig up old bones,' said Aroha. 'You need to forgive.'

There was pain in Larissa's voice as she tried to be heard. The night of the abuse by Paul was brought up.

'Why did you wait so many years to tell us?' asked Klaus.

'I blanked it out. But when I told you, you dismissed it.'

'We didn't know how to deal with it,' said Aroha. 'We didn't want anything like that to happen to either of our children. I'm sorry.'

'I'm sorry too. You need to forgive, Larissa,' added Klaus.

Larissa wasn't ready to forgive yet. She had a tiger to kill.

When she walked back into her room, music videos were still playing on her computer, selecting themselves. She saw a post on social media that had a picture of a gun. At the same time, a music video to *Wake Me Up Before You Go-Go* started playing and the word 'bang' stood out, so she watched the video. The last time she remembered hearing that song was when she had listened to music with Ava in the 1980s. She went into a trance-like state watching the video, noticing the words 'Choose Life' on the white T-shirts. She felt certain she had seen the video before.

Larissa pulled on her new blue suede boots. Her room was a mess because she had pulled items out of the wardrobe and desk. A roll of dog poop bags decorated with tiny paw prints was on the floor. She grabbed some bags and the two prisms – the tear drop prism and the Xoe angel. She found a big rock in the garden and grabbed the sledgehammer and walked to the front of the property.

Larissa wanted to get as far from the house as possible, so any evil spirits would not come back into the house, if they were released while destroying them. These ideas were not completely unique to Larissa, as she remembered how an evangelist had claimed jewellery had screamed from demonic forces, when he had struck it with a hammer.

While people gathered around outside Kuini's house, Larissa was outside in her dressing gown and boots with a sledgehammer, to smash the angel of death and the teardrop prism. A teardrop prism just like Ava used to have in her bedroom. She lay a bag with pictures of butterflies on the rock to catch any fragments. Then she lay the dog poop bags containing the ornaments on top.

As the prisms smashed, she said, 'I choose life, not death,' while she listened to *Wake Me Up Before You Go-Go* on a continuous loop. Suicide had flashed through her mind. She'd had suicidal thoughts when she was depressed and also when she was extremely agitated, like now. Everything was going very fast, like a rollercoaster about to come off the tracks.

The little fragments were contained in the dog poop bags which she tied in a knot then disposed of in the wheelie bin. The butterfly bag was now tatty but she wasn't finished with it yet.

Larissa felt an urgency about destroying symbolic objects – Daniel's life depended on it. Her mission from God.

Everything felt symbolic to Larissa. All of her jewellery, her car, various pictures, and the personalised number plates from her car in Australia. She had kept them as a reminder of something she had achieved on her own: starting an award-winning business. But now they reminded her of being attached to Australia. They were limited edition pet charity personalised number plates with the words 'Can't live without my cat' and a silhouette of a black cat.

Larissa didn't need Raja now. Just in case there were any spirits attached to the image, she decided to destroy the photograph, as well as any other objects that stood out to her. It was something that was frequently done in church and youth group in the 1980s. Burning records, cassettes, books, anything the church declared was demonic.

She decided to destroy the calcite egg and a little ceramic jewellery box from Australia that looked like a smooth, grey rock with a colourful lizard on top of it. She had discerned that the calcite egg was a bad egg. She took the egg near the woodshed, put it on a wooden stump and hit it with the sledgehammer. It smashed apart. The lizard jewellery box went flying several metres, but after a few attempts, it was smashed apart too. The objects did not scream nor burst into flames like the stories she had grown up with.

She felt anxious that Diana was also a bad egg as she was now contaminated by death and the toilet, even though she had been disinfected and then submerged in water to lift *tapu*, which is any spiritual connections associated with an object, in Maori spirituality. She hit Diana with the sledgehammer but the jade was very hard and she made only a small dent. After hitting Diana a few times, she decided she would have to get rid of her another way.

She paced around anxiously and went through the cupboards and shelves of the garage which Klaus kept very orderly with labels on everything. She gathered together a hand drill, a small handsaw, a hammer, nails, screws and linseed oil. She also found a box of with some children's poster paints and brushes like the ones she'd painted with at kindergarten. She chose a pot of red and a pot of white paint and a bristle paintbrush.

The fire was going as it was the middle of winter. Larissa was still wearing her pyjamas and purple dressing gown. Her hair was lank and greasy and she needed to shower and she could smell the odour of stress on herself. But she was too busy to shower yet. She had too much to do. She was very driven by a sense of urgency.

She looked at her jewellery that had been soaking. The string from the tiger's eye pendant had now shrunk, too short to wear after being in the water for hours. The way it was wrapped around the ornament reminded Larissa of a noose. Larissa interpreted this as a sign that she needed to destroy the tiger's eye pendant. She put the fire and ice maternity ring aside to keep as it represented the bond she had with her twins. She took several items to the garage, along with the lemon sunshine soap bought recently. The bars of soap had stamped into them 'Made in Australia.'

Larissa was listening to music with a portable player as it helped relieve some of her anxiety. It also helped her to stop analysing and to go with her instincts.

Larissa walked fast back to the woodshed. She hastily poured *Onyx Panther* nail polish over the outside of the *Magnetic* nail polish so the contents of the bottle could not be seen. In Larissa's mind, the black nail polish was cancelling out the magnetic attractive forces of the *Magnetic* nail polish. She painted out the names on the perfume bottles.

Larissa went to the garage and sat on a wooden nail box, using another nail box as a table. It was something she had done as a young child with Kat, playing with some of Klaus's hand tools. She had selected the exact same tools from her childhood memories.

She took the photo of Raja and saw that it had been sealed in from the back as it had been framed professionally. So she smashed the front with a hammer. A tiny fragment of glass cut her finger. 'You bit me,' she said quietly. She removed the shards of glass with bare fingers, remembering how it felt when she had to go to the toilet after her haemorrhoidectomy – like jagged glass ripping her apart. Like Snowball had been ripped apart.

Then she drilled holes into the photograph, winding the handle of the hand drill like the egg-beater when she had baked as a child. 'See no evil; hear no evil; speak no evil; smell no evil,' she said as she drilled into the tiger's eyes, ears, mouth and nose. She used the saw to roughly cut the defaced picture in half then tossed it into the fire, which roared.

She scraped the words 'Made in Australia' off the lemon soap and then hammered nails into it. She felt that she needed to urgently change her car's name from 'Lemon' to 'Sunny' to stop the visions of her dying with Lemon. Just like she had urgently needed to change her name from 'Heni' to 'Larissa' to stop the flashbacks of sexual assault.

She tossed the soap into the butterfly bag which was now damaged from being hit by a sledgehammer on a rock. She had felt like her own name change was transforming into a butterfly. A vulnerable butterfly that was yet to fly, with broken wings.

She tore the canvas off the photograph of the black and blue fairywren from Australia and threw it into the fire.

She took a canvas from a painting she had tried to do but didn't like. It was of autumn trees in a park in brown and green. Aroha had suggested she try painting as she had enjoyed it when she was younger. But Larissa declared it to be the ugliest painting she had ever done. So it had sat in the garage for months.

She put it on an easel and looked at the two paints she had pulled out of the cupboard. *Red over white or white over red?* She pondered briefly. To her at that moment, red symbolised blood and white symbolised innocence. *White as snow*, came to mind as she remembered Snowball and also how a preacher had said we are all so filthy we are like dirt in the snow. She had never felt good enough and Christianity had reinforced that belief.

Larissa went into a trance, listening to music to stop her analysing. She chose red. She painted 'Mouse', Heni Victoria Hertz', 'Desiree,' and 'Larissa Flight' in red over the painting. She was acknowledging that she had suffered. Why did she still have to suffer?

Then she picked up the white paint. 'White as snow,' she said as she remembered Snowball, who had suffered too. She wanted to try paint over and make it look like a fresh blank canvas. She painted the white when the red was not quite dry so it mixed together to make pink. Like an abstract pink rose on a white background. It made Larissa remember her romance with Kent.

Then Larissa used the saw to cut the wooden frame of the canvas. She ripped it and burned it in the fire, trying to burn away all the pain. The flames licked up high towards the chimney.

Unable to crack Diana, she smothered her into silence in pot of thick white paint. Larissa removed the silver 'healing' ring with the green glass leaves. She thought of Ziggy and Tripod buried with trees planted over them.

She was anxious that the silver was connected to the silver identity bracelets she had given the twins just before she'd left Australia. She was worried they were cursed too and connected to death, because silver tarnishes. Larissa used pliers to twist the ring and cut it before it was smothered in the pot of white paint too. She felt she had to urgently tell the twins to destroy the jewellery.

She removed the black onyx ring from the finger she'd used to yell 'fuck you!' when she'd driven around in anger at high speed. It too, was engulfed by the white paint. She smashed the tiger's eye pendant with a hammer and stuffed the broken fragments into the pot of paint. She put the items she'd destroyed but could not burn into the bashed up butterfly bag then discarded them.

She searched her room and found some medical records that had travelled from New Zealand to Australia and back again. The medical report stated that three internal haemorrhoids six centimetres long had been excised from 3 o'clock, 6 o'clock and 11 o'clock. 'My anus is not a clock-face!' she said as she tore the records up then burned them in the fire.

Recovering from that surgery had been the worst physical pain she had experienced. Far worse than the kidney trauma, childbirth and skiing accident combined. But it was nothing compared to the psychological suffering she had endured.

Late into the night, Larissa continued to destroy objects. She grabbed a knife from the kitchen.

She stabbed the tiger pyjamas that had been soaking in the bathtub to make sure the tiger spirit was dead – the same pyjamas she had been wearing when she had been visited by a frightening spirit. She squeezed out the water and wrapped the hot-pink dildo in the shredded fabric. The wheelie bin was nearly full.

Then she remembered the possessed cat port bottle from the morgue that had been converted into a winery. The twins were only four years old at the time they had visited the winery and they had mimicked wine-tasting with water in a wineglass. They had spat water into the barrel after swishing it around in their mouths.

Larissa phoned Richard. She hadn't spoken to Richard since before she was hospitalised. She felt anxious talking to him and spoke very fast. She gave him instructions to dunk the children's silver jewellery she had gifted them in water and then destroy them. Also to get rid of the port bottle if he still had it. Her voice was pressured – she was speaking fast and urgently. Richard interpreted the conversation as friendly but rather eccentric.

When she got off the phone, she looked at her cat tattoos – were they cursed too? As a child, she had been told that tattoos were cursed. Did she need to get the tattoos removed? She couldn't afford professional removal. She imagined herself cutting them off with a knife.

She looked at the cat on the number plates with the word 'can't'. 'I *can* live without my cat,' Larissa said. Memories of Snowball's suffering had haunted her for decades. It was part of why she had wanted to become a vet. She wanted to try to save animals. To try to ease their suffering. But the vet clinic environment had been too triggering. Even the pet sitting. Finding out pets she had developed a bond with had died.

She went back to the garage, still in her pyjamas and dressing gown, still sweating much more than usual and with greasy hair. She found another pot of thick white paint and a spatula. Rosebud followed her with a concerned look on her face. Most people wouldn't be able to tell different expressions on a cat's face but

Larissa could. It was mostly in the eyes. Rosebud followed Larissa into the garage then to the laundry.

Larissa went outside and shut the laundry door. Rosebud looked through the glass and her face seemed to be pleading *No, please don't!* Larissa felt that Snowball was visiting again, as Rosebud. Snowball needed to let go of her attachment to Larissa and go beyond Rainbow Bridge to Cat Heaven. As far as Larissa was concerned, cats did go to Heaven.

'Snowball, go! You are no longer attached to me! It's time for you to go!' said Larissa as she smeared thick white paint on the black cat on the number plates and the 't' in 'can't' with a spatula. When she looked up, Rosebud was gone.

After finally showering and then being knocked out by medication for some sleep, Larissa woke up ready to change her car's name. She washed her car slowly in a trance-like state, listening to *Sunny*, a song she remembered playing on the record player when she was a young child. Then she invited Aroha and Klaus for a renaming ceremony.

Larissa allowed Aroha to say a short prayer and then Larissa anointed Sunny with linseed oil. Anointing with oil was something she remembered from church in her childhood. Larissa chose the linseed oil because it reminded her of the smell of the wood putty she had sniffed on Klaus's bench when he had carved the plaque for Kat's grave out of wood because Kuini and Lindsay could not afford a headstone.

Then, for the first time in years, Larissa allowed Aroha and Klaus to pray for her. She felt like they were fully accepting her as part of their family if she believed in God too. Larissa had a confession to make but she felt so much shame.

'I was going to hang myself on that hook outside with the belt from my dressing gown.'

'When was this?'

'About six months after I got back from Australia. Because I was in so much pain.'

'Thank you for telling us,' said Aroha. 'Thank you for not going through with it.' Klaus and Aroha hugged Larissa tightly.

Larissa had another confession to make.

'I had sex in your house. I broke your 'not under our roof' rule.

'When was that?' asked Aroha.

'When I was off my medications. When you went on holiday.'

'Rules are meant to be broken,' said Klaus. Larissa felt relief. Klaus and Aroha had very strict beliefs about sex. Their beliefs were that sex was only between a man and a woman within marriage. It had been a constant source of conflict that Larissa had broken the rules prescribed by the church.

Angelica visited and said that it was not a good idea for Larissa to have cortisol surging through her body and that she needed to relax. Her medication was still being increased to try to get the mania under control and to help her get some rest. Angelica explained to Larissa that there was a risk of sliding into psychosis which was losing touch with reality.

As the medication was increased and as Larissa was able to get some sleep, she started to question her recent belief in God. She would later learn that hyperreligiosity is often part of mania.

Over the next few days, after Larissa's confessions, Klaus and Aroha were both angry. 'She lied to us! How dare she invite men into our house! Why are you so rebellious, Larissa! You've always been rebellious!'

Larissa started crying. 'I tried to be good but it's never enough for you. I'm a rotten egg,' she said. That's why she felt she had to symbolically destroy the 'bad' eggs. The calcite egg represented young Heni who was smashed apart by trauma and felt defective. The jade egg represented adult Heni who was more resilient, yet still felt damaged and unable to have a voice.

Aroha started to soften. 'You're not a rotten egg,' she said.

'I feel like I've been a rotten egg since the sexual abuse, and I cracked open a bad egg, baking a lemon Madeira cake, and then Lemon the chicken was killed,' she said. 'I can't do anything right. I can't please you. Whatever I do isn't good enough. I'm not good enough!'

Aroha and Klaus sat down to listen. For the first time ever, they intently listened. Previously they would tell Larissa how she needed to get right with God, and turn from her wicked ways, before she burned in hell forever like Kent.

'I feel like I'm cursed and contaminated, and that's why everyone I love dies,' Larissa continued. 'I'm scared I won't cope when you and Daniel die.'

Aroha and Klaus continued to listen.

'I felt like you dismissed me. Dismissing me felt almost as traumatising as the abuse.'

'We're sorry for dismissing you,' said Aroha. 'I don't know what else we can do. You need to forgive.'

'For yourself more than us,' added Klaus.

After smashing up the eggs and the symbolic objects and feeling a release with doing that, Larissa felt she was finally ready to forgive.

'I forgive you for dismissing me when I told you about the abuse.' It was very hard for her to say. She also found it hard to say the words 'I love you,' even to her children.

Larissa remembered all the links and patterns with her pets and symbolic objects. Smashing symbolic objects had felt therapeutic. Even when she was extremely unwell, she was self-aware. It felt like a process of internal transformation.

Aroha, Klaus and Larissa hugged.

'I think I've gotten rid of nearly everything from Australia,' said Larissa. Some of the few items left, were her camera that was struck by a snake and her laptop. She didn't want to get rid of them yet as she couldn't afford to buy new ones. Also she didn't want to get rid of her new blue suede boots. One of the songs she had listened to was *Blue Suede Shoes*. She saw several links and associations with memories in the lyrics, just with all the other songs that came to mind that she'd heard over several decades.

Even though she couldn't actively recall most of the lyrics, when she looked up a song, even from a string of three or four words, some of the lyrics in the song were related to the current themes that she was processing. Listening to the songs while doing some form of creative expression helped her to process the emotions which were linked to painful memories.

Larissa still felt very anxious about the few remaining items – they were all linked in her mind. Literally everything linked in some way back to trauma in a complex web – songs, objects, places, names, smells. All potential triggers. Larissa accepted Aroha's offer to pray for things, including her laptop, camera and boots and anoint them with oil, even though she was sceptical about prayer.

Larissa saw Dr Eric Wright again. This time she wore her blue suede boots.

'Now that I've seen you in mania, I'm very confident that your diagnosis of bipolar disorder is correct,' said Eric. 'It is unusual for a patient to be self-aware that they are unwell, though.'

'Yeah it's kind of weird. It's like I can go outside my own body and observe myself. I think making the videos of myself over the past month helped me to see myself from another perspective.'

Eric and Angelica nodded in agreement.

'Yes,' said Angelica. 'You asked for help. It's amazing how much difference addressing the sleep deprivation has made.'

'I know what if feels like when I'm sliding quickly and about to fall off the cliff. Falling off the cliff really hurt last time.'

'You're already starting to sound more organised in your thinking and your speech,' said Eric.

'It still feels like I can see the future. It feels spiritual.'

'Your mood is still elevated. Those will be associations that you see,' said Angelica. 'You are more aware of links and patterns than most other people.'

'I was afraid my boots would kill you,' said Larissa, laughing. 'So I didn't wear them to my appointment when you had the flu.'

Eric laughed. 'You know that's irrational, don't you?'

'Yes, but it felt so real. I felt very spiritual to the point of being superstitious. I started believing in God again even though I'm more agnostic, leaning atheist usually.'

'That could be one of your indicators of when you are unwell.'

'There you go, believing in God is a mental illness,' joked Larissa, nudging Aroha. Aroha sat there looking unimpressed. She didn't like it that since taking the medications, Larissa was now questioning her temporary renewed belief in God.

Aroha believed that this diagnosis of 'bipolar affective disorder' was a spiritual affliction, not mental illness and that if Larissa believed enough, God would heal her. Yet, she had taken her daughter to the psychiatrist when Larissa requested, despite conflict with her beliefs.

God had not healed Heni years ago when she had sincerely believed in God. God had not prevented Heni from being sexually abused after she had invited Jesus into her heart. God did not stop Kat from dying from cancer. As far as Larissa was concerned, God either didn't care or didn't exist.

Back home, Larissa was cutting up a pineapple when Aroha brought up the topic of Larissa needing to believe in God and what the Bible said.

'Blessed are those who smash babies on rocks?' asked Larissa.

'The Bible doesn't say that.'

'It does so. It's one of the Psalms.'

'You're taking it out of context.'

'That's always the excuse. Taking it out of context. How do you put that into context?'

'The people were bad and deserved it.'

'Just like with God killing all the innocent babies and children all through the Bible? Like drowning them in a flood?'

'Evil people deserved it. God made a promise with a rainbow not to flood the world again.'

'A promise not to kill life with a global flood that there is no scientific evidence for taking place?'

'What is it with you and rainbows?'

'I like colour and nature. Rainbows are refraction of light through water droplets. I made my own as a kid with the garden hose. '

'Sin is why there is so much trouble in the world. If you confess and believe, God will heal you.'

'God didn't bother to heal me when I believed. I cannot accept that child cancer is a punishment for all future generations after two people ate a piece of fruit because a talking snake told them to. Speaking of fruit, this pineapple is delicious – so juicy and sweet.'

As Larissa's short-term memory was impaired, Aroha managed her medications for several weeks, until Larissa was able to organise and take medications on her own. She was instructed to keep increasing the doses until she reached mood stabilising levels over the next few months. She was still not well enough to work or to drive.

She alternated between an elevated mood, and then a crash into depression.

Aroha took Larissa to town, during a high. Larissa was listening to her music in the store. Larissa danced and sang, *'(You drive me) Crazy.'*

'You drive *me* crazy,' replied Aroha.

When depressed, her energy was very low and it was hard to cling to hope and keep going. It was hard for her to speak at all when she was depressed or shut down. She would go from being feisty in the elevated moods to withdrawn in the depressed moods. The sudden mood crashes were hugely distressing.

Larissa was overwhelmed when attempting to do any basic administrative tasks. Her brain wouldn't function well enough to be able to follow online instructions or complete a form to apply for a benefit. It was difficult for her to even complete a sentence as her mind forgot what she had done a few seconds ago.

Larissa longed to be independent, not to have to rely on people to help her fill out a form or to help her remember the instructions for taking her medications.

For several weeks after starting a heavily sedating antipsychotic which Eric hoped would also act as a mood stabiliser at higher doses, Larissa woke up suddenly in the early hours of the morning in a panic, with her heart pounding and feeling like she was going to throw up. She felt like she was drowning and was gasping to breathe. She felt pressure and pain in her chest.

Eric said that these were not side effects he was aware of but he expected any side effects to ease within a month. He said he thought perhaps the symptoms were more trauma related. Larissa was instructed to keep increasing the dosage of medication.

The weight Larissa had rapidly lost when off medications quickly went back on. Larissa told Angelica it felt like her brain was burning up rocket fuel during the mood crashes from mania into depression and she strongly craved ice-cream and chocolate.

Angelica strongly recommended that Larissa resume walking to regain fitness and to help counteract the weight gain from the medications. Larissa often took her camera which now had a broken on/off button. She would have to take the battery out to turn the camera off.

That was how it was with the night medications. They were like turning her off for the night. She was either fully on with mania or off, being knocked out by medications, with no in between. It was more difficult to go walking when she was depressed but she tried to persevere with walking at her own pace, faster when she was in elevated moods, slower when depressed.

Larissa went walking by the lake and she wound up in a gully full of bees. She took photographs of the bees on the light purple wildflowers. She remembered how Kent had said that when he died, he would come back as a bee. Larissa felt at peace watching all the bees. A little cat who looked just like her cat Tommy, who was run over by a truck when she was a teenager, greeted her. It felt like Tommy was visiting, even though she knew it was another very affectionate cat.

When Tommy had been run over, Heni had sat in bed so anxious that she felt like she was going to throw up. She had heard the truck before Aroha and Klaus took a shovel down to the road and told her not to come to the road. Tommy was buried under a rose bush.

Larissa walked past a house where a pallet of glass had been dropped while being lifted up onto a balcony. Just the day before, she had seen the pallet of glass sitting on the ground and taken a photo of it. She took another photo of the scene – the wooden palette with a logo of a beeswax was dangling from the balcony and the glass was on the ground. The men at the site were very upset that she was watching and told her that it was 'not nice to take photos of unfortunate events'.

Larissa had difficulty getting her words out but she managed to ask if all the glass was broken. The men seemed to calm down and told her that the outside pieces of glass had broken but the inside pieces were still intact after falling from a height. Larissa couldn't help but feel that she had caused the glass to fall. That she was hexed. That it was still all her fault that bad things happened.

19. Storms

Larissa was walking around town. Her complexion was glowing with minimal makeup. She was wearing a long indigo dress she'd bought when in the psychiatric unit, which emphasised her bust which was even fuller than usual with the weight gain from going back onto medications.

Part of town was blocked off with a triathlon event.

I wonder if Nate's competing? Seconds after that thought, she saw Nate walking towards her wearing his cycling gear. Nate was very goal orientated with his walking, just like with sex. Larissa stopped to glare at him. He glanced her way and said 'Hi' then quickly looked away and then almost sprinted into a store.

'Go on then, act like you don't know who I am,' Larissa goaded him.

Irritated and bold, Larissa followed Nate into the store. Nate disappeared behind some suspended bikes. Larissa waited at the other end of the bikes then stepped out as Nate walked past.

'Are you in the habit of using people?' she said as Nate charged right past, as though Larissa wasn't there. A sales assistant stifled an amused smile.

Nate charged out of the shop and vanished from view. He'd disappeared so quickly that Larissa figured he'd either sprinted away or ducked down to hide behind some cars. If Larissa hadn't been on medications, she probably wouldn't have been able to suppress the impulse to yell, 'Coward!' The confidence she had been attracted to was all fake. Just like with Richie. Then she realised for the first time that Nate had used her but she'd used him too.

At Larissa's next psychiatric appointment she couldn't stop looking at Eric and smiling. Eric smiled back. Larissa felt temporarily infatuated with him.

'How are things going?' asked Eric, smiling more than usual because of Larissa's glances and smiles.

'I'm a little high,' replied Larissa, still smiling.

'It's okay to be a little high,' said Eric. 'As long as you're in control of it. Your speech is much more organised than before.'

Larissa told Eric that the nocturnal panic attacks had eased and that she was still seeing patterns, which felt significant to her. 'It's like I can still see the future.'

'Coincidences.'

'Hundreds of coincidences then,' insisted Larissa in a defiant tone. 'Things that happen at exactly the same time. Several times every day.'

'Yes, all coincidences.'

'I've been wondering if I should date.'

'I don't recommend it while you're vulnerable.'

'What about social media?'

'Don't put stuff on social media when you're in mania because you may say things you don't really mean when you look back at it later. Try writing in a journal instead.'

'Can I drive yet?'

'Yes, but not if you're feeling the effects of sedation or mania or fatigue. Only if you can focus well enough to drive safely.'

It had been months since Larissa had driven her car. Going driving with Sunny felt like a small amount of freedom and independence. She booked a doctor's appointment to get a renewed medical certificate so she could keep receiving a benefit until she could work again.

'You still have pressure of speech,' observed Dr Keyes. Larissa felt she had to speak urgently as her mind raced faster than her mouth could keep up. Her sentences would sometimes come out scrambled or with missing or substituted words, going off on tangents.

'Everything flashes through my head like a video on fast forward,' said Larissa, very quickly. It's quite weird as all these words and images flash through my head and then I see them, so it's like I can see the future. I felt I had to walk down the alcohol section of the supermarket and even though I rarely drink alcohol, it was like I recognised all the logos and names from other things I'd seen the night before. Similar logos and words from music videos. Is that flight of ideas?'

'Flight of ideas is when someone jumps from one thing to another and another, even in the same sentence, which is hard for others to follow.'

'I've been having memories flashing into my mind as images and words in rapid succession. Then I see those same things the same day in real life. Often at exactly the same time. At first it made me feel panicked but now I'm realising that they are actually linked in some way.

'Angelica, the mental health nurse, said it's because I see patterns, which feels like I can see the future. I think of an ambulance and then I see one seconds later. It's like a net that's coming to the surface with lots of corks bobbing and I can't squash it down anymore. All the connections go back to trauma.'

'You are insightful and have an ability to analyse so you can step outside of yourself and try to make sense of it.'

'I went to the library and looked through historical newspapers,' said Larissa, very fast, while jiggling her legs and tapping her fingers. She fidgeted more in repetitive motions when her mood was elevated or when she was anxious. 'I flicked through them very fast. I've been figuring out missing links. It's weird because it's like I've seen everything in the newspapers before.'

'Take care when going back to the past. It could trigger something very big. And make sure you come back to the present. You've still got the crisis line number in case you need it? Your mood still seems elevated. If you feel like you're losing control, contact the crisis team.'

Larissa was glad Dr Keyes didn't judge her and took the time to explain things. Dr Keyes and Angelina actually explained more about bipolar disorder than Dr Eric Wright.

That was the frustrating thing about all the years she had been sent to psychiatrists – they focused on dispensing medication and if she seemed to look better from the outside, they decided she was fine, when she wasn't fine on the inside. They didn't actually tell her much about her diagnosis.

At the library, Larissa requested to look at newspapers from the 1980s. The librarian brought out newspapers from the archive room. Larissa flicked quickly through the pages at a rate of about one second per page. Certain things jumped out at her, while everything else was a blur.

Sometimes, she'd pause to take a photo of anything of interest. Her short-term memory was extremely impaired, so taking photos helped her to feel like she was allowed to forget, knowing that she could refer to the photos later if she needed to.

In the newspapers there were people she recognised, new businesses opening, birth and death notices, the town's first set of traffic lights and diggers laying pipes for the town sewage system. All of these were familiar. She saw the death notice for Kat in the same year that the town sewage system was still being installed. The paper reminded her that Kat's funeral had been on Daniel's birthday, so the anniversary would be in a few days time. She had blanked that out.

She saw the launch of the rescue helicopter that had uplifted Ava to hospital. Then she saw a memorial notice for Paul. She paused to read it. It said he was remembered and loved by family and friends.

Aroha and Klaus had refused to tell Larissa any more details about when she was abused, so she concluded from how her mind had linked it with Kat's death that she must have been no older than eight years old. She now had Paul's date of birth and date of death.

Her mind was unable to do any mental arithmetic so she tried doing calculations on her phone. She concluded that he was around fifteen when she was eight years old. Even though he had seemed older, more like seventeen.

Can't charge a dead man. Remains an allegation. Larissa didn't know how she could get closure. Contacting his sister didn't give her closure. His mother might be in more pain if she knew. She closed the newspapers.

Larissa purchased another bottle of nail polish, *Golden Dewdrop*, to add to her growing collection. She usually only wore nail polish when her mood was elevated. Just like she only ever wore perfume in mania. The more elevated her mood, the brighter the colours with more layers.

She had painted messy, miniature, symbolic abstracts on her fingernails and toenails, representing colours of flags, logos, patterns, moods and symbolism.

She removed the multicoloured layers with nail polish remover. The separation of colours on the cotton pads resembled chromatography. Then, she painted spring flowers and butterflies in bright colours over a background of *Golden Dewdrop*: shimmery gold with a hint of violet.

Klaus and Aroha announced they were going away for a few days so Larissa would be on her own. For the past month, she had been managing her own medication which was still difficult because of her short-term memory issues.

Larissa was restless. She opened a drawer and pulled out a chess game and some cards. She put a black pawn, a black queen and a white king on the chess board with some playing cards, including a red diamond. She started assembling objects from around the house, trying to represent some of the hundreds of links going through her mind like a complex web.

She soon filled the dining room table. She pulled an atlas off the shelf, and opened it to Australia and put it on a chair away from the table. She was creating a massive still life and visual mind map. The still life filled the table and spilled onto the floor.

She went into the garage, opened the cupboards and found jumper leads. She connected them to a kitchen stool. The jumper leads were meant to represent her heart being restarted when she had nearly died after her surgery. Plus her attempts to revive her broken heart. Most objects had more than one meaning.

Over the next several hours, she assembled hundreds of objects from around the house. She opened a cupboard and found a wooden box containing the compass that Klaus had given her before Kat died. Inside the box was the Silver Star lifesaving award she had earned many years ago. She hung the compass in her window where the prism had been, to represent a moral compass. She also found two paua shell dolphin broaches – one with silver and one with gold.

To her still life, she added the glass bottles she had purchased from the opportunity shop. To the bottle that was shaped like a conical flask, she added two marbles, an AA battery and purple glitter, and then rested a larger marble on top as a stopper. She added a plastic pendant she had found, that looked like a Maori carving in an infinity symbol. She included a bottle of shower gel, which had the word 'magical.'

After assembling all the objects so that they told a complex story in her mind, she dragged in a tall ladder from the garage. Despite heavy sedation after another dose of medication, she climbed up the ladder to take photos of her still life from up high, representing how in mania, she could see things from a different perspective, even though there was a danger of falling.

It was the night before the anniversary of Kat's funeral. She lit the fire and was watching the flames in a trance-like state. She held down the shutter button to take multiple photos in quick succession. Suddenly, she became very anxious as there appeared to be a cat in the flames – the shape of a skull with cat ears, a body and a tail. She looked back at the photos to confirm what she saw.

The rational explanation was that the cat was an optical illusion from the shape of the flames and the smoke, but at that moment in time, Larissa was very anxious that there was a demon in the fireplace. Especially after remembering how, growing up, Aroha had claimed that various objects around the house had demons in them and had ordered they be burned in the fire.

Larissa went to her room to take her night medication. She had been keeping track with a chart because she was now on over a dozen pills per day, spaced throughout the day and still increasing. The same medication that previously, just one tablet of which would knock her out within minutes.

She accidentally tipped the pills out all over her desk and because her short-term memory was so impaired, she did not know if she had just swallowed the pills or was yet to take them. Her mind was struggling to have any focus at all.

She managed to call the crisis number to ask for advice. They told her that she sounded very confused, so they sent an ambulance as Larissa was too sedated to drive to the hospital. Larissa was disorientated and having difficulty standing, so the hospital staff insisted on a wheelchair. She felt relieved when they went past room eight and instead went to room nine. We're going to do an EEG to check your heart. Does any part of your body hurt?'

'My anus hurts,' said Larissa. Her sphincter muscles were in such a tight painful spasm, like a leg cramp, only concentrated in her anus like after the surgery. That happened sometimes when she was extremely anxious.

After Larissa had been kept in overnight for observation for a queried accidental overdose, Daniel took her home and started helping her tidy up. It had been very easy to pull things out but now it was very difficult to try to put things back. Larissa's brain could see multiple links like a network but had extreme difficulty with organising words into sentences or objects back into designated spaces.

Klaus and Aroha arrived home. 'What is this mess?' exclaimed Klaus with stress in his voice. He needed the house to be immaculate with everything in its exact place.

'It's a still life,' said Larissa.

'It's a mess!' Klaus picked up the jumper cord leads, 'How dare you go through our stuff!' He went pale and clutched at his chest. 'I think I'm having a heart attack!' he whispered. The ambulance made a second visit to the house, this time for Klaus. After tests were run, it was concluded that Klaus had suffered from a panic attack, triggered by the stress of the house not being organised exactly as he needed it to be.

An urgent family meeting was called with Daniel and Angelina in attendance.

'I'm too old to deal with this. I can't handle the stress,' said Klaus. 'I'm going to have a heart attack. She's going to have to live elsewhere.'

'I could see what she was trying to do,' Aroha tried to defend Larissa. 'She was trying to do something creative.' But Klaus wouldn't have it. He needed to have his house, his castle, arranged in a particular way. His way. Everything lined up, neat and tidy, clean, labelled and organised. But that was not how Larissa's brain worked. It was stressful for her to try to please Klaus.

'You're going to have to pack your bags,' said Klaus.

'I'm a burden!' cried Larissa with distress in her voice. 'I may as well kill myself right now because no one wants me anyway!'

Larissa was crying and was exhausted. Too exhausted to keep fighting to stay alive.

'You're not a burden,' said Aroha gently. 'It's not your fault that someone hurt you when you were six years old.'

'You mean Paul? What do you mean I was only six years old?' Larissa went from feeling despair into in a state of panic. Her fight or flight response was intensely activated instead of her usual response of shutting down with triggers. Her heart was racing.

'Yes,' nodded Klaus wearily. 'You were very young.'

'Daniel?' Larissa asked anxiously. 'What do you remember?'

'I think I was still seven, so you must have been six, maybe even five. I remember Paul yelled at us that night.'

Angelica took Larissa away from the others as she was pacing the room, in an extreme state of hypervigilance and restless agitation.

'I can't remember him yelling, but yelling is one of my triggers. His body seemed like an adult's.'

'It can seem like that way when you're a young child. What is it that upsets you so much about finding out how young you were, Larissa?' asked Angelica.

'Then he must have only been thirteen or maybe even twelve. I was abused by a child! He was younger than my children are now!'

After several minutes alone with Angelica to self-regulate, using controlled breathing while listening to calming instrumental music, she told Angelica, 'it makes more sense that I was six because it was a picture book that he read to me and I was learning to spell. Whereas I could read the Bible and children's novels when I was eight.'

Klaus and Aroha made the decision that it was too stressful for them to have Larissa continue to live with them, so Daniel allowed Larissa to move in. Larissa packed her few belongings, feeling so very sad. Aroha let Larissa keep the two paua dolphin broaches.

Larissa placed the silver dolphin into a purple storage container. She took a photo of the dolphin in a sea of purple, then posted it to her page on social media with a caption: 'Alone in the corner, upside down, trying not to drown.' Even though she found social media at times to be toxic, there were some people who did seem to acknowledge her feelings.

Aroha gave Larissa some purple and yellow flowers, encouraging her to plant them in the garden for spring. Larissa drove down to the cemetery and buried the lifesaving award in the children's memorial garden. She put the purple flowers on top without removing the plastic container. She planted the yellow flowers in the garden at home and watered them by making a fine spray with the hose like she used to do as a child to form a spraybow.

Larissa woke up in the middle of the night, energised. She put on the purple ball gown she'd bought when in the hospital. She took out the new 'virgin' student acrylic paints she'd purchased from the six primary and secondary colours of the painting colour wheel – red, green, yellow, purple, blue, orange.

She listened to *Funeral for a Friend/Love Lies Bleeding* on a loop, which she found to be an increasingly mood elevating and energetic piece of music. She felt euphoric as she danced and painted an abstract in bright colours without white and black. She tried not to blend them to make brown. She put the opposite colours on the colour wheel next to each other so they seemed extra intense. Her brush strokes were messy.

The symbolic abstract was of a rollercoaster which represented DNA unzipping as well as Paul's jeans unzipping. The top half of the zip also represented mania, which was suddenly cut off so there was a crash. The bottom half of the zip slid down into depression. Fireworks were exploding near the top. Flames of fire licked up from the bottom.

The open zipper reminded her of a mouth and she painted brightly coloured shapes, representing vomit. She developed a vomit phobia after a boy called Paul vomited on the netball courts at school. After that, she'd felt so repulsed by the sight and smell of vomit that she'd suddenly lost her netball skills. She'd started zoning out and dropping the ball. She'd stood there looking vacant when the ball hit her in the head. The other girls in the netball team had called her 'dummy' and 'klutz' so she quit.

Even though she was painting in a euphoric, trance-like state, intensity was captured in the painting, which symbolised trauma and bipolar disorder in abstract with bright colours. What she was painting about only briefly flashed through her mind, so she was not re-traumatised.

Then, feeling much calmer, and using fine brushes, she started another small painting with a completely different mood and style. It started with a Catherine Wheel firework spinning, which was how her brain felt. Then she painted over it her ruby heart engagement ring and the tips of a compass. The ring looked like an abstract eye.

Over the North compass tip, she painted a triangle which represented a delta symbol, meaning 'change' or 'difference'. Then, the triangle was transformed into the head of Lemon the chicken, adding flapping wings to transform Lemon into an angel. She added a gemstone to cover Lemon's head.

She decorated the ring with loops of fine golden cord to represent *Wonder Woman's* lasso, compelling one to tell the truth. She added other Greek symbols including a lowercase lambda, reflected and transformed. Then she painted 'arohanui' which means 'farewell' in Maori language on the side and glued pieces of broken paua to represent islands.

Aroha came to visit. 'That looks interesting,' she said, pointing to the *Love Lies Bleeding* painting. 'Very bright and colourful.'

'I also did this one,' Larissa said, holding up the miniature painting which was now quite ornate with various symbols and reflective sequins and imitation gemstones. As soon as Aroha saw the painting, she became critical.

'The Devil has a foothold on you, Larissa. It's been proven that brains can grow horns if you hold bitterness in your heart.'

'What a load of rubbish.'

'What's it mean?' Aroha said, still in a critical tone.

'I won't tell you if you're going to judge me. I won't paint.'

'Let me pray for you.'

'I don't want your prayers.'

'Tell me what it means,' said Aroha, trying to sound less judgemental in her tone.

'It's called *Kathryn Wheel Angels*. It means empathy for people who have lost their children and pets. Thank you for judging – not.'

Aroha seemed to calm down and told Larissa to keep painting. It had been many years since Larissa had painted and Aroha didn't want to stop Larissa from painting, even though it made her feel uncomfortable that Larissa painted with abstracted symbolism which was like a secret code. But that was how Larissa felt safer. Painting in disguise, to avoid being judged.

Larissa had been having lucid dreams since starting the medications. Some dreams were beautiful, some weird and others frightening. Usually she couldn't remember dreams. Some dreams were sleep hallucinations, as she was aware of strange sensations in her body when she was in a halfway state between being awake and asleep. It was often accompanied by sleep paralysis where she was unable to move or speak.

She only had one recollection of that happening before she had the breakdown, when she had told her parents she had been abused by Paul. She had been lying on her front to nap then was temporarily paralysed while she felt the pressure of a cat's feet walking up her back. At the same time, the door blew wide open in the wind, jarring Heni fully awake.

The light bulb flickered in a sudden electric storm. Heni had felt anxious. People in the church had insisted demons inhabited Heni and her house, which made her feel more anxious.

'I was lying on the bed and a demon peeled me off the bed and I felt myself floating,' said Larissa to Eric, describing her recent sleep hallucinations. 'The demon took me over to the mirror and tried to get me to look in the reflection at his red eyes. Then I realised that I was still lying face down on my bed and that the demon was Paul,' said Larissa.

'Then another time, a dead tree wrapped itself around me from behind, like a creepy hug. I felt electricity going through my arms to my fingertips as its dead branches grew and I could not speak. It was terrifying. The dead tree with the haunting branches was Paul.'

'Lucid dreaming can be a side effect of the medication,' said Eric. 'The meds are not stabilising your moods as much as we hoped – you've been alternating between mania and crashes.'

'When I'm crashing, I have intense cravings for ice-cream,' said Larissa. 'It's like my brain is burning up like rocket fuel. I'm already putting on weight from these meds. They suck.'

'What do you suggest we try then?'

'I don't know. You're supposed to be the expert,' Larissa said sarcastically.

'*You're* the expert.'

'What?'

'You're the expert on how the medications make you feel.'

'They all make me feel like crap.'

'Which medications have you already tried?'

'I can't remember.'

'That's not very helpful.'

'I have trouble remembering names. You should have it in your records what I've been on.'

'I'm doing my best to keep you alive right now,' said Eric with frustration in his voice for the first time.

'I will probably recognise if you say their names. The meds aren't getting to the root of the problem anyway, which is addressing the trauma.'

'We have referred you to a trauma psychologist but there may be a long wait, perhaps a year or more. You will need to be more stable to cope with the therapy. Let's try another adjustment. I will be away for a month, so you will see a locum.'

Larissa saw the locum psychiatrist who said to Angelica, 'Does she always talk this much?' Larissa thought that was rude. She couldn't help that her speech alternated between extremes of not talking at all to talking excessively. She wasn't doing it on purpose. The locum prescribed a more aggressive change in medications than Eric.

'Your moods are not stable, so it is as if you are sitting on a chair with no sides and swinging from one side to the other between mania and depression. We don't want you to be like some of my clients who ran down the street naked or jumped off a building because they believed they could fly,' he said.

Larissa didn't tell him that she had jumped off the wood shed when she was younger, wanting to feel like she was flying. She had also walked around a forest naked, to feel one with nature.

When Eric returned, Aroha was concerned so she attended Larissa's appointment.

'My medications were stuffed up and I was really sick,' said Larissa. 'I crashed into a depression. We called the helpline and they told me I should have only been on half the dose. So I've reduced the dose.'

'She was stumbling around and slurring her speech like a drunk person,' added Aroha.

'There's no sign of that now. It's in the past. Let's focus on the way forward,' said Eric, matter-of-factly.

'So it doesn't matter that I crashed really hard into depression?'

'You weren't given a toxic dose. You had an unpleasant reaction but the doses weren't lethal.'

'I've been severely depressed.' Larissa was feisty now. Angelica sat with wide eyes as Larissa argued with the psychiatrist.

'Pharmacy error,' Eric said dismissively.

'Pharmacy error? Psychiatrists never make mistakes?'

'Yep, pharmacies make mistakes all the time. As I said, it's in the past. You're fine. Let's move forward.'

'I've had to fight against acting on suicidal urges. If it had been someone else who wasn't so determined to try to survive, they could have committed suicide. It does matter. To stop it happening to someone else!'

This time, Eric didn't retort immediately. He sat there quiet, with his pen flicking against Larissa's thick file of medical records.

'I'd like a copy of the locum prescription to show to the pharmacy please,' Larissa said in a calmer, yet assertive voice.

'Sure thing,' said Eric. He flipped back to the locum script. He started to scrutinise closer. 'There are three errors in the script and he shouldn't have started you on such a strong dose with you being so sensitive.'

'So what are you going to do about it?'

'I'll talk to my manager,' said Eric. *Eric has a manager?* Larissa thought, incredulously.

She finally felt heard.

The appointments with Eric were short but Larissa continued regular counselling sessions with Angelica until she could finally be seen by a trauma psychologist. Neither Eric nor Angelica wanted to address trauma. They wanted to wait for a specialist.

Angelica explained that when Larissa avoided intense emotions by shutting them down, her anxiety would increase. Larissa was usually able to completely segregate her thinking and feeling.

'The meds are like putting a bucket under the Huka Falls,' said Larissa. 'They hardly do anything.' She remembered the roar when she had visited the Huka Falls as a child.

'That's a good analogy to help us understand,' said Angelica. 'Does the Huka Falls represent the intensity of your emotions?'

'Yes. Usually I can't feel my emotions but when I'm manic, all my emotions come out intensely at once. It's like the emotions were frozen but then they thawed and became tidal waves. I think the emotions need to come out though, rather than be suppressed with the meds. I don't want to feel like a zombie.'

'You are very insightful,' said Angelica. 'We can ask Eric to use the medications to help you manage episodes rather than to try to suppress the bipolar, if that's what you want. We need to get you stabilised enough to cope with trauma therapy. I've applied for you to be seen by a trauma psychologist. It seems you've been figuring out creative ways on your own though that help you in the meantime.'

'It's scary to feel my emotions, but I want to feel them. Even if I can't feel them, I've been able to express them creatively. The emotion of anger scares me the most. I hardly ever feel anger and then if I do, it's usually very distressing.

'Unless I'm manic – then it can feel energising and even exciting. The energy is starting to feel like a dam releasing and then building up again rather than a continuous powerful waterfall.'

Larissa dyed a white rosebud from the garden by splitting the stem and immersing it in food colouring to become a rainbow rose like the rose buds Kent had given her years ago. She had also woven roses on stems out of flax after Aroha had shown her how.

This time she didn't need music to ease her anxiety. She was going to face her fears of cemeteries without the music but with her rainbow rose and bouquet of flax roses. She drove to the cemetery after taking a photo of a tui, feeding from a flax flower in the front garden that morning.

For the first time, she found Ava and Kent's graves together at one end of the cemetery, with their smiling faces on the headstones. She put the rainbow rose on Kent's grave. Larissa had buried the lifesaving award at the polar opposite end of the cemetery in a children's garden. She wanted to retrieve it to give it to Ava.

She walked to the children's garden and then saw Paul's grave a few metres away. She didn't remember ever seeing his grave before. It was right by the place where she had felt very emotional and buried the lifesaving award and put the punnet of purple flowers on top.

There was a photo of Paul on the headstone with his red hair, unsmiling. She didn't really recognise him as she had blanked out most of his face. She felt nothing for him but disdain. 'Fuck you,' she said as she stood on his grave. Aroha had told her that it was disrespectful to stand on graves.

She grabbed a stick and walked to the nearby children's garden and pulled out the plastic planter tray of purple flowers, still alive, that she'd put in the garden weeks before. The roots were very constricted in the plastic container. She started digging with the stick. 'I wanted it for you, Ava,' she said, starting to feel emotional.

At that moment, she saw a glistening of metal. She picked out the award and saw she had painted a gold star in nail polish before she had buried it. She walked to Paul's grave and tossed the plastic container on his grave. Empty rubbish, that's all he deserved.

She knew exactly where Kat's grave was, amongst the adult graves near the toilet, remembering from the only time she had been to a cemetery as a child. It still had the wooden plaque that Klaus had carved many years ago. She planted the flowers with their roots free to grow and stabbed the 'stem' of a flax rose into the ground like a stake.

Then, still holding the stick, she walked with purpose back to the opposite end of the cemetery to Ava's grave. She felt overcome with emotion and buried the lifesaving award behind the headstone under an ornament of a bird.

'Thank you for teaching me what love is, my friend,' she said as tears streamed down her face. 'Love isn't romance or sex. It's a non-judgemental friend who inspires me to keep living.'

She had felt like Ava was an angel, looking over her these past few months, keeping her safe when she felt terrified that something was trying to kill her. Ava's courage had inspired Larissa to stay alive.

Larissa walked over to the edge of the cemetery where there was a cliff. On the way, she passed graves of people she recognised even if she didn't know them personally. Some, she knew, had died from suicide, some from cancer, one from domestic violence, some from accidents. One was the recent grave for Maxine, Daniel's apprentice, and another was Kuini's. Some graves were of babies who had been alive for only hours after being born.

Larissa put flax roses on some of the graves. She still did not understand the meaning of suffering and why good people died before their time. Religion had given her little comfort, and only more anxiety. Despite not understanding suffering, and religion being inadequate in explaining it, she now she felt more at peace about the death of her three friends.

A tui sat on one of two pine trees at the edge of the cliff and started to sing. She remembered how that morning, she'd taken photographs of a tui that had visited the garden. She tossed the stick like a spear between the two pine trees. She'd had a significant emotional release and felt calmer in her mind at that time.

It was hot now and as Larissa went back to her car, a notification came through on her phone. It was a letter from Richard's lawyer stating that Larissa was dangerous so Richard would not be sending the children for Christmas, for their own safety.

The letter quoted some information Richard had gleaned from social media, such as Larissa posting the photo of the dolphin broach to represent how lonely and depressed she had felt. The letter said that Larissa would need to provide access to her medical records for a decision to be made.

Larissa went to an appointment with Eric.

'We do not release medical records to lawyers or anyone else. Not even to you. The best I can do is to provide a letter stating there is no risk of you harming your children. But his lawyer will need to make a formal request directly to me.' Eric gave Larissa his business card. 'I don't usually give out my email address.'

Larissa forwarded Eric's instructions to Richard's lawyer.

That evening, an electric storm was brewing after a hot, humid day. Thunder was rumbling in the distance. Larissa could feel the static in the air. She emailed Richard. 'You think I'm a potential murderer?'

'Who knows what you're capable of. You're nuts.'

'You really think I would murder the twins?'

'Maybe. They shouldn't be around a crazy bitch like you. I've got pages and pages of evidence against you.'

'Evidence? What evidence?'

'Your friends on social media are not really your friends.'

'Your evidence is spying on me on social media? I never even mentioned your name. You're a fucking arsehole! I am no longer afraid of you. You know I've been waiting for months to see the kids. I am not going to murder them because my diagnosis has changed from depression to bipolar, you fuckwit! I had the bipolar all along, even when you met me. Go on, waste your money on lawyers you big crybaby!'

Larissa felt energised as she told Richard what she thought of him at that moment in time in several impulsive, ranting emails, as the lightning struck outside her open window. To mock him further, she painted a few quick abstracts, one using a hammer and the other using a knife and fork for some of the strokes. One resembled glass shattered by a bullet. The other represented a cemetery with monsters at one end and angels at the other.

She posted the paintings to social media with a cryptic message, knowing Richard would see them. 'Some dickwad believes I will murder my children because I have been diagnosed with bipolar disorder. Here are my crime scenes – Exhibit A and Exhibit B. Lock me up and throw away the key!'

After feeling a tremendous release, she resumed painting her *Ava Angel* painting. She had started from the shape of a hex-nut, representing feeling like a 'nut' from a 'hexed' six-year old girl combined with an 'X' from opposite corners. She had drilled small holes in a square piece of mdf board and inserted small nails to navigate if she got lost in paint. She'd smeared the board with thick medium compound to provide textured shapes.

The top half of the hex-nut spelled 'AVA', looking like two mountains and a valley. It was reflected below. The V and its reflection looked like a number 8 made into an hourglass with abstracted yellow dolphins top and bottom.

An eagle-like figure looked like it was flying head on – facing fears. The eagle had curled feet like koru and it was holding a green net to save the bottom dolphin from drowning. The other dolphin looked like it was held up by a water fountain.

After her email fight with Richie, the air felt cleansed by the electric storm. She put the song, *Confident* on a continuous loop.

She started to go into a trance and to go with her instincts as she painted. Various thoughts and emotions would briefly pass into her head but would swirl away. She was just observing as the thoughts and feelings came and went. Angelica had taught her to observe her thoughts and emotions without judging them as good or bad.

She could see flashes of lightning out the window and could sometimes hear thunder above the beat of the music. Sometimes a mood storm was needed to clear the air.

She covered over most of the lifesaving ring with swirling layers of paint. She 'cut' the net by painting over it. She was letting go of the green and the gold. Letting go of the pain of Australia. The dolphin would learn to swim again and navigate the rough ocean. She painted soft, blurred turquoise and blue with hints of violet representing swirling seas.

She painted the two V shapes into red hearts like mirrors struck by lightning. It resembled a dog's face, so she added whiskers. When she flipped it upside down, it looked like a monster's face with spades for eyes, a big nose and a mouth, that was also a dolphin being held down, trying not to drown. The dolphin in the net now looked like it was a parachute. The painting was like an optical illusion that could be viewed upright or upside down. The wings of the eagle also looked angel wings.

She finished the artwork with metallics to bring out the textures, including a treble clef and a bass clef, representing music. Music had been her salvation. She couldn't bear to listen to music for a long time in all her pain, but once she started again, listening to music from different eras, the glacier started thawing and the rivers started to flow.

She removed all the nails with pliers and replaced them with brass pins to finish.

'What's changed?' asked Aroha when she visited the following day. 'It's like a huge weight has been lifted off your shoulders.'

'I told Richard what I thought of him and called him an arsehole for not sending the kids over for Christmas.'

'Good. I hope you also told him that he's a dick.' It was rare for Aroha to use swear words.

She asked her family what they saw in the *Ava Angel* painting. They all said, 'An angel'.

She asked Daniel what he saw when it was flipped upside down. He replied, 'I see a monkey!' They both laughed. Where Larissa saw a monster, Daniel saw a monkey.

Angelica advised Larissa that Richard had forwarded Larissa's ranting emails to Eric.

At her next appointment, Eric said, 'That's why I don't like giving out my email address. Richard decided he didn't need a letter after all.'

Larissa emailed Richard, 'My psychiatrist said you don't need a letter. So the twins are coming over?'

'They were always coming over. I just know how you like to play games.'

'The twins are coming over. That's all I need to know.' Any further communication was only about organising the twin's travel, matter-of-fact, no emotion and minimal contact.

20. Exhibitionist

For several months, with multiple medication adjustments, Larissa rapid-cycled into mania then crashed into depression. To try to anchor herself in the storms of the extreme mood shifts, Larissa continued to paint abstracts.

Klaus was trying to support Larissa's need to make a therapeutic, creative mess. He provided old gloves and a big worn-out paintbrush and laid out recycled cardboard. Klaus strained the rust out of tins of old enamel paints in the garage using recycled stockings. He had sheets of recycled cardboard and mdf board Larissa could paint on.

Larissa was feeling extreme hyperarousal energy with restlessness after learning that Richard had married Vanessa. She couldn't feel emotion, just a frantic energy that she needed to give expression to somehow.

Larissa listened to *Don't Stop Me Now* and painted fast. She slapped paint on messily with old brush then drizzled paint from recycled foil cat food containers. On a large piece of corrugated cardboard, she roughly painted an abstract red and yellow submarine volcano surrounded by blue erupting into a black sky. She felt trippy as she watched the paint rippling over the corrugations when she tilted it. She called the messy painting *Eruption Under the Sea*. It represented rage she could not feel, yet could still express creatively.

On another piece of cardboard, she painted dark blue and then a black arrow drizzled in red and yellow, pointing forward with the feathers of the flaming arrow turned into curved koru. Then she drizzled over lighter blue and white in the shape of an infinity symbol which also looked like a mask. She called the painting *Outer Space High*.

On a piece of mdf board, she turned a black and blue koru shape into a wave set against a red sky drizzled with yellow. She called it *Crashing*. It represented crashing from mania into depression.

Making a mess in creative ways was a tremendous release. She drizzled some remaining paint onto two boards. To one board, she attached old hex-nuts, rope and ribbon to spell out *NUTZ*. To the other board, she attached dozens of screws to spell *Screwed*. She wove red ribbons and black and white wool connecting the letters, highlighting the words 'wed' and 'ewe'.

Painting abstracts in a trance-like state to music helped her to express intense emotion, even if she could not access feeling emotions as identifiable emotions, but rather as hyperarousal energy. She did not have to feel emotions as emotions to express. Dancing also gave her release, but not as intensely as messy visual art. She felt more freedom slapping on paint messily than trying to paint something realistically. Trying to paint realistically made her anxiety about perfectionism start to flare up.

Late into the evening, Larissa listened to music while calmly scratching out an eye with scissors after scribbling crayon underneath then painting brown over the top representing shit. Scratch paintings was something she had done at school as a child. She scratched out a paua coloured iris with a pupil shaped like a pawn piece and keyhole representing secrets. She scratched out the reflection of a window as a highlight and called it *Payne*.

Larissa bought an inexpensive, round wooden chopping board, a small hammer and tiny brass nails. She hammered the nails in part way. Then she connected colourful embroidery threads between the nails in a seemingly random pattern, but it was actually a koru curling around to the centre. She called it *Koru Network* and it was representing her brain with multiple colourful connections.

While she was connecting thread, she sat alone at the dining room table listening to *Unchained Melody,* quietly shedding tears because she missed her twins. Then she remembered some scenes from the movie *Ghost*. She remembered Whoopi Goldberg's entertaining acting. At that exact same moment, Daniel walked past and put a newspaper on the table. It was an advertisement for *Sister Act*, with a woman dressed up as a nun. Larissa didn't recall seeing the newspaper before.

The next day, Larissa decided to buy a lottery ticket as a test. To see if she could really see the future or whether it was just that she saw patterns and meaningful coincidences.

She walked to the shop and along the way, digits from her childhood phone number jumped out at her from electrical posts and vehicles. She had never been able to remember sequences of numbers, other than her childhood phone number which had a visual pattern. On the way, she listened to *Spinning Around*.

When she arrived home, she painted an image of how her brain felt, on fire and spinning around like the Sun but trying to move forwards, even though she was going around in circles. She swirled on green and blue paint and then streaked on red and yellow, thickly with a little makeup spatula she had found. She called it *Spinning Orbit*. While painting *Spinning Orbit*, she decided she was going to have an art exhibition. To give herself a sense of meaning and purpose, with a 'ridiculous' goal.

The lottery was drawn and she had only selected half the correct numbers and did not win a prize. She concluded that she would not feel happy winning money anyway. Instead, she applied for a Community Arts grant. She pitched her idea as a Community Arts exhibition of process art as therapy, raising awareness about bipolar disorder. She called the proposed exhibition *Spinning Orbit* after the painting that inspired the idea for an exhibition. The application was for art materials and gallery exhibition fees. To her surprise, her application was accepted and a grant was approved, to be used within one year.

All Larissa's artwork looked like it had been done by different people, depending on her mood shifts. The only common theme was that most of it was in bright colours. Some of the paintings looked as if they had been done by a child. She did a series of crayon drawings with purple dye in an intense mixed mood episode – symptoms of mania and depression together. Mixed episodes and crashes were especially stressful. Larissa felt internally agitated and she scribbled out her trauma with crayon on several pieces of paper.

She listened to *Another Brick in the Wall* and scribbled secrets about her childhood trauma. Then she picked up a black crayon and scribbled in overlapping circles to cover up everything she had written. Like the record player playing scratched records when she was a child in the seventies. Getting stuck and repeating over and over like her trauma. She frantically scratched in games like noughts and crosses and hangman. She washed over the black crayon with purple dye.

It was very dark, unlike all the colourful paintings she had done. To Larissa, black mainly represented 'survivor'. Then she drew a keyhole and outlines of bricks in a wall with a glue stick and sprinkled purple glitter over the glue. She called it *Memories Remain*.

On another piece of paper, she frantically scribbled brightly coloured crayons, feeling irritable as she expressed her trauma in multiple layers, hiding most of what was written beneath. She used such force, that the yellow crayon snapped in half. Only if one were to look very carefully, some words could be made out. 'I will', 'can', 'he stole my innocence', 'believe me'.

She washed over the crayon with dye, staining the paper purple. Then when dry, she used a glue stick to mark out an 'X' and then she transformed it into a butterfly, sprinkling it with purple glitter. She called it *Rebirth*.

On a larger piece of paper, she wrote *Was ist Liebe?* in crayon and drew abstract symbols representing bonds, neurotransmitters, energy, wavelengths, waves of the sea, music, colour, pets and DNA. She drew a full circle rainbow and wrote 'Aroha' under 'Liebe'. She wrote 'can't' and crossed out the 't'. She washed it over with purple dye.

She messily wrote on several other pieces of paper, listening to *Purple Rain*. She drew a crayon rainbow bridge with a white cat and a black dog and a stick figure person standing on top and a river under the bridge. On one side of the rainbow was a sun with an angry face. On the other were tear drop shapes in blue and red. Very messily, she scrawled, 'So exhausted but can't sleep.'

After several months, medication changes and art works later, Larissa's mood was no longer rapidly cycling between extremes of mania and severe depression but now hypomania and moderate depression. She was starting to feel more in control of her mood episodes.

Creative expression with abstracts helped her to process trauma without re-traumatising herself. Sometimes, she didn't feel emotions in a trance. At other times, she felt intense emotions. Painting helped calm her racing mind.

She purchased canvases for the exhibition and continued to paint through the ups and downs. She observed that trauma processing happened during the mood shifts. Many of the paintings had multiple hidden layers.

She also filled over a dozen journals with frantic writing and sketches. When she was manic, she preferred unlined scrapbooks and brightly coloured felt-tip pens. One of the scrapbooks had a picture of *Wonder Woman* on the front.

Her writing was barely legible and she found visual mind-maps and quick sketches more efficient in making sense of the numerous connections in her mind than to try write full sentences. When her brain was too scrambled for words, painting was easier.

Alexandria and Xavier visited for Christmas and flew back to Australia all too quickly. The Christmas and New Year period was very difficult for Larissa and she felt terribly lonely.

She started talking to a man on a dating site to distract herself. He was over a decade younger than Larissa and seeking a sexual friendship. Michael was a twenty-nine-year-old chef.

When they met, Larissa noticed Michael talked really fast like he also had pressure of speech.

'Do you have bipolar as well?' asked Larissa.

'I don't think so. I get anxious, especially meeting people. Are you creative? I love creativity,' said Michael. 'I take great photos and I love being creative with food.'

'Yes, I'm creative. I like taking photos too.'

'May I kiss you?'

'Sure,' said Larissa. Michael was socially awkward yet he was a very sensual and passionate kisser.

'You can't fall in love with me. We can't fall in love,' said Michael. 'I'm not ready. Just sex and friendship. No romance.'

'Fine by me,' said Larissa flippantly. 'Who needs romance?'

Larissa and Michael sexted over the next few weeks as Michael refused to talk on the phone. When her mood was elevated, Larissa sometimes found sexting to be arousing until she got bored with it. Or triggered.

'Will you be my dominatrix?' asked Michael.

'I'm not a dominatrix,' replied Larissa.

'Can I pretend you are? Tell me what to do. I'll do anything for you my mistress, my queen and goddess.'

'Meet me.'

'Where? You can't come to my place. I have flatmates.'

'Then we'll get creative. Meet me by the lake,' Larissa instructed. She specified a location secluded in native bushland by the lake where few people visited. 'I'll be wearing a sundress without a bra and panties.'

Michael was very excited to see Larissa again. Larissa's mood was elevated yet she acted cool, calm and collected. She felt in control of it. She had painted her nails with a fruity neon colour to express her current mood.

Occasionally they passed other people. When no-one was in view, Larissa walked ahead of Michael then she lifted up the back of her dress to reveal her curvaceous bare bottom, then dropped it again.

'Wow, oh wow,' gasped Michael. Larissa felt confident and smiled as other people walked past seconds later. Then when they disappeared from view, Michael and Larissa kissed and groped each other. It felt deliciously forbidden.

'That is so hot,' gushed Michael. 'If there weren't other people around, we'd so be having sex right now. Would we be having sex?'

'We could have sex right here.'

'What? How? There's people around.'

'At night. We could come back at night.'

It took Michael a few weeks to have the courage to meet Larissa in person again. In the meantime, another antipsychotic was added to Larissa's medications which made her feel terrible. Her mood plunged and her libido was annihilated. Still she met Michael for sex outdoors at night as he was very eager. They skinny-dipped in the lake under moonlight which felt delightfully sensual.

Then after their swim, they had sex. For the first time ever, Larissa faked an orgasm to please Michael as he was anxious about his sexual performance. The sex was disappointing; she felt depressed and conflicted and didn't want to see him again, despite having developed feelings for him.

She didn't want to have to please men. She was annoyed at herself and at Michael because he had pressured her into not using a condom.

Michael was confused because Larissa was now irritable and avoidant about sex. Michael said he couldn't be just friends because he could only think about Larissa in a sexual way, even though they both admitted to having feelings. They parted ways. Larissa battled a depressive episode for more than a month.

To process her confused feelings about Michael, and after watching water being released from a dam beneath a road, she painted *Release*. Controlled stripes in the colours of traffic lights against a blue background swirled as they escaped on the other side of the road which had a splat on it, representing an accident.

She streaked patterns with the prongs of a fork and painted deconstructed energy equations and symbols which looked like they spelled 'eve' and 'Hz for Hertz'. An 'e' in 'eve' also looked like 'o' so she added an L to spell Love. So the painting said 'Love hurts.'

When she saw Eric again, her main complaint was that she struggled to get up in the morning.

'You're hung over from the meds,' said Eric. Larissa had never been drunk so she didn't know what being hungover from alcohol felt like. Yet she was hungover every day.

'I can't live like this. It's screwing up my hormone levels. My blood test shows my prolactin levels are over seven times higher than the upper limit. I feel like crap. My GP says I'm overweight now which raises risk of heart disease and diabetes.'

'We only take prolactin into consideration if there are clinical symptoms. It's weighing up risks versus benefits. Being more stable with moods versus some extra weight.'

'Why am I on two antipsychotics? The second one makes me feel depressed and even more tired. It's constipating and I can't orgasm on it.'

'We can wean you off it if you want. Your mood stabiliser is also sedating. We can move most of the dose to the evening.'

'I want to be on as minimal meds as possible. I'd rather have moderate ups and downs than to feel like a hungover zombie all the time.'

Larissa went through another month-long depressive episode, adjusting to weaning off the second antipsychotic. But after she came through that, plus taking most of her medications now in the evening, she felt much better in the mornings.

Larissa finally saw a psychologist who agreed with her diagnosis of bipolar 1 disorder. She also diagnosed post-traumatic stress disorder (PTSD) and social anxiety disorder. The psychologist said that the childhood sexual abuse trauma and the adult sexual assault trauma had both contributed to PTSD. Without the trauma, with her other experiences, she would likely have developed anxiety, but not PTSD.

Her presentation was the childhood form of PTSD with mainly avoidance and shut downs. Her social anxiety was currently mild as she was managing it with skills she had learnt over the years. Part of her social anxiety was fear of negative evaluation from others.

Larissa was referred to a specialist trauma psychologist to treat the PTSD. Sandy Dawn agreed with the diagnoses and explained to Larissa that young children will often go into a freeze and shutdown state instead of fight or flight when faced with a threat. Much like a hedgehog rolling up into a ball instead of running away or attacking.

Larissa had tried to avoid triggers as much as possible, but then her anxiety increased. When she was unable to avoid, when triggered, Larissa tended to freeze and shut down. Splitting up her emotions, her body sensations, her memories and her thoughts were all part of how PTSD presented for her. She could talk about trauma without expressing the emotion, because she shut the emotion down.

'You've been doing a lot of processing on you own in creative ways. Continue to do it, just don't go too fast,' said Sandy. 'With therapy, we aim to reduce the impact of PTSD triggers and integrate your body and mind, thoughts and emotions.'

There was a long process to go through to access funding for continued therapy. Otherwise, Larissa simply could not afford it.

'How are you moods currently? You seem very low,' asked Sandy at another appointment.

'This past week, I keep having intrusive thoughts of being hit by a truck.'

'Do you feel like you will act on those thoughts?'

'It's something distressing I see every time I see a truck. That I am being hit by a truck and badly injured and perhaps killed. I want it to stop.'

'Do you have have an active plan for suicide?'

'No, but when I have had intentions, it has come on suddenly. I was just trying to make the intense distress stop. Like when I nearly put the tweezers in a socket and picked up the belt from my dressing gown to hang myself.'

'When else have you had suicidal ideations?'

'When I've been faced with homelessness. It feels too unsafe for me physically and emotionally to be homeless.'

'Is suicide your plan B?'

'Yes. But I don't tell anyone because it upsets them.'

After her appointment, Larissa stared at the abstract she had started with yellow on one side and green on the other – Australian colours. It had sat on her easel for a week. She didn't analyse as she painted. She listened to music to override most of her analytical thinking. Thunder was rumbling in the distance and the storm was getting closer.

She listened to *It Must Have Been Love* on a continuous loop as she painted and cried hard. It was the first painting during which she cried and cried but the music and colour helped her to get it out without being overcome by the intense emotion. She painted spikes in Payne's grey, stabbing from the green into the yellow.

She used a knife to smear red paint over the yellow, representing bloodshed, pain and suffering. Then she darkened the whole painting with glazes of Payne's grey. She sobbed and sobbed. She painted a lightning strike separating the red and the green.

After she felt that she had cried enough, she changed the music to *Feather Theme* from the *Forest Gump* movie. The lightening strike was now also an abstract tree, so she painted golden leaves, bringing it back to life and pushing the pain to the background. She named the painting *Healing a Broken Heart*.

After that, the intrusive thoughts and visions of being hit by a truck stopped.

Then she painted another abstract with a knife, like colourful grasses bending but able to spring back. She called it *Resilient in the Storm*.

At her next appointment with Sandy, Larissa was feeling more in the middle with her mood. She took a painting she had done the night before while listening to *Don't Speak*.

'Who is this?' asked Sandy, curiously.

'This is Snowball. She's the final painting for my exhibition. What do you see?'

'Well, people will have their own interpretations, but it looks to me like Snowball is trying to communicate. She has such big eyes and she looks like she is trying to say something.'

'It's kind of childlike and her ears are a bit wonky,' said Larissa.

'I like her ears. I think she is twiddling her ears like cats sometimes do. Like picking up signals.'

'Snowball was my childhood cat who suffered terribly before she died. Even though she was white, I painted her in Payne's grey, representing pain, with magenta streaks in her eyes, representing blood. Then I painted her with spikes of titanium white for strength because titanium is a metal with high tensile strength. I make associations with the names of paints as well as symbolic colours. I painted her with extra large eyes to represent a child. Snowball is also a metaphorical self-portrait of me as a child.'

'Oh wow, Snowball is also a metaphor for you? There is so much depth and creativity in how your mind works. Snowball is finding her voice. What is Snowball wanting to say?'

'Snowball wants to say that one time was bad enough. Don't dismiss. Listen.' Larissa was holding back tears and there was emotion in her voice as she said that.

'That's a very powerful message. You communicate so much through your art. You've done a lot of trauma processing on your own in creative ways. I want to help you continue that process. Hopefully, the approval for further sessions will come though soon.'

Larissa started a part-time job. A few hours per day helping a small business owner with manufacturing and dispatching orders for natural massage balms containing manuka beeswax. The labels were all applied by hand. Larissa wanted to be able to work full-time but her energy levels and ability to focus still fluctuated.

One day, Larissa was in the car with Aroha. They drove past a house surrounded by scaffolding and covered in plastic.

'That house looks like it's covered in a giant condom,' said Aroha.

'Well, technically it is an erection,' replied Larissa with a smirk.

Aroha laughed.

Larissa was getting her art ready for her first solo exhibition. A gallery was receptive to the idea of exhibiting process art as therapy for mental health. The local community newspapers interviewed her and she was on the front page.

'*What if people recognise me?*' she worried. People did recognise her. They told she was courageous and that it was 'a cool thing to do'.

'Does having an art exhibition mean you're an exhibitionist?' quipped Daniel.

'Wouldn't you want to know?' replied Larissa, sarcastically.

Leading up to the exhibition, Larissa was feeling anxious. Klaus and Aroha helped with transporting the artworks. Forty-five pieces including drawings and paintings to go onto the walls and several more drawings and extracts from her journals and photos showing her creative process. Larissa decided not to put prices on any of the art, as she didn't want people to judge them as not good enough. Snowball was not for sale, as Larissa wasn't ready to let go of her yet.

Two artists who had previously had exhibitions walked through just after all the paintings were up.

'These are so colourful. It must be wonderful to see them all together.'

'You like them? I didn't think they were actually any good.'

'Yes, they're incredible. It's like putting your soul on the walls, isn't it?'

'I've disguised what my paintings are about by using bright colours and abstraction.'

'You have still captured moods and emotions and expressed in a way that feels safe to you. I think what you are doing is inspirational.'

'What if no one comes? What if too many people come? I don't like crowds.'

'I'm sure people will come and see. It's completely normal to have a variety of emotions with the exhibition process.'

Eric, Angelica and Sandy came to the opening night and they all said they were proud of Larissa. Despite her anxiety, Larissa was all smiles and even gave a short speech. Over the week-long exhibition, despite her fatigue, Larissa spent a few hours each day at the gallery painting, while visitors looked around. There were several comments on Snowball with her striking eyes.

A woman burst into tears when she saw *Payne*, the eye scratched in brightly coloured crayon through shit-brown paint. She said she had also had PTSD and she was overcome with emotion as soon as she saw it. She said Larissa's art communicated feelings that words could not express.

During the week there were more visitors. 'I love *SCREWED*. *NUTZ* is brilliant too. I like your humour,' commented a man visiting with his wife. 'The ribbons on the R of *SCREWED* looks a bit like a suspender belt', he added.

'How do you know I didn't intend it to be that way?' Larissa replied with a half-smile. Larissa didn't tell him that after the exhibition, she was going to destroy *SCREWED* because of the painful emotions associated with it, even though she had made it as a joke. Larissa was in disbelief when two offers were made for *SCREWED*. Just because she didn't like some of her own art, someone else did.

'Why did you call this one *Tiger Bunnies*?' asked another visitor, pointing to an abstract that started off in green and gold and had smears of white and blue and slashes of red.

'Because when I look from it at certain angles, I can see an abstract tiger and some rabbits,' replied Larissa. 'I didn't intentionally put them there, they just showed up.'

'Oh wow, I can see them now too.' The visitor put an offer on the painting.

During the exhibition, Larissa painted a turquoise eye with an iris in colours of a paua shell but with more depth, on a white background. She added purple eyeshadow and painted long lashes in Payne's grey. Then she added teardrops. She called it *Healing Tears*. Then she painted red lips in a flirtatious smile, on another canvas, in a similar style. So, the eye and lips were disjointed, yet could go together.

As she was adding the final touches to *Flirty*, a man with a boy and a girl walked in.

'I love this one with the kite,' the man said. 'We have literally just been out flying kites, haven't we?' His children nodded but didn't say anything.

'*Hot Air Rise Above It,*' the man said reading the name tag. It was a cartoon-like painting with a grumpy looking toad in the earthy colours Larissa usually avoided using, a bright yellow sunflower wearing headphones, an earthworm working hard to turn compost into fertile soil and a kite flying high in the air. The toad had bloodshot eyes and was smoking a cigarette. Several people had commented on how it would make a good children's book cover, minus the cigarette.

'That toad kind of looks like Mum,' said the boy with a hybrid Kiwi-Aussie accent. The man looked like he was trying to suppress a laugh.

'Is it a cane toad?' asked the girl, also with a hybrid Kiwi-Aussie accent.

'Yes, it is,' replied Larissa.

'The twins are visiting from Australia,' said the man.

'I have twins who live in Australia too,' said Larissa. 'How old are you?'

'Twelve.'

They looked around quickly then went outside. The man took his time browsing.

'This one really stands out,' he said, standing in front of *Ava Angel*, rubbing his beard.

'I've had two offers on it already and a lot of people want to know what it means. It means something to me but I think people can have their own interpretations. Most people say they see love and an angel. What do you see?'

'I see violence.' Larissa recoiled slightly but then she was curious.

'Really? You're the first person to say that.'

'Yes, I see violence. My name is Oliver.' Larissa started visibly trembling when Oliver said his name.

'What makes you think violence?' she managed to choke out the words.

'The swirling chaos. Is that an axe I can see?' Oliver pointed to a shape. Oliver seemed harmless. He seemed like a nice, friendly man with a gentle voice. Larissa felt conflicted about what she felt and what she observed.

'That's a Maori fish-hook. It means safe travel over water. To me, the swirling is turbulence of the sea. My paintings are metaphors for how I've felt.'

'I'm a paramedic. I'd like to talk more but the kids are waiting. Text me if you'd like to talk.'

Larissa pushed away the few alarm bells that went off and accepted his invitation to stay in touch. She was lonely and he seemed like he was a good listener.

They texted then spoke on the phone. Oliver didn't judge Larissa for having bipolar disorder. His children had gone back to Australia and he was alone again in his house. He lived in Manuka. He said he wasn't just after sex and that he was open to love.

Larissa accepted his invitation for a dinner date. Apart from her discomfort over the triggering associations with his name and a few things he had said, she was interested in getting to know him. Possibly because he seemed so interested in getting to know her. Men had not done that before. Not since Kent. She craved emotional-intellectual intimacy more than physical intimacy.

At the end of their first date, they shared their first kiss.

Then a text came through from Michael.

'Are you seeing anyone?'

'Yes.'

'I'm ready for a committed relationship. I really want to see you again.'

'Who was that?' asked Oliver.

'Just some guy I used to see semi-casually.'

'I want to date you exclusively with no one else on the scene.'

'We haven't fallen in love yet,' said Larissa.

'I like you. If we continue to see each other, then I'll need to be your one and only.'

Larissa replied to Michael that she was not interested and not to contact her again.

Larissa started spending the occasional night at Oliver's house. She felt somewhat anxious being under such heavy sedation after taking her evening medications. She hadn't told him yet the details why, but she emphasised to Oliver to not touch her in a sexual manner while she was sleeping.

'Of course, I won't do that,' he said.

They took a sensual bath together.

'Do you prefer being called Oliver or Ollie?' Larissa asked.

'People I am close to call me Ollie.'

'What can I call you?'

'You can call me Ollie.'

'Is it horrible dealing with lots of dead people in your job?'

'I have a lot of respect for the dead. At least they don't puke on me or throw a punch at me.'

'I couldn't do what you do.'

'I've just always wanted to help people. It's challenging but I love my job. The hardest part is when children are hurt or die.'

'That would be very difficult. How do you deal with it?'

'Sometimes, I've come home and had a cry to just release the tension.'

'I don't often cry. It's like my feelings get stuck. But then when I do cry, it is a huge release.'

'My ex cheated on me then took my kids away, so it's hard for me to trust a woman.'

'What would be scarier for you? Jumping out of a plane or falling in love?' asked Larissa.

'Both terrify me but I think jumping out of a plane as I'm open to the possibility of falling in love now,' said Ollie. 'I already have feelings for you.'

'I kinda feel like the elevated moods have helped me face my fears. When I'm manic, I feel daring, experimental, beautiful, sexy, attractive, intelligent, gifted and worthy.'

'You are all those.'

'I want to face my fears and attempt skydiving again. Somewhere I can see the mountain and the lake.'

'That would take a lot of courage. What would be scarier for you? Falling in love or jumping out of a plane?'

'Falling in love. I'm still healing from the hurt.'

'I think we're both still healing.'

After a few initial sessions with Sandy, the trauma psychologist, everything had ground to a halt. Finally, nearly a year later, Sandy contacted Larissa for another appointment.

'I'm sorry this has taken so long,' she said. 'The people who make the decisions about funding tried to blame your symptoms on bipolar because they were not familiar with the childhood presentation of PTSD. Also, they tried to say the trauma in Australia wasn't their problem. Here is the letter of approval for treatment.'

Larissa felt overwhelmed with emotion as she read the letter. It said: 'Your injury of Post-Traumatic Stress Disorder has been approved for therapy'.

'What are you feeling right now?' asked Sandy.

'That I was dismissed for so long, but I'm starting to feel heard,' replied Larissa.

'I advocated very strongly for you. I know you are a vulnerable person.'

'Thank you.'

Larissa visited her parents. 'Thank you for bringing me back to New Zealand. I miss my kids so much but I know that could have been me dying on the crane above the hospital.' Larissa was tearful. 'Homelessness was too scary.'

'I know you would not have survived,' said Aroha gently, embracing Larissa in a hug.

'That's what parents do,' said Klaus. 'We haven't always been perfect parents but we did our best.'

When the twins visited again, Larissa talked to Alexandria.

'Did you really think I was going to kill you when I restrained you that time?'

'No. I just didn't know how I got there, that's all. I was startled.'

'You were hitting and kicking me during a meltdown.'

'I don't remember most of what happened during meltdowns.'

'Do you still struggle with meltdowns?'

'No, I get a bit frustrated at times but I handle things better now.'

'I haven't always been the best parent. I have tried my best.'

Talking to Sandy, the trauma psychologist, took the pressure off her relationship with her family, enabling her to talk about more ordinary, daily life things.

She was seeing Sandy weekly and still doing most of the processing on her own in between. Some of the processing happened somatically, such as the bizarre sensations in her body during sleep hallucinations, which were less frequent now.

She no longer needed to see Eric and Angelica unless she needed another medication review. Her GP was now writing the scripts for her medications.

She didn't want the bipolar to be completely suppressed, as she observed that processing of trauma and emotions took place during the mood shifts. It was an uncomfortable process, but the frozen emotions were continuing to thaw and starting to flow.

Larissa continued to work part-time. She saved up for something important. She was ready to face one of her biggest fears.

21. Above Rainbow Bridge

One thing Larissa's friendships with pets taught her was to be present in the here and now. That was something Larissa struggled with. She was either grieving about the past, anxious about the future, shut down from trauma or high with mania.

Larissa trusted pets more than humans. Pets listened to her without judging her. Larissa was starting to believe that she was worthy of love. To her, a pet's purpose is to love and be loved. Pets didn't need extravagant lifestyles or numerous possessions. They needed a home, food and someone who cared.

The painting of Snowball was on her bedroom wall, reminding her that her purpose was to express her voice. Larissa had sold several paintings at the exhibition, despite her considering them all to be 'process' paintings and not fine art. She used the money from the sales to buy a new camera with a functioning on/off button and without a scratched lens.

Larissa didn't want the bipolar to be flat-lined. She came to a compromise with Eric to be minimally medicated. She was instructed how to do a temporary medication adjustment at the first signs of mania.

Crashing from mania was like crashing in her skydiving accident. Plus there was the fallout of impulsive and reckless decisions made along the way in mania. The goal was to prevent mania and severe depression. If starting to go into mania, she could bring it under control more quickly and safely on medications.

Short bouts of hypomania, an elevated mood less intense than mania was acceptable for Larissa and her clinicians as long as she was now self-aware, safe and in control of it. Moderate depression was no fun but the episodes were shorter lasting and less severe than previously, typically lasting a few weeks at most rather than several months or even years.

Moderate depression was was more tolerable for her than being overmedicated until she felt like a zombie. It had been hard for her to feel her emotions, and she wanted to be able to feel.

Not being medicated at all had too high a risk of things spinning out of control. She monitored her moods carefully and she was aware when she was hypomanic. Others around her gave feedback and she was starting to recognise for herself early indicators of mania such as pressure of speech – which internally felt like a distressed urgency to be heard with an internal feeling of pressure.

Mania also tended to flare during big PTSD triggers. She had a minor medication change during those times to be sedated to sleep to quieten down mania.

During the elevated moods, Larissa felt like she could face her fears. She felt like there was a purpose to it. As long as she felt in control of it, Eric and Sandy were supportive with her decision to be minimally medicated. She also saw things from a different perspective when she was elevated yet still able to see the ground. The key was to land safely again, even though landing could be a bit rough.

During a hypomania episode, she had extra energy, felt confident and ready.

Larissa sat in an aeroplane strapped to a skydiver. She closed her eyes, controlled her breathing and hummed to ease her anxiety. Just like she did to get through panic attacks.

Just as they exited the plane, she had flashbacks of her wedding day with Kent calling out, 'I've got your back,' and 'I love you.'

Larissa screamed during the free-fall, then went quiet as her parachute deployed. Her terror turned to peace, then to somewhere between joy and euphoria, yet she was still present.

As she glided down to Earth, she saw a richly saturated full-circle double rainbow framing the peak of Mount Whakapono standing tall in a violet-grey sky. The darker the sky, the more intense the rainbows. *Mount Whakapono. Mount Believe.*

Larissa observed and felt more than she thought. *There was never a Rainbow Bridge. Not an arch but a full circle. Was ist Liebe? What is love?* Larissa felt like she knew the answer. She felt like Kent and Ava were with her again. Plus Kat and her beloved pets, including Snowball, Zoey, Tripod and Ziggy.

It felt spiritual, only she she was in touch with reality and able to see the ground, despite being up high. Like hypomania – a moderate high, not as extreme as mania.

Bipolar mania was exhilarating yet had much more risk of crashing and dying than skydiving. Larissa still didn't understand suffering but she wanted to believe there was a purpose to the mood episodes and the shutdowns. With the mood shifts, she had started processing trauma that had been frozen for decades.

Ollie was waiting on the ground. 'I'm so proud of you!' he exclaimed enthusiastically.

Larissa was all smiles and talking fast. The adrenaline rush felt similar to the energy of mania.

'I screamed the first part. I think I needed to get the screaming out. I saw something incredible – a double full circle rainbow! They can only be seen from up high in rare conditions. Hopefully it was captured on video so you can see. I felt so calm after the chutes opened. Felt so magical. I'll try to explain to you what it was like, if only I can find the words.'

As they drove to the lake, *Amazing* was playing on the stereo. They parked near the lake.

'I'm falling for you, Larissa,' said Ollie, clutching Larissa's hands. 'I'm falling in love with you.'

'I don't feel like I'm falling. I feel like I'm growing in love. Growing like a plant that is getting ready to bloom. I'm grounded yet high at the same time.'

Love felt different this time. Larissa felt ready to open her heart to love again. Although she had never stopped loving. She loved Aroha and Klaus and Daniel. She loved her children Alexandria and Xavier. Although they were far away, they were close in her heart. Along with her angel friends who had inspired her to face her fears and to live with purpose and courage.

Thank you for reading *Pet Purpose: Your Unspoken Voice*.
Look out for the sequel, *Soar Purpose: Will Be Heard.*

Art

Rainbow Pi (back cover) was painted by Xanthe during a mania episode, while sedated by medications for bipolar disorder. It is a visual mind map. If a picture tells a thousand words, a symbolic, metaphorical visual mind map tells over 94,000 words (after over 10,000 words were culled).

Rainbow Pi was painted to calm Xanthe's racing mind in mania, while sedated by bipolar medications. It helped simplify the main themes for *Pet Purpose: Your Unspoken Voice.*

Creative expression processed shut down emotions, which was therapeutic. The paintings and other artworks were also visual mind maps in metaphor. Some of Xanthe's art was described in *Pet Purpose.*

Xanthe has had two solo art as therapy exhibitions, *Spinning Orbit* and *Speak.* All artworks are linked to each other and to this story. Both the artworks and writing the novel have played a key role in processing trauma and shutdown emotions. *Snowball* (cover image), was painted in acrylics on canvas.

Pet Purpose is the essence of Xanthe's story after being pulled apart, filtered, distilled then put together creatively. Painting with words.

See *bipolarcourage.com* for Xanthe's art and her creative process.

References

Popular culture references are mentioned in some chapters of *Pet Purpose*. Titles of songs and instrumental music are in italics with preferred artist. Some readers may be curious to look up the lyrics or listen to the songs to try work out why the author chose to mention them in the storyline. (Clue: mood and/or lyrics).

1
Rainbow Bridge – poem – Paul C. Dahm
Somebody to Love – Queen

2
Hangman – board-game - Milton Bradley (1970s)
Operation – board-game - Milton Bradley (1970s)
Wonder Woman (original TV series 1970s with Lynda Carter)
The Muppet Show (TV series 1970s)
Rainbow Connection (Kermit the Frog/Jim Henson)
The Muppet Movie, 1979

3
Total Eclipse of the Heart – Bonnie Tyler
Broken Wings – Mr Mister

4
That'll Be the Day – Buddy Holly
White Wedding – Billy Idol
The Rain Must Fall – Yanni
Fly Away – Lenny Kravitz
Truly Madly Deeply – Savage Garden

6
In These Arms – Bon Jovi

7
Bring Me to Life – Evanescence

10
Wrecking Ball – Miley Cyrus (music video)

Live at the Acropolis (album) – Yanni

11
Hysteria (studio album) – Def Leppard
Pour Some Sugar On Me – Def Leppard

13
Arlandria – Foo Fighters

14
Live at the Acropolis (album) – Yanni

15
Addicted to You – Avicii/Audre May
Stronger – Britney Spears
So What – P!nk
Wonder Woman (2017 film)
Is She With You? - Wonder Woman (2017 film) - Hans Zimmer, Junkie XL
Roar – Katy Perry
Feel – Robbie Williams

16
The Power of Love – Dalton Harris, James Arthur; Frankie Goes to Hollywood
Friend of a Wounded Heart – Wayne Watson
Gone Away – The Offspring
Danger Zone – Kenny Loggins
Dangerous – Roxette
Is She With You? - Wonder Woman (2017 film) - Hans Zimmer, Junkie XL
Feel – Robbie Williams

17
Wonder Woman (2017 film with Gal Gadot); 1970s TV series (with Lynda Carter)
Running Away – Delta Goodrem
You're My Best Friend – Queen
Over the Rainbow – Israel Kamakawiwo'ole
I Can See Clearly Now – Jimmy Cliff
Under Pressure – Queen & David Bowie
Defy You – The Offspring
Bohemian Rhapsody – Queen

Jesus Loves Me – Anna Bartlett Warner, William Batchelder Bradbury

18
Kiss from a Rose – Seal
Daniel – Elton John, Bernie Taupin
Wake Me Up Before You Go-Go – Wham – music video
Sunny – Boney M, Bobby Hebb
Blue Suede Shoes – Elvis Presley
(You Drive Me) Crazy – Britney Spears

19
Love Lies Bleeding/Funeral for a Friend – Elton John, Bernie Taupin
Lasso of Truth – William Moulton Marston, Wonder Woman character
Confident – Demi Levato

20
Don't Stop Me Now – Queen
Unchained Melody – Righteous Brothers
Whoopi Goldberg acting in Ghost (film) and Sister Act (film)
Spinning Around – Kylie Minogue
Another Brick in the Wall Pt 2 – Pink Floyd
Purple Rain – Prince
Wonder Woman (Justice League merchandise)
It Must Have Been Love – Roxette
Don't Speak – No Doubt
Feather Theme – Forrest Gump film – Alan Silvestri

21
Amazing – Aerosmith

About the Author

Pet Purpose: Your Unspoken Voice is a first novel by Xanthe Wyse, inspired by her own story which she felt safer to tell as semi-autobiographical fiction, rather than full memoir. Xanthe changed her name legally, after her former name became a trauma trigger, for similar reasons to the character in *Pet Purpose*.

Xanthe was diagnosed with bipolar affective disorder (type 1), post-traumatic stress disorder (PTSD) and social anxiety disorder in her forties. Prior to that, she was diagnosed with major depressive disorder and generalised anxiety disorder since her early twenties. She has experienced the full mood spectrum from severe depression to mania. She wanted to highlight bipolar mania in *Pet Purpose* as it is so misunderstood.

Writing and editing *Pet Purpose* has taken seven years since conception. The original idea was a story about her bond with pets. After more life-changing experiences, including episodes of severe mania, Xanthe decided to make the focus complex trauma, as well as keep a pet theme.

Xanthe struggles with short-term memory (even forgetting what she named her characters) as well as having difficulty with organising words, so others can understand. Editing and proof-reading took over a year.

She wrote *Pet Purpose* out of order, while processing trauma and managing bipolar disorder. The initial writing was a release, but it would have been mostly incoherent to others. Then, she arranged what she had written into a timeline. Then, she rewrote the whole story to flow.

Friends helped with reading the drafts for feedback and proofreading.

Rewriting and editing took a long time, trying to organise words so they could be understood by others. Xanthe frequently added words in the middle of a sentence, omitted words, swapped words, repeated parts of a sentence and repeated sections.

When her brain was too scrambled or racing too fast for words, she painted her story in metaphor instead. *Pet Purpose* was a very challenging goal that gave Xanthe a sense of meaning and purpose.

Xanthe is writing the sequel, *Soar Purpose*. She lives in New Zealand and is mother of an adult son.

Xanthe's website is: *bipolarcourage.com*

Made in the USA
Coppell, TX
09 May 2021